Gender Equality a

Beyond Empowerment

_____

To access a presentation delivered by Stroma Cole as well as an interview with her, please visit http://www.cabi.org/openresources/94422

Gender Equality and Tourism

Beyond Empowerment

Edited by

Stroma Cole

University of the West of England, UK

CABI is a trading name of CAB International

CABI
Nosworthy Way
Wallingford
Oxfordshire OX10 8DE
UK

CABI
745 Atlantic Avenue
8th Floor
Boston, MA 02111
USA

Tel: +44 (0)1491 832111
Fax: +44 (0)1491 833508
E-mail: info@cabi.org
Website: www.cabi.org

Tel: +1 (617)682-9015
E-mail: cabi-nao@cabi.org

A catalogue record for this book is available from the British Library, London, UK.

Library of Congress Cataloging-in-Publication Data

Names: Cole, Stroma, editor.
Title: Gender equality and tourism beyond empowerment / edited by Stroma
   Cole, University of the West of England.
Description: Wallingford, Oxfordshire, UK ; Boston, MA, USA : CABI, [2018] |
   Includes bibliographical references and index.
Identifiers: LCCN 2018002401 (print) | LCCN 2018012785 (ebook) | ISBN
   9781786394439 (ePDF) | ISBN 9781786394446 (ePub) | ISBN 9781786394422 (pbk
   : alk. paper)
Subjects: LCSH: Tourism--Employees. | Women--Employment. | Tourism--Social
   aspects. | Women--Travel--Social aspects.
Classification: LCC HD5716.T64 (ebook) | LCC HD5716.T64 G46 2018 (print) |
   DDC 331.4/133--dc23
LC record available at https://lccn.loc.gov/2018002401

ISBN-13: 978 1 78639 442 2 (paperback)

Commissioning editor: Claire Parfitt
Editorial assistant: Emma McCann
Production editor: Shankari Wilford

Typeset by SPi, Pondicherry, India
Printed and bound in the UK by Severn, Gloucester

Contents

Contributors

Fiona Eva Bakas is a critical tourism researcher with a PhD in tourism and gender (Otago University, NZ, 2014) and an MSc in ecotourism (Portsmouth University, UK, 2004). With 20 years of varied work experience in academia, the tourism industry and corporate businesses, she is currently a postdoctoral researcher on CREATOUR, a project on creative tourism in rural areas in Portugal. Fiona is an associate of the non-governmental organization (NGO) Equality in Tourism. E-mail: fiona.bakas@ua.pt

Stroma Cole is a senior lecturer in international tourism development at the University of the West of England. Stroma combines her academic career with action research and consultancy, most recently looking at tourism and water rights in Indonesia. She is a director of Equality in Tourism and was the chair of Tourism Concern (2006–2012). Stroma is an activist researcher critiquing the consequences of tourism development. E-mail: Stroma.Cole@uwe.ac.uk

Isis Arlene Díaz-Carrión holds a PhD from Universidad Complutense de Madrid, Spain, on the link between gender and rural tourism in Veracruz (Mexico). She has over 15 years of experience as coordinator, scientist, professor and project lead in gender and tourism as well as in sustainability and tourism. She has worked in Mexico and Spain in universities and training schools. Isis works at Facultad de Turismo y Mercadotecnia-Universidad Autónoma de Baja California, Tijuana, Mexico. E-mail: diaz.isis@uabc.edu.mx

Marília Durão is a research fellow at the University of Aveiro, Portugal, and has been granted a doctoral scholarship by the Portuguese Foundation for Science and Technology (FCT). She holds a Master's degree in tourism planning and management from the University of Aveiro, where she is currently a PhD candidate in the tourism doctoral programme.

Lucy Ferguson is a researcher and trainer in gender equality. Since completing her PhD in tourism and gender in 2007, she has produced a number of publications on the topic. She has worked as a consultant at the United Nations World Tourism Organization and at UNWomen, and is a Director of Equality in Tourism. She has delivered gender training to Kuoni Travel and responsibletravel.com, and has written on working with the private sector on these issues. E-mail: lucyjferguson@gmail.com

Wendy Hillman is a senior lecturer in sociology in the School of Nursing, Midwifery and Social Sciences, at CQUniversity, Australia, Rockhampton campus. She holds a PhD in sociology from James Cook University, Australia. She continues to pursue her passion for Nepal, where she currently researches the amelioration of poverty in women through transformative tourism and social entrepreneurship. E-mail: w.hillman@cqu.edu.au

Heather Jeffrey is a lecturer in tourism studies at Middlesex University, Dubai, United Arab Emirates. Heather's research interests lie in tourism and social inequalities, and her PhD research focused on women and tourism in Tunisia. Heather tries to blog and tweet on these themes and you can follow her here: www.huffingtonpost.co.uk/author/heather-jeffrey or on Twitter @H_L_Jeffrey. E-mail: H.Jeffrey@mdx.ac.uk

Belén Martínez Caparrós has recently received her MSc in sustainable development in practice from the University of the West of England. Her research focuses on gender equality and how patriarchy shapes women's agency in different cultures. She is particularly interested in how societal norms inhibit women's empowerment and how challenging these norms can improve the impact of development projects focusing on achieving gender equality. E-mail: belen.martinez.caparros@gmail.com

Daniela Moreno Alarcón got her PhD in 2017 in tourism and gender from the Faculty of Political Science and Sociology, University Complutense, Madrid, Spain. She is a director of Equality in Tourism. Since 2009, she has gained broad international project/research experience fostering gender mainstreaming within tourism policies around the world. She has proposed concrete recommendations tailored to the context of tourism and gender, alongside identification and promotion of good practices in gender and tourism. E-mail: daniela@equalityintourism.org

Meghan Muldoon is a PhD candidate at the University of Waterloo in Waterloo, Canada. Her thesis research in South Africa involved learning about issues of gender, race and relations of power in tourism in the townships. Prior to choosing a life in academia, Meghan worked with women and youth living in unplanned urban settlements in East Africa, as well as with women experiencing homelessness in Canada. E-mail: mmuldoon@uwaterloo.ca

Kylie Radel is a senior lecturer in marketing and tourism with the School of Business and Law, at Central Queensland University, Australia. Her research seeks to advance tourism as an agent for transformation and sustainable economic and social opportunity. She is currently working with rural and remote women tourism enterprises in Nepal and Fiji. Indigenous tourism, qualitative methodologies and business education are her principal foci. E-mail: k.radel@cqu.edu.au

Paola Vizcaino Suárez, originally from Mexico, is a lecturer in the Faculty of Management at Bournemouth University, UK. Her research focuses on the critical perspectives of women in tourism, including gendered work, empowerment, gender-aware policies and knowledge production in Latin America. She holds a PhD in tourism studies from Universidad Autónoma del Estado de México and an MA in tourism management and planning from the University of Alicante (Spain). E-mail: lvizcainosuarez@bournemouth.ac.uk

Hazel Tucker is associate professor in tourism at the University of Otago, New Zealand, and specializes in the area of tourism's influences on socio-cultural relationships and change. As well as conducting a longitudinal ethnographic study in Turkey focusing on gender, host–guest interaction and World Heritage, Hazel publishes on colonialism/postcolonialism, tours and tour guiding, and emotional dimensions of tourism encounters. Hazel is an Associate Editor for *Annals of Tourism Research* and an associate at Equality in Tourism. E-mail: hazel.tucker@otago.ac.nz

Fiona Eva Bakas, Carlos Costa, Marília Durão, Inês Carvalho and Zélia Breda are tourism academics researching gender in tourism as part of the GENTOUR II Project (2012–2015). This was a nationwide project that aimed to evaluate the role of gender within tourism labour structures, and investigate the potential played by networks and internationalization to promote forms of gender equality and to introduce innovative forms of economic growth. All authors worked together at the Aveiro University Tourism Department, which Carlos Costa heads, and are all part of the GOVCOPP (Governance, Competitiveness and Public Policies) research unit.

Foreword by Margaret Byrne Swain

This dynamic collection about gender equality and tourism engages the moment we are in, being developed just as the #MeToo movement began to propel issues of gender disempowerment into public discourse through social and mainstream media. Events in Hollywood triggered a global response to chronic sexism, gender inequality, sexual harassment and assault. A hashtag erupted using the same phrase developed in 2007 by African American activist Tarana Burke to name her non-profit organization supporting harassment and assault victims (Garcia, 2017). As this synergy became known, so have multiple intersecting oppressions of race, class, ethnicity, gender, sexuality, age and ability come into focus. We see these intersections in this chronicle of women producers of tourism, including guides, managers, handicraft artisans, entrepreneurs and service workers from around the world.

People of many backgrounds in many nations have recently registered their disgust with hegemonic toxic masculinity, making personal reports and promoting daily documentation of political and economic reckoning. In at least 85 countries versions of #MeToo, some with local names such as 'Balance ton porc', or 'Expose your pig' in French have suddenly arrived, while struggles against harassment and assault have simmered for 'years, decades, centuries' (Zacharek et al., 2017), millennia. Guarded apathy as in Italy or entrenched victim blaming and state censorship as in China created added barriers, yet still the reports persisted.

With this and the world-wide Women's March in early 2017 there has been a surging interest in just what 'feminism' means, and recognition of efforts already in place among working poor, unions, non-governmental organizations (NGOs), civil groups and, yes, governments to combat patriarchy, to change our societies, our cultural ideologies, our world. It's too early to know if the #MeToo revolution is a true crack in patriarchy's defences, a harbinger of transformation, or if we will revert back to continued old orders and neoliberal controls. From all walks of life, including the entertainment and service industries directly related to hospitality and tourism, people in elite positions as well as those with no financial security or representation have found the power to tell their stories. #MeToo became a very timely intersection of hubris and historical moment with the following deeply engaging book on gender equality and tourism, moving beyond empowerment rhetoric.

Gender inequality was a coherent issue in tourism studies by the mid-1990s, and later intersected with other variables of difference including race, class and sexuality. Dimensions of power, cultural relativity and the near-universality of patriarchy have shaped our analysis. Where we often have been stuck is at the 'what next' step, asking how to transform what is unequal, harmful, this book takes up the question of how to mobilize beyond talk of empowerment within the realm of tourism. Passion, competency and some outrage shape these essays. Chapters presenting academic case studies and analysis are counterbalanced by lived stories of gender in tourism. We hear commonalities among women workers in distinct environments and with diverse responsibilities as they seek out tourism connections with visitors, and variation in their navigation of sexism and harassment due to gender relations and ideologies. It is the collection's geographic variety, featuring African, Asian, European and Latin American nationalities, that brings into focus a multiplicity of potential culturally specific ways to be empowered, transforming gendered inequality. This is in direct contrast to accidental gender mainstreaming policy by various development agencies, equating empowerment with obtaining (any) paid income by women. In these cases, praxis is missing, putting theoretical ideals into practice. It may seem ironic that this book about gender equality only portrays women's efforts to find power within tourism work; however as demonstrated, context is critical and complicated.

Stroma Cole's Introduction provides three axes of empowerment processes: agency, autonomy and authority, all of which women are often found to be lacking in comparison to men in terms of economic, psychological, social and political relations (Scheyvens, 1999), as well as other divisions of socially sanctioned and culturally validated power. Her discussion brought to mind a scene in the 1989 film *Cannibal Tours* in which a Papua New Guinean woman forcefully speaks out about tourists being too cheap to buy her handicrafts when she needs the money in order to feed her kids and send them to school. Scornfully she notes any money that men earn they spend on themselves, often for getting drunk.

This brings me back to the 'P' word – patriarchy. What if it were not a given, but rather a relic of the past? What if the Women's March and the #MeToo movement represented change, transforming gender relations towards equality? This may be way too optimistic, although it is good to think about. Certainly with reference to tourism, the evidence provided in this collection gives hope that women and men are capable of sustained equitable relationships, and that women can become acknowledged for their work and worth. Reading through this book also raised another of my favourite topics: the position of women researchers as agents of transformation for gender equality in the communities they work in by their very presence and by the questions they ask (Swain, 2004). Some of the authors here touch on their agency, while organizations such as Equality in Tourism (http://equalityintourism.org) and Women Academics in Tourism (WAIT) promote activism in tourism and networking, also addressing gender issues within our field.

Returning to Stroma's framing and final points reflecting on tourism, changing masculinities and gender-based violence, she has noted that an artificial divide between paid and unpaid labour, and the disvalue of care work is a driver of gender inequality in all human interactions. Tourism production and consumption are based within numerous gender scripts of expectations and values dictated by local and global norms as well as capitalistic structures. One powerful perspective is that we will only have transformation towards gender equality when boys are taught how to be different men, to balance gender relations and re-align identities. To do this successfully, girls also need to learn to be different women, to negate consensual patriarchy and complicit misogyny. This book documents hope for the future.

References

Garcia, S.E. (2017) The woman who created #MeToo long before hashtags. Available at: https://www.nytimes.com/2017/10/20/us/me-too-movement-tarana-burke.html?emc=edit_gn_20171207&nl=&nlid=83619912&te=1&_r=0 (accessed 26 February 2018).

Scheyvens, R. (1999) Ecotourism and the empowerment of local communities. *Tourism Management* 20(2), 245–249.

Swain, M.B. (2004) (Dis)embodied experience and power dynamics in tourism research. In: Phillimore, J. and Goodson, L. (eds) *Qualitative Research in Tourism: Ontologies, Epistemologies and Methodologies.* Routledge, London and New York, pp. 102–118.

Zacharek, S., Dockterman, E. and Edwards, H.S. (2017) Time Person of the Year: the silence breakers: the voices that launched a movement. Available at: http://time.com/time-person-of-the-year-2017-silence-breakers (accessed 26 February 2018).

Acknowledgements

This book would not have been possible without the contribution and support of many people. First and foremost I'd like to thank the contributors to this book, both the academic authors and the women who have shared their stories – without your efforts and dedication this book would not have been possible. Thank you to my colleagues, especially Tricia and Dani at Equality in Tourism for your enthusiasm and support of this project. I'd also like to thank Claire Parfitt and the team at CABI for their help in the successful completion of this book. Last but not least I'd like to thank Brian, Mira and Toby for your patience and under-standing over the past year, while I worked on this book.

1 Introduction: Gender Equality and Tourism – Beyond Empowerment

Stroma Cole*

University of the West of England, Bristol, UK

The Origins of This Book

The ideas fuelling the creation of this book arose from submissions to a conference organized by Equality in Tourism (http://equalityintourism.org), an organization dedicated to ensuring women always have a voice in global tourism, and Yeşil Valiz (http://yesilvaliz.org), which was to be held in Turkey in 2016. Sadly, the conference had to be abandoned due to the violent political events that took place at the time – reminding us just how fickle the tourism endeavour is! However, from the ashes, the abstracts, together with an engagement with some of our associates at Equality in Tourism, became discussions, and the book was born.

Drawing on the theme of gender equality in tourism, this book aims to identify the main obstacles to women's advancement in the tourism industry, and to discover and share successful strategies to overcome them, drawing on case studies from all over the world. All the authors contributing to this book are proudly feminist and, with the exception of Chapter 3, have used qualitative methods to give depth and feeling to the women's stories they present. All of us have used positionality and reflexivity to reflect our engagement with subjectivity. Many of the authors are not writing in their first language and this book has the privilege of bringing Spanish-speaking and Latin American scholarship to the English-speaking world. Interlaced between the chapters are stories from women who work in tourism.

Why Gender Equality?

Gender is a system of cultural identities and social relationships between females and males (Swain, 1995), characterized by unequal power and norms that determine an unequal distribution of resources, work, decision making, political power, and the entitlement of rights and obligations in both the private and public spheres (Thierry, 2007). The study of gender as a pertinent issue within tourism began receiving academic interest and systematic investigation in the 1990s (Swain, 1995; Figueroa-Domecq *et al.*, 2015). Although on the agenda for 30 years, women continue to face injustice, and it remains the case that while women make up between 60 and 70% of the labour force (Baum, 2013), they are far more likely than men to be found in lower-paid, unskilled jobs. Women face discrimination, occupational segregation, are undervalued, stereotyped

---

* E-mail: Stroma.Cole@uwe.ac.uk

and not promoted, given less training than men and struggle more with work–life balance (Wong and Ko, 2009). They tend to have unskilled or semi-skilled work in the most vulnerable jobs, where they are more likely to experience poor working conditions, inequality of opportunity and treatment, violence, exploitation, stress and sexual harassment (Baum, 2013). In a sample of 78 tourism companies, women only made up 15.8% of board members, and over 20% of tourism companies had no women on their boards (Equality in Tourism, 2013). Furthermore, the tourism industry draws on and reinforces gender inequalities through its reliance on the 'embodied attributes of the worker, and his/her ability to perform emotional labor' (Webster, 2010, p. 188).

Empowerment and Beyond

Institutional responses suggest that women can be empowered by tourism. According to the World Tourism Organization (UNWTO) 'tourism can empower women in multiple ways, particularly through the provision of jobs and through income-generating opportunities in small and larger-scale tourism ... enterprises'. And '...tourism can be a tool for women to unlock their potential ... and thus contribute to the UNSDG 5: Achieve gender equality and empower all women and girls' (UNWTO, 2015). However, the rhetoric is frequently overstated and the global hegemonic masculinity that gives agency to capitalism (Swain, 2002) frequently results in a lack of control and powerlessness. This book's critical analysis of women in tourism from different stakeholder perspectives, from international non-governmental organizations (INGOs), national governments and managers, as well as workers in a variety of fields producing tourism, explores the continuing power imbalances and injustices women experience and sheds some light on how to overcome them.

While using the framework of empowerment this book takes a critical view of how empowerment is understood and, while building on 'the nascent research line

that examines gender-tourism-empowerment' (Panta and Thapa, 2018, p. 22), it points to why empowerment, as it has been hijacked by the neoliberal agenda, is missing the point. Empowerment as so frequently conceptualized deals only with productive and not reproductive labour, and fails to address the structural inequalities that lie at the base of societies built on patriarchal symbolic and normative codes. Entrenched gender discrimination practices of patriarchal cultures and structures that are internalized and socialized are constantly replicated. Transformation for women will only happen when the structural inequalities in society are laid bare and overcome.

The following sections of this introduction are structured to first introduce the reader to the development and empowerment literature, before moving on to review studies of tourism and empowerment. In the third section some critical reflections are explored.

Development and Empowerment

Empowerment is a relatively broad concept lacking a single clear definition (Trommlerova et al., 2015); it has experienced growing importance and become one of the most elastic buzzwords in the international development lexicon (Cornwall, 2016) with over 29 definitions (Ibrahim and Alkire, 2007). 'Empowerment has become a very popular concept across various fields of study particularly those dealing with development and politics. Its use in both scholarly and practice literature has been so wide that many authors no longer care to define it in terms of how they use it. It is as if the meaning is clear and without dispute, yet it is a highly loaded concept' (Lenao and Busupi, 2016, p. 54). However, 'women's empowerment' remains a central objective of international development (Mosedale, 2014). While its use started in the 1980s and 1990s as a radical approach concerned with transforming power relations in favour of women's rights and greater equality between women and men (Cornwall, 2016) it runs the risk of becoming an empty-shell mantra for governments,

INGOs and NGOs. Empowerment was about transforming gendered inequality, but has come to mean providing income for women (or perhaps even to increase the labour force and provide businesses with cheap employees to exploit).

Accepting the term has a longer history (Batliwala, 2010). Scholars commonly use one of two models that explore aspects of empowerment. Friedmann (1992) put forward three kinds: psychological, social and political, whereas Rowlands (1997) used 'power to' ('generative or productive power'), 'power with' (collective power of a group) and 'power within' (strength based on self-acceptance and consciousization). While each of these might be seen as a distinct exercise of agency (Trommlerova *et al.*, 2015), I explain empowerment with three As:

* Agency – the ability to make things happen, the capacity to initiate action.
* Autonomy – the ability to make choices, self-governance, to decide for oneself and being able to have a role in public life.
* Authority – to be respected, listened to and be looked up to.

Common to all three conceptualizations is that empowerment is a process. 'Empowerment relates to processes of change. In particular, it refers to the processes by which those who have been denied the capacity for choice gain this capacity' (Kabeer, 2017, p. 650) and we are talking here about meaningful or strategic choices.

Women's lack of agency comes from entrenched gender discrimination practices of the patriarchal cultures and structures in society that are acculturated and socialized (Munar *et al.*, 2015). As gender operates through the unquestioned acceptance of power, many women are not aware of the possibilities of equality; they accept their subordinate position as the only option. Cultural norms surrounding gender roles frequently deny that inequalities exist or that such inequalities are unjust. Norms are internalized and responses are automatic and habituated, maintaining and reproducing patriarchy. Systemic, and unconscious for the majority, inequality is pervasive and reinforced throughout societies, and begins

very early as demonstrated in this video (https://www.facebook.com/BBCStories/videos/10155357926475659). It is reproduced through education systems including in the Western 'developed' world, as can be seen in these videos: (https://www.youtube.com/watch?v=Z1Jbd4-fPOE; https://www.youtube.com/watch?v=6syQC4rc_W0); and continues through to the top of tourism businesses as discussed here (https://www.youtube.com/watch?v=ibjEVtseGbU).

While I cannot do justice to all the discussion on empowerment in the development literature, a number of debates are pertinent to the arguments germane to a critical analysis of tourism gender and empowerment. These debates are overlapping and interconnected, so, for ease of discussion, I have separated them into four broad themes here:

1   Drivers or determinants of empowerment

A number of studies have looked at what empowers, what are the drivers or determinants? For example, Trommlerova and colleagues' (2015) study in The Gambia concluded that age, health and marital status correlated with empowerment. According to Syed (2010) such correlations that have been identified are specific and limited. Deeper studies have far more nuanced conclusions. For example, Kabeer explored the economic pathways to empowerment in Bangladesh. She concluded 'paid work outside the home, … may have brought greater voice and influence in family and, for some forms of work, reduced domestic violence, but it also subjected women to more physically demanding and personally demeaning forms of work and greater difficulties in reconciling their domestic and earning responsibilities' (Kabeer, 2017, p. 661).

2   Conceptualization and measuring empowerment

Although evidence suggests there is no one-size-fits-all recipe for empowerment

(Cornwall, 2016), attempts have been made to measure it, for example, the United Nations Development Programme's (UNDP) Gender Empowerment Measure. However, as Syed (2010) discusses, these measures have inherent biases. First, the capitalist bias – they only measure productive labour. With a narrow focus on those incorporated into paid work, the quality of the work, the double burdens associated with that work and the ignorance of the importance of reproductive labour are not considered, but are significant (and will be discussed in further detail in relation to gender and tourism). Syed also alerted us both to an elite bias in the metric, for example, female members of parliament are counted but not females on local councils, and a secular bias, as religious choices and commitments were not taken into account.

3 A shift from power

In the early formulations of empowerment, economics did not feature. '… all efforts to conceptualise the term … clearly stressed … a socio-political process, that the critical operating concept within empowerment was power' (Batliwala, 2010, p. 124). Over time, 'it has been "mainstreamed" in a manner that has virtually robbed it of its original meaning and strategic value' (Batliwala, 2010, p. 126). The UN's sustainable development goal (SDG) on why gender equality matters (UN, 2016) states: 'Women's and girls' empowerment is essential to expand economic growth and promote social development. The full participation of women in labour forces would add percentage points to most national growth rates – double digits in many cases'. This is a clear example of how the power has been removed from empowerment. As Cornwall (2016) discusses, 'it is commonplace for contemporary "empowerment" initiatives to begin and end with increasing women's access to resources. The underpinning assumption of this being that once women have access to economic resources, they will be able to make changes in other areas of their lives' (Cornwall, 2016, p. 356). This may or may not happen. Earning money does not necessarily lead to increased equality or overcoming injustice.

4 Issues of context

(i) Universalist versus context specific: As Swain (2016) discusses, there is a forever unresolved dialectic between the particular and the universal. The tensions between universal and specific ideals and between universal rights such as freedom from violence and the need for cultural diversity, for example, a woman's choice to wear a veil, remains unresolved (Moghissi, 2002). (ii) Levels of analysis: As Syed (2010) discusses, factors at a number of levels affect empowerment. At the macro level empowerment is affected by political and legal frameworks; at the meso-organizational level by business and institutional arrangements; and at the micro-individual level by a host of intersecting variables such as race, age, ethnicity and ability. Oxfam (2017) has released a composite index for measuring empowerment based on a framework that recognizes three levels where change can take place: personal, relational and environmental. Changes at a personal level refer to changes taking place within the person – changes in how the person sees herself. Changes at the relational level refer to changes in the relationships and power relations within the woman's surrounding network. This includes, for example, changes within the household, the community, markets and local authorities. Finally, changes at environmental level take place in the broader context such as social norms, attitudes and the beliefs of wider society; as well as formal changes in the political and legislative framework.

There is agreement that context is critical and what empowers one woman might not empower another: there are no one-size-fits-all recipes for empowerment. And empowering experiences in one area of a woman's life do not automatically translate into greater capacity to exercise agency and transform power relations in another part of her life. While a number of authors have emphasized dignity and self-esteem/pride and self-worth as central to empowerment (Rowlands, 1997; Scheyvens and Lagisa, 1998), this is at the micro-individual level and does not challenge systemic inequality or structures of patriarchy necessary for transformative change. Batliwala suggested 'the goals of women's empowerment are to challenge patriarchal ideology; to transform the structures and institutions that reinforce and perpetuate gender discrimination and social inequality' (Batliwala,1994, p. 130). As Cornwall (2016) explains, empowerment is fundamentally about changing power relations, and involves building critical consciousness of inequalities and injustice to generate the impetus to act together to change society.

Gender Equality, Tourism Development and Empowerment

We have Regina Scheyvens' (1999) paper to thank for bringing ideas of empowerment to the tourism academy. A few articles (Di Castri, 2004; Cole, 2006; 2007; Pleno, 2006) and Sofield's (2003) book followed in the first decade of the century, but the topic has received considerable attention in the past few years. While nearly all authors have used Scheyvens' (1999) four-part model of economic, psychological, social and political empowerment, there have been two recent additions. Ramos and Prideaux considered the need to add environmental empowerment, explained as 'the community's ability to gain power to protect and preserve the surrounding ecosystem' (Ramos and Prideaux, 2014, p. 465), while Heimtum and Morgan (2012) included political, personal, cultural and spiritual empowerment, without explaining what each meant. Exceptions to the use of Scheyvens' framework have included Walter (2011) and Trans and Walter (2014), who used Longwe's (2002) framework that examines empowerment through welfare, access, conscientization, participation and control. Any divisions of empowerment are difficult as it is multifaceted and experienced in different ways by different women and at different levels.

Some tourism scholars have attempted to measure community empowerment through tourism. Boley and McGehee (2014) developed the residents' empowerment through the Resident Empowerment through Tourism Scale (RETS), and Boley et al. (2015) tested its cross-cultural application in Japan. A further paper (Boley et al., 2017) used data from the two previous studies to explore gender differences. They found that in Virginia, USA, women felt more empowered by tourism, whereas in Japan no gender differences were reported. Strzelecka (2017) demonstrated that residents' emotional bonds with places and nature influence some dimensions of psychological and social empowerment. Ramos and Prideaux (2014) used mixed methods, including Likert scale questions, to develop a wheel of empowerment scale, to explore empowerment among a Mayan community in Mexico. While the highest scores were for psychological empowerment, overall the research suggested tourism was not empowering the community. Tensions between the generations led to low social empowerment and even lower political empowerment. However, gender differences were not explored.

An increasing number of studies suggest that tourism brings some economic empowerment to some women (Stronza, 2005; Cole, 2006; Pleno, 2006; Tucker and Boonabaana, 2012; Feng, 2013; Tran and Walter, 2014; Moswete and Lacey, 2015; Knight and Cottrell, 2016; Panta and Thapa, 2018; Movono and Dahles, 2017). In fact, only Ramos and Prideaux (2014) found tourism did not bring economic empowerment. This privileging of economic empowerment over other forms of empowerment reflects the shift away from power observed in the development studies literature. As Ferguson (2011) discusses, most tourism development policies and programmes are limited in their conceptualization of women's empowerment being simply economic and failing to consider its multidimensional, multi-level aspects. However, the value of financial independence should not be underestimated. As Moswete and Lacey describe, in Botswana, 'female empowerment is expressed in terms of freedom from economic dependency on men and society,... which afforded the freedom to make choices, purchase land, build homes, pursue additional business interests, provide for their families, educate their children, travel, and engage socially with a wide range of people including foreign tourists' (Moswete and Lacey, 2015, p. 614). Increased earning power not only brings increased status, but also peace of mind, as Tao and Wall (2009) found among Massai women who invest in cattle, which can be sold in times of need.

A large number of the above studies also draw attention to the fact that while women may earn, in some cases a pittance – but essential income – for example, among the Mukono of Uganda (Tucker and Boonabaana, 2012), their tourism work is in addition to their present workload. This double burden, so often ignored in the policy literature that advocates tourism for women's economic empowerment, results from not including domestic and caring services or reproductive labour. The importance of domestic and subsistence agricultural work is ignored. Women's involvement in tourism frequently repeats these same types of jobs but also involves intangible (also unpaid and therefore undervalued) emotional work through hospitality, smiling, and making guests comfortable and safe.

The second most commonly reported form of empowerment is psychological or individual, resulting from increased self-esteem, greater self-confidence and pride. Self-esteem is important, as Pleno explains, 'having high self-esteem is important as it provides courage to try new things and the power to believe in oneself, as well as the capacity to respect others and be respected' (Pleno, 2006, p. 152). The 'power within' in the form of increased confidence and self-esteem frequently came from meeting people outside family networks, speaking with outsiders/tourists or through socializing with other members of ecotourism/community-based tourism groups at meetings or facilitated training sessions (Panta and Thapa, 2018). Self-esteem and confidence are the building blocks for further forms of empowerment. In the case of women in Vatuolalai, from minor economic

empowerment, hotel workers' confidence grew and they opened their own businesses, which over time, with increased respect, led to participation in decision making, and increased autonomy and control over their lives (Movono and Dahles, 2017).

Social empowerment comes from collectivity, 'power with' as Rowlands (1997) called it. It includes pride, normally associated with individuals, but as my (Cole, 2007) study of the Ngadha, in eastern Indonesia, showed the group became proud of their identity, and group identity gave them power. Moswete and Lacey (2015) show how what is psychological empowerment for some is social for others. Social empowerment most frequently relates to community cohesion confirmed or strengthened by tourism (Strzelecka, 2017). The importance of networks for many of the women was a critical element of their empowerment (Tucker and Boonabaana, 2012).

Political empowerment, the core element of empowerment is of course the hardest to achieve. It starts for many women when they gain power to make decisions relating to an ecotourism- or community-based tourism project, for example, in the ecotourism project in Bohol, the Philippines (Pleno, 2006). The women in the ecotourism project in Vietnam discussed by Tran and Walter (2014) increased in self-confidence, became more aware of their status and rights, and became active leaders in the project. However, beyond the project men were still preferred leaders over women and still had control over the distribution of the benefits from the project. Furthermore, despite increased awareness of their rights women still had to put up with, usually alcohol-induced, male violence. One recent study from Fiji reported that through tourism the women disrupted cultural barriers and became 'office bearers in the village council, heads of respective development committees and advisory roles at the provincial level demonstrates that women ... were well placed in positions of authority and control over their affairs and that of the greater community' (Movono and Dahles, 2017, p. 689).

Gender Equality in Tourism: Beyond Empowerment

So women's empowerment through tourism is possible but why is it still so rare (or rarely reported)? Why is it given so much lip service by international organizations but so little support through policy and action? Why do women make up the greatest number of workers in tourism, while still doing the majority of reproductive labour, but still have so little control? Hopefully, the chapters in this book will go some way to shedding more light on the critical issue for tourism (and development more broadly). Some considerations that would seem critical include:

1   Tourism is business

As well as being an aspect of international development, tourism is about business. Most of the studies that have examined the gender–tourism–empowerment nexus have been about small-scale developments in Less Economically Developed Countries (LEDCs). Patriarchal norms, structural inequality, glass ceilings and gender pay gaps exist just as much in tourism as in other industries on a global scale. While the introduction of gender equality measures in the tourism industry is in its infancy, Chapter 4 finds that there is an increasing awareness of the value of such measures being in place. Indeed, Bakas *et al.* find that, even though the implementation of gender equality measures is often perceived as the responsibility of the state, gender roles play a significant part in this process. The finding that women who are top-level managers are more likely to implement gender equality measures than male managers, shows that women are more aware of the need for gender equality measures. Furthermore, it suggests the need to change stereotyped perceptions of gender roles, which is the root of the problem, if real progress in achieving gender equality and empowerment through tourism is to be made. The nature of the tourism business also makes it a special case for a number of reasons:

- It is fickle, which can have grave impacts on women's efforts, see, for example, Tucker's Chapter 11.
- The Othering, and romanticization of women hosts as expressed in both Chapters 11 and 7, and the glamour associated with some tourism employment, for example, in the airline industry (Baum, 2012), hides lived realities.
- The interlinkages with other sectors mean that the gendered consequences of tourism can be felt through many avenues: water in Labuan Bajo (Cole, 2017); textile production in Tunisia (see Chapter 9); and land in Nicaragua (Moreno, 2017), for example.

2   Importance of context

As Feng explains: 'In order to fully understand gender dynamics in tourism, it is important to contextualize such analysis with the particular historical and sociocultural factors in a given locality and against the backdrop of the global economic trend' (Feng, 2013, p. 11). Hazel Tucker's Chapter 11 brings into view a longitudinal, generational focus on women in tourism contexts, exploring Turkish doll-makers' desires to break free from producing souvenirs. Meanwhile, Jeffrey's Chapter 9 explores how colonial history, religion and politics have shaped Tunisian women's identity and equality, with consequences for tourism employment.

3   Local conceptions

Only two studies, Knight and Cottrell (2016) and Panta and Thapa (2018), have explored empowerment from the participants' perspectives. While total equality and equal power may be the end goal, the journey is long and we need to understand where the priorities for local women lie. Barnett and Cole (2017) uncovered how in Tanzania women put freedom from gender-based violence above economic empowerment, equality in the domestic sphere or leadership in their considerations of empowerment. In Chapter 7 Muldoon used a PhotoVoice methodology to explore the complexity of women's involvement in tourism. The female township residents in South Africa found themselves at once empowered as community entrepreneurs, the passive recipients of tourists' support, and advocates in disrupting tourists' conceptions of African women as victims. In Chapter 8 the meaning of empowerment that the Nepali women attach to their emancipatory journeys is that of being answerable to and for themselves, for their own destiny and in charge of their own purpose in life.

4   Barriers and facilitators

While patriarchal norms lie at the base of women's struggle for agency, autonomy and authority, when it comes to the steps to use tourism as a tool for empowerment there are a number of specific hurdles to overcome. Many of these barriers are well known, such as the lack of information – about tourism (Cole, 2006), business development (Panta and Thapa, 2018) and about women's rights. The lack of start-up capital (Moswete and Lacey, 2015), centralized control (Cole, 2006; Moswete and Lacey, 2015) and lack of land ownership/land rights (Ramos and Prideaux, 2014; Moreno, 2017; Moreno and Tovar, 2015) are important constraints.

We also know that NGOs and local organizations have been critical in kickstarting women's empowerment, providing training, and forums to socialize and develop self-confidence. Policy and strategies at global and national levels can act to either facilitate or not women's empowerment through tourism. As Moreno Alarcón (Chapter 3) discusses, the development of a tourism action plan on gender and tourism needs to be done from a feminist perspective. A strategy and mindset to mainstream a gender perspective and, as a consequence, to reduce gender inequalities is required rather than investing in women's projects per se. Giota's story (p. 12) from Greece, and Vizcaino Suárez's chapter from Mexico (Chapter 5) both underline the cultural and institutional barriers to women's empowerment through tourism. Certainly, 'Women need to be more meaningfully involved in the formulation, implementation and review of tourism policy'

(Moswete and Lacey, 2015, p. 615). However, many women not only overcome the lack of support mechanisms, but, despite their poverty, support their communities and empower other women themselves, as the Nepali women in Chapter 8 demonstrate. One of the greatest barriers is the 'shadow of sexual assault' as discussed by Martínez Caparrós, in Chapter 6. Changing the patriarchal norms that blame women for the violation of women's safety and force women to take responsibility not to put themselves in danger is critical to achieving gender equality.

5   Empowerment is a slow process

Empowerment is not a static phenomenon, it is a dynamic process that requires gradual, multiple and often seemingly contradictory processes of negotiation (Tucker and Boonabaana, 2012). In many cases, the journey is not direct but requires small iterative steps. It requires shifts in culture of gender norms, roles and existing inequalities. Tourism creates spaces for negotiating power, as Vizcaino Suárez discusses in Chapter 5, subtle negotiations have taken place to redefine work, gender and identity for individuals, but changes at the community level have occurred at a much slower pace. As Díaz-Carrión shows in Chapter 10 entrepreneurship in tourism can build social capital through increased financial security, improved networks, increased self-confidence and overcoming social isolation, but it is not a linear process. Cultural change doesn't happen overnight but, given that there have been over 20 years of gender and tourism studies highlighting the issues, many could ask why, for many women, there has been so little change.

6   Women outside tourism

Nearly all the studies about gender equality and women's empowerment explore the experiences of the women involved in tourism but this is necessarily only a subsection of the community and we know tourism can affect women in the same destination variously (Swain, 1995). Studies have largely neglected those not involved in tourism. Cole's (2017) study shows how while tourism in Labuan Bajo, Indonesia, may empower a tiny minority of women and improve their gender relations in private, the consequences of tourism development are challenging the human rights of the majority. The study explores how the intersectionality with other factors including ethnicity, socio-economic status and life stage had important bearings on women's experiences of tourism. As Knight and Cottrell (2016) found, the empowerment of some led to a loss of dignity, freedom and well-being of others. Movono and Dahles (2017) refer to the 'consequences of empowerment' and point out that the empowerment of women has led to wider effects, including more drinking by the men. Tran and Walter (2014) had similar findings. As Moreno Alarcón discusses in Chapter 3, the focus of gender equality needs to go beyond the women who work in tourism. Only then can tourism be an ally – theoretically and practically – to help end gender inequality and the disempowerment of women.

7 In relation to men

If women's empowerment is about gender equality, it is necessarily relational to men. However, as Feng (2013) discusses, changed gender norms or flexibility in the gendered division of labour, improved roles or changed status need to be situated in the interactive relations between men and women. Women can appear more autonomous when compared to themselves previously through having cash income from tourism, but she points out that women undertook 'men's work', but men did not engage in 'women's work', and that the role of sacrifice for 'ideal households' fell on women rather than on men. In several chapters, the problem of the double burden is emphasized. As discussed in Chapter 5, in Metepec, Mexico, the burden of care and domestic work still falls on women, despite their tourism employment (Vizcaino Suárez). As discussed by Martínez Caparrós in Chapter 6, self-confident Ladakhi women, who are proud of their ability to overcome gender norms in the public sphere, do not challenge deeply institutionalized roles of cooking and childcare, and undertake this on top of their tourism work. While changes in social reproduction as a result of tourism have been discussed in the literature (Ferguson, 2010), for the majority of women it seems that the gender stereotypes are stubborn, change is slow, subtle and being constantly negotiated.

Absent from this book are the male stories. While acknowledging a fuller understanding of masculinities is required, and that gender equality is about changing men's roles as well as women's, there has not been the space to include their perspective here. The chapters and stories that make up this book explore women's stories of empowerment beyond the hijacked neoliberal conceptualizations of economic improvement, to highlight the structural inequalities that prevent true gender equality. Institutional patriarchy within international as well as national government and local structures provides policy barriers that women struggle against. The artificial divide between paid productive labour and unpaid reproductive labour and the lack of value given to care work are recurrent themes and significant obstacles to achieving gender equality. The collection points to the slow and small changes that women are making and how women are using the transformations tourism brings to their advantage. This book is a collection of stories of how women, despite prejudice and stereotypes, are gaining agency and autonomy by using tourism to shift gender relations.

References

Barnett, T. and Cole, S. (2017) Empowering women farmers in Tanzania. Unpublished report. UNCTAD, Geneva.
Batliwala, S. (1994) The meaning of women's empowerment: new concepts from action. In: Sen, G., Germain, A. and Chen, L.C. (eds) *Population Policies Reconsidered: Health, Empowerment and Rights*. Harvard University Press, Boston, Massachusetts, pp. 127–138.

Batliwala, S. (2010) Taking the power out of empowerment – an experiential account. In: Cornwall, A. and Eade, D. (eds) *Deconstructing Development Discourse; Buzzwords and Fuzzwords*. Practical Action Publishing in Association with Oxfam, Oxford, UK, pp. 111–122.

Baum, T. (2012) Working the skies: changing representations of gendered work in the airline industry, 1930–2011. *Tourism Management* 33(5), 1185–1194.

Baum, T. (2013) International perspectives on women and work in hotels, catering and tourism. *International Labour Organization Working Paper*. ILO, Geneva.

Boley, B. and McGehee, N. (2014) Measuring empowerment: developing and validating the Resident Empowerment through Tourism Scale (RETS). *Tourism Management* 45, 85–94.

Boley, B.B., Maruyama, N. and Woosnam, K.M. (2015) Measuring empowerment in an eastern context: findings from Japan. *Tourism Management* 50, 112–122.

Boley, B.B., Ayscue, A., Maruyama, N. and Woosnam, K.M. (2017) Gender and empowerment: assessing discrepancies using the resident empowerment through tourism scale. *Journal of Sustainable Tourism* 25(1): 113–129.

Cole, S. (2006) Information and empowerment: the keys to achieving sustainable tourism. *Journal of Sustainable Tourism* 14(6), 629–644.

Cole, S. (2007) *Tourism, Culture and Development: Hopes, Dreams and Realities in Eastern Indonesia*. Channel View Publications, Clevedon, UK.

Cole, S. (2017) Water worries: an intersectional feminist political ecology of tourism and water in Labuan Bajo, Indonesia. *Annals of Tourism Research* 67, 14–24.

Cornwall, A. (2016) Women's empowerment: what works? *Journal of International Development* 28, 342–359.

Di Castri, F. (2004) Sustainable tourism in small islands: local empowerment as the key factor. *INSULA-PARIS* 13(1/2).

Equality in Tourism (2013) Sun, sand and ceilings: women in the boardroom in the tourism industry. Available at: http://equalityintourism.org/sun-sand-and-ceilings-women-in-the-boardroom-in-the-tourism-industry (accessed 26 February 2018).

Feng, X. (2013) Women's work, men's work: gender and tourism among the Miao in rural China. *Anthropology of Work Review* 34(1), 2–14.

Ferguson, L. (2010) Interrogating 'gender' in development policy and practice: the World Bank, tourism and microenterprise in Honduras. *International Feminist Journal of Politics* 12(1), 3–24.

Ferguson, L. (2011) Promoting gender equality and empowering women? Tourism and the third Millennium Development Goal. *Current Issues in Tourism* 14(3), 235–249.

Figueroa-Domecq, C., Pritchard, A., Segovia-Pérez, M., Morgan, N. and Villacé-Molinero, T. (2015) Tourism gender research: a critical accounting. *Annals of Tourism Research* 52, 87–103.

Friedmann, J. (1992) *Empowerment: the Politics of Alternative Development*. Blackwell Publishers, Oxford, UK..

Heimtum, B. and Morgan, M. (2012) Proposing paradigm peace: mixed methods in feminist tourism research. *Tourist Studies* 12(3), 287–304.

Ibrahim, S. and Alkire, S. (2007) Agency and empowerment: a proposal for internationally comparable indicators. *Oxford Development Studies* 35(4), 379–403.

Kabeer, N. (2017) Economic pathways to women's empowerment and active citizenship: what does the evidence from Bangladesh tell us? *Journal of Development Studies* 53(5), 649–663.

Knight, D. and Cottrell, S. (2016) Evaluating tourism-linked empowerment in Cuzco, Peru. *Annals of Tourism Research* 56, 32–47.

Lenao, M. and Busupi, B. (2016) Ecotourism development and female empowerment in Botswana: a review. *Tourism Management Perspectives* 18, 51–58.

Longwe, S.H. (2002) Spectacles for seeing gender in project evaluation. Available at: www.genderevaluation.net/gem/en/understanding_gem/longwe.htm (accessed 13 March 2017).

Moghissi, H. (2002) *Feminism and Islamic Fundamentalism: The Limits of Postmodern Analysis*. Zed Books, London.

Moreno, D. (2017) Tourism and gender: an essential approach in the context of sustainable and responsible tourism development. Unpublished PhD thesis. University Complutense of Madrid, Spain.

Moreno, D. and Tovar, N. (2015) Reflexiones y propuestas para un turismo responsable con enfoque de género. En Foro de Turismo Responsable (ed.) *¿Equidad de género en el turismo? muchas sombras pocas luces*. Foro de Turismo Responsable, Madrid, pp. 65–104.

Mosedale S. (2014) Women's empowerment as a development goal: taking a feminist standpoint. *Journal of International Development* 26, 1115–1125.

Moswete, N. and Lacey, G. (2015) 'Women cannot lead': empowering women through cultural tourism in Botswana. *Journal of Sustainable Tourism* 23(4), 600–617.

Movono, A. and Dahles, H. (2017) Female empowerment and tourism: a focus on businesses in a Fijian village, Asia Pacific. *Journal of Tourism Research* 22(6), 681–692.

Munar, A.M., Biran, A., Budeanu, A., Canton, K., Chambers, D., Dredge, D. and Ram, Y. (2015) The gender gap in the tourism academy: statistics and indicators of gender equality, while waiting for the dawn. *Tourism Education Futures Initiative (TEFI), Report I.* Available at: http://tourismeducationfutures.org/tefi-gender-in-the-tourism-academy (accessed 12 March 2018).

Oxfam (2017) How do we measure women's empowerment? Available at: https://views-voices.oxfam.org.uk/gender/2017/05/measure-womens-empowerment (accessed 26 February 2018).

Panta, S.K. and Thapa, B. (2018) Entrepreneurship and women's empowerment in gateway communities of Bardia National Park, Nepal. *Journal of Ecotourism* 17, 20–42.

Pleno, M.J.L. (2006) Ecotourism projects and women's empowerment: a case study in the province of Bohol, Philippines. *Forum of International Development Studies* 32, 137–155.

Ramos, A. and Prideaux, B. (2014) Indigenous ecotourism in the Mayan rainforest of Palenque: empowerment issues in sustainable development. *Journal of Sustainable Tourism* 22(3), 461–479.

Rowlands, J. (1997) *Questioning Empowerment: Working with Women in Honduras.* Oxfam Publishing, Oxford, UK.

Scheyvens, R. (1999) Ecotourism and the empowerment of local communities. *Tourism Management* 20(2), 245–249.

Scheyvens, R. and Lagisa, L. (1998) Women, disempowerment and resistance: an analysis of logging and mining activities in the Pacific. *Singapore Journal of Tropical Geography* 19, 51–70.

Sofield, T.H.B. (2003) *Empowerment for Sustainable Tourism Development.* Elsevier Science, Kidlington, UK.

Stronza, A. (2005) Hosts and hosts: the anthropology of community-based ecotourism in the Peruvian Amazon. *NAPA Bulletin* 23, 170–190.

Strzelecka, M. (2017) Place attachment and empowerment: do residents need to be attached to be empowered? *Annals of Tourism Research* 66, 61–73.

Swain, M. (1995) Gender in tourism. *Annals of Tourism Research* 22(2), 247–266.

Swain, M. (2002) Gender/Tourism/Fun(?): an introduction. In: Swain, M. and Momsen, E. (eds) *Gender / Tourism/Fun?* Cognizant Communications, Putnam Valley, New York.

Swain, M.B. (2016) Embodying cosmopolitan paradigms in tourism research. In: Munar, A.M. and Jamal, T. (eds) *Tourism Research Paradigms: Critical and Emergent Knowledges.* Emerald, Bingley, UK, pp. 87–111.

Syed, J. (2010) Reconstructing gender empowerment. *Women's Studies International Forum* 33, 283–294.

Tao, T.C.H. and Wall, G. (2009) Tourism as a sustainable livelihood strategy. *Tourism Management* 30(1), 90–98.

Thierry, A.R. (2007) The elephant in the room: gender and expert-led poverty reduction. *Management Decision* 45(8), 1359–1376.

Trans, L. and Walter, P. (2014) Ecotourism, gender and development in northern Vietnam. *Annals of Tourism Research* 44, 116–130.

Trommlerova, S., Klasen, S. and Lessmann, O. (2015) Determinants of empowerment in a capability based poverty approach: evidence from The Gambia. *Courant Research Center: Poverty, Equity and Growth – Discussion Papers* No. 147.

Tucker, H. and Boonabaana, B. (2012) A critical analysis of tourism, gender and poverty reduction. *Journal of Sustainable Tourism* 20(3), 437–455.

United Nations (UN) (2016) Gender equality: why it matters. Available at: www.un.org/sustainabledevelopment/wp-content/uploads/2016/08/5_Why-it-Matters_GenderEquality_2p.pdf (accessed 26 February 2018).

UNWTO Tourism and the Sustainable Development Goals. Available at: https://www.e-unwto.org/doi/pdf/10.18111/9789284417254 (accessed 16 April 2018).

Walter, P. (2011) Gender analysis in community-based ecotourism. *Tourism Recreation Research* 36(2), 159–168.

Webster, J. (2010) Clerks, cashiers, customer carers: women's work in European services. In: Howcroft, D. and Richardson, H. (eds) *Work and Life in the Global Economy: A Gendered Analysis of Service Work.* Palgrave Macmillan, London, 185–208.

Wong, S.C. and Ko, A. (2009) Exploratory study of understanding hotel employees' perception on work-life balance issues. *International Journal of Hospitality Management* 28(2), 195–203.

World Trade Organization (UNWTO) (2015) Gender equality. Available at: www.un.org/sustainabledevelopment/gender-equality (accessed 26 February 2018).

Giota's Story: Behind the Mountains

Panagiota Stefanopoulou

My name is Panagiota Stefanopoulou and I am 41 years old. I was born in Dortmund, Germany, to Greek parents, and went to Greece with my mother and two sisters when I was 6 months old. My father, who was a miner, stayed behind to work in Germany. After studying tourism management in Larisa, I worked in the hospitality industry up until 2004. It was then that I visited Zagori, Epirus, with a friend with the initial intention of creating a workshop using traditional looms. Zagori does not have many permanent inhabitants, schools, hospitals or bakeries, and is mainly a winter tourism destination with limited livestock farming. I worked in the booming tourism industry there for a few years. Tourism work is highly seasonal in Zagori and so in some months everyone seems to want you to work for them but in other months no one wants to give you any work.

Whilst working, I also learnt how to process sheep's wool, dye it with natural, homemade dyes, weave it on traditional looms, knit and felt. In 2009 I tried to get a 'cottage industry' licence, but the law said that you could only get such a licence if you had an underage child at home or a house-bound elderly person. Instead, I used a state subsidy aimed at increasing female entrepreneurship, and in 2010 I opened my shop/workshop. It is called 'ANO KATO', which means 'messy, in disarray' or 'up and down' in Greek.

On this journey there were various people who helped me get where I am. Some were people within the system and some were people whom I spoke to about my vision and they simply did what they could to help. I am a woman but I am not determined by my gender, as I want to be seen primarily as a human being. All this entrepreneurial process has made me strong but power does not have a start, a middle and an end. As a result of my involvement in both work-

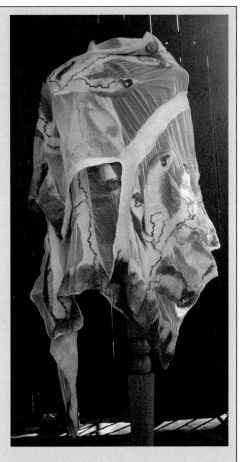

Fig. S1. Giota's felt scarf.

shops and making handicrafts, I feel I have gained on various levels. I get a material satisfaction because I receive a monetary reward for my work, and I also get a soulful reward as the buyer of my services (workshops or handicrafts) has understood the path that the tourist product made in order to reach the consumer's hands. It is important for me that the tourist feels like they are taking a part of me with them. This exchange makes me feel empowered to continue creating and offering my knowledge to any visitor who may be interested in what I do.

In my efforts to cooperate with hotels or travel agencies, I discovered something very sad: most of these professionals have no training in how to operate as a touristic entity. They believe that the tourist product is only the buildings, beds and food. I, on the other hand, recognize that the tourist product is made up of a succession of 'hoops' that are linked together to form the full tourism chain. A tourist should be able to taste the whole tourist product, which I perceive as a combination of the geographic area's natural characteristics, the area's infrastructure, the area's culture and the area's people. Despite Greece being a country that receives more than 18% of its gross domestic product from tourism activities, there is a lack of tourism education.

The juxtaposition between self-perception and societal perception is a barrier that I face on a daily basis in the place where I have chosen to live and work. The small mountainous village society that I eventually became a member of is made up of a few permanent residents and visitors with family ties. All these people could not understand why an educated, unmarried woman like myself had chosen to live in a remote place like their village and work as a cleaner. The first thing that they thought was that I was of 'free morals' and available to any man who wanted me. As a result of this mentality, there were various efforts to evict me from the village. Twice I found myself in court because my dogs were perceived as noisy. Apart from the constant looming fear of eviction, I was constantly sexually harassed by the villagers. Since I didn't respond to their advances, this made them more aggressive. However, the years passed, I continued to live in the area and, not only that, eventually I opened a fully fledged tourism business! What a scandal!

As well as making and selling felted items, I also organize seminars for children and adults on various felting techniques. I recently started organizing seminars for primary schools in the area with the title 'Red thread tied and wrapped on the spinning wheel', a programme that has been approved by the Greek Ministry of Education.

My workshop address is ANO KATO, Elati, Zagori, Epirus, Greece. Facebook: ANO KATO.

2 Gender Equality and Tourism: The Global Policy Context

Lucy Ferguson*

*Instituto Complutense de Estudios Internacionales,
Universidad Complutense de Madrid, Madrid, Spain*

Introduction

At the global level, a wide range of international agreements exist to ensure continual advancement towards gender equality and women's empowerment. The broadly accepted strategy for achieving these goals is gender mainstreaming, which involves 'ensuring that gender perspectives and attention to the goal of gender equality are central to all activities – policy development, research, advocacy/ dialogue, legislation, resource allocation, and planning, implementation and monitoring of programmes and projects' (UN Women). While progress has been slow and is contested at multiple levels, gender mainstreaming has become ubiquitous throughout the majority of public institutions worldwide (Hafner-Burton and Pollack, 2002). Moreover, a gender equality strategy can be found within the ministries of the majority of sectors in a wide range of countries. Guidelines, research and policy advice on gender equality are conducted by the representative global bodies of a range of sectors – see, for example, the World Health Organization (WHO), the Food and Agriculture Organization (FAO) and the United Nations Educational, Scientific and Cultural Organization (UNESCO), for education.

In contrast, tourism has proved highly resistant to gender mainstreaming. There is no globally agreed policy statement on tourism and gender equality (Ferguson, 2011). Very few countries have developed policies or strategies on gender equality in tourism, with the exception of Mexico, Nicaragua and Cape Verde (see Chapter 3 by Moreno Alarcón, this volume; also Vizcaino-Suárez *et al.*, 2014). In stark contrast to other comparable sector-specific or issue-specific international organizations – such as WHO or FAO, for example – the UN World Tourism Organization (UNWTO) has no guidelines, policies or programmes on gender equality. As outlined in detail below, other than producing the Global Report on Women in Tourism 2010 and commissioning the second edition in 2018, the UNWTO has not done any work on gender issues, despite the findings and recommendations emerging from that report. Similarly, other large multilateral institutions such as the World Bank have no explicit work on gender equality in tourism. While gender has been listed as a key theme in a number of World Bank projects (see, for example, Ferguson, 2010 on Copán in Honduras), there has been little concerted effort to make links between the Bank's work on tourism and its work on gender equality. Similarly, the International Labour

* E-mail: Lucyferg@ucm.es

Organization (ILO) has paid little explicit attention to gender and tourism, with the exception of its Working Paper on the topic International Perspectives on Women and Work in Hotels, Catering and Tourism (ILO, 2013). In terms of the private sector, gender issues have made little impact. A handful of tourism companies – such as Kuoni Travel and Responsibletravel.com – have conducted limited gender equality training or explored gender issues in their work. However, as argued by Ferguson and Moreno (2016), working on gender equality with the tourism private sector has proved highly challenging.

This chapter explores why there is such a substantive disconnect between global policy and practice on gender equality, and its glaring absence in the tourism sector. The governance of tourism spans public, private and semi-private organizations. As such, it is difficult to establish clear authority and responsibility for gender equality in the tourism sector. Indeed, there have been few attempts to map how gender issues are taken into account in tourism governance. In order to address this, here I review the gender dimensions of tourism policy in international organizations – focusing primarily on the UNWTO. In terms of international organizations, the key institution for our purposes is the UNWTO, based in Madrid. Achieving UN specialized agency status in November 2003, UNWTO is the only international institution existing solely to promote the spread of the tourism industry across the globe. Its role can be understood in a number of ways: as a campaigning organization for the tourism industry; as a donor for tourism development projects; and as the primary source of research and statistics on global tourism.

In a visit to UNWTO headquarters in Madrid in April 2006, then UN Secretary-General Kofi Annan argued that 'tourism really has the potential of opening up economic space for people around the world', reinforcing the role of the institution as a driver of the global tourism industry. In contrast to other UN agencies with intergovernmental status, UNWTO continues to be 'open to partnership with other actors in the realm of tourism, particularly those in the private sector'.[1] Although nominally separate from the World Travel and Tourism Council (WTTC) – made up of over 100 chief executives of major airlines, hotel chains, cruise lines and catering companies – UNWTO nevertheless has a large number of private sector members (see Cole, 2016 regarding the gender bias in the WTTC). Following recent work on the reorientation of the UN from a public sector to a more market-oriented organization, the presence of private industry interests in UNWTO does not conflict too dramatically with the overall outlook of the UN. However, UNWTO remains the only specialized agency to allow members from the private sector in its decision-making framework. As an intergovernmental agency, the main body of UNWTO is made up of 150 Member States and more than 300 Affiliate Members, predominantly but not exclusively private sector organizations.

The chapter develops in two main sections, covering two periods of gender policy and practice in UNWTO – 2007–2012 and 2012 onwards. Following this, the concluding section explores why there is such a persistent gender gap in tourism policy, and proposes steps to address this. In line with the spirit of this book and broader commitments to reflexivity in feminist politics, I situate myself within this chapter as both a researcher and practitioner. I have produced a number of publications on the gender dimensions of tourism as a development strategy, and engaged with trying to change tourism policy as a consultant at UNWTO and in brief trainings with private sector organizations. The chapter is motivated by my frustration at the limited inclusion of gender as a serious issue at the macro level, and continued resistances – both explicit and implicit – to change. At the time of this book going to press, I am currently working as the Lead Consultant to produce the second edition of the Global Report on Women in Tourism, funded by UNWTO, UN Women and GIZ. It is hoped that this chapter will generate further support to challenge tourism organizations to work in substantive ways for gender equality.

Gender Initiatives at UNWTO 2007–2012

Within the institution, gender falls within the remit of the Ethical and Social Dimensions of Tourism Programme, where it is just one of several areas that the small team are concerned with, along with accessible tourism, intangible cultural tourism, protection of indigenous peoples and the protection of children. As such, there are limited resources with which to develop and promote a strong gender agenda. Gender equality as a concept was not widely visible in the organization until 2007. Those within UNWTO with a concern for gender issues managed to take advantage of the theme of World Tourism Day 2007: 'Tourism Opens Doors for Women' in order to raise the profile of gender issues in the institution. As part of this event, a roundtable involving a broad range of participants was held with the express purpose of exploring the relationship between this theme and the Millennium Development Goals (MDGs), setting up a work agenda for the future. In 2008, UNWTO signed a Memorandum of Understanding with UN Women (then UNIFEM) in 2008, with the aim of 'harnessing tourism's potential to contribute to gender equality and women's empowerment'. This included an Action Plan to Empower Women through Tourism, as set out in Box 2.1.

A shared budget was negotiated, which was used to work on three different products – the Global Report on Women in Tourism, the Women in Tourism Empowerment Programme, and the Gender and Tourism Portal. First, UNWTO and UN Women jointly produced the Global Report on Women in Tourism 2010. The report was launched at ITB Berlin in March 2011, and includes key findings, case studies and recommendations for increasing gender equality in the tourism sector. The recommendations are organized by theme and by key stakeholder groups, as set out in Boxes 2.2 and 2.3 below.

The report highlights the importance of re-evaluating the indicators at least every 3 years in order to assess how effective policy actions are in improving the situation of women in tourism. Following the publication of the report, UNWTO signed a renewed framework agreement in October 2011, with a commitment to 'build on the findings of the Global Report to generate momentum for tourism's active contribution to equality and women's empowerment, as well as to develop a gender mainstreaming strategy

---

Box 2.1. Action Plan to Empower Women through Tourism, 2008.

The UNWTO/UN Women collaboration follows an Action Plan with a number of specific activities:
1. Set up a multi-stakeholder taskforce.
2. Initiate a triennial joint report on the participation and status of women in tourism industry.
3. Establish a portal to serve as a global network for knowledge sharing.
4. Build international awareness about opportunities for women in tourism.
5. Call upon UNWTO members to take vigorous steps to support gender mainstreaming in national development processes, so as to achieve women's equality in the tourism sector.

Box 2.2. Global Report on Women in Tourism 2010 main recommendations by theme.

Employment. Increase awareness of the important economic role that women play in the tourism industry. Strengthen legal protection for women in tourism employment; such protections include minimum wage regulations and equal pay laws. Improve maternity leave requirements, flexible hours, work-from-home options, and arrangements for childcare.
Entrepreneurship. Facilitate women's tourism entrepreneurship by ensuring women's access to credit, land and property as well as providing appropriate training and resources to support women's enterprises.
Education. Promote women's participation in tourism education and training and improve the educational level of women already working in different areas of the industry through a targeted and strategic program of action.
Leadership. Support women's tourism leadership at all levels: public sector, private sector, and community management by establishing leadership programs at the national level and in large and small-scale tourism enterprises.
Community. Ensure that women's contribution to community development is properly recognized and rewarded by taking into account women's unpaid work and by monitoring tourism activities carried out in the household and in the community.

Box 2.3. Global Report on Women in Tourism 2010 main recommendations for stakeholders.

Private sector. Promote gender equality and women's empowerment as fundamental components of Corporate Social Responsibility activities, in line with the Global Compact-UN Women Women's Empowerment Principles.
Public sector including tourism policy-makers. Take proactive steps to mainstream gender in tourism policy, planning, and operations.
International organizations and civil society. Call on governments, the international community, civil society organizations and the private sector to protect women's rights in tourism and to monitor progress in the empowerment of women through tourism. Collaborate with UNWTO-UN Women to develop programs and projects dedicated to promoting gender equality and women's empowerment through tourism.

for the public and private members of the tourism sector'.[2] Planned activities at this time included the Women in Tourism Empowerment Programme and the Tourism and Gender Portal.

The second part of the 2008 co-funding commitment between UN Women and UNWTO was the development of the Women in Tourism Empowerment Programme (WITEP) (http://ethics.unwto.org/content/women-tourism-empowerment-programme-witep). The purpose of WITEP is to 'set a precedent for establishing tourism as a tool for the promotion of gender equality and women's empowerment, using gender analysis and gender training to tackle inequality and gender-based discrimination in the tourism industry'. The programme focuses on promoting women's economic empowerment in tourism through partnerships with hotel chains and other stakeholders. This will involve 'improving employment/entrepreneurship opportunities for women by facilitating their access to jobs and/or participation in supply-chains, and by creating possibilities for career advancement'.[3] WITEP has four main components: Employment Skills; Supply Chain; Career Advancement; and Gender Awareness. The focus of WITEP is primarily on women's economic empowerment. However, the Gender Awareness

component includes gender equality training for management and communities, expanding the notion of empowerment to a broader conception. The UNWTO website states that the pilot implementation phase of WITEP is currently being designed and UNWTO's Ethics and Social Responsibility Programme is in negotiation with a series of potential partners from the public and private sector.

Finally, the collaboration between UN Women and UNWTO proposed the development of a Tourism and Gender Portal, which would 'create a global reference point on tourism and gender, providing resources, information, and a space for awareness-raising and dialogue. The overall aim of the Portal is to contribute to the improvement of women's role in tourism worldwide, by providing a global forum for exchanging information and ideas'. The Tourism and Gender Portal was expected to have five main sections: Awareness-raising and Communication; Good Practices; Training and Empowerment; Networking; and Research and Resources. However, as stated on the UNWTO website, the Portal is currently still in a 'conceptual phase'. The website states that the Portal will be developed after the pilot of WITEP has been carried out, subject to securing external funding.[4]

A further activity to mention during the period 2007–2012 is the UNWTO Regional Commission for Africa Seminar in June 2012, for which the theme was 'Responsible Tourism: Opportunities for Women and Youth', in Calabar, Nigeria. The seminar 'explored the ways in which the tourism sector can improve conditions for women and young persons throughout the region, and, in so doing, benefit the tourism trade at large, view towards enhancing tourism's positive effects on the economic and social development of Africa. The Seminar gathered policy-makers, representatives of the tourism industry, communities engaged in/interested in tourism development, women's cooperatives, educational institutions, non-governmental organizations (NGOs) and civil society organisations.'[5] The event focused on three key areas: forging women leaders in African tourism; strengthening entrepreneurship in

Africa's tourism sector; and capacity building and community development. Women leaders from different areas of African tourism and politics presented on a range of issues. The author of this chapter was UNWTO's invited consultant for facilitating the event. In my concluding comments, I outlined the key challenges and opportunities that were identified during the seminar. Following the event, a collaboration proposal was developed, which recommended the development of an Empowerment Programme for African Women and Youth in Tourism. It was also agreed that 'UNWTO should provide ongoing technical support and establish itself as a reference point for communication, exchange and information in this area'.[6]

Assessing UNWTO's Work on Gender Equality Since 2012

Based on this overview of UNWTO's work between 2007 and 2012, it is now necessary to critically evaluate the extent to which the joint commitments made by UN Women and UNWTO in 2008 and re-affirmed in 2011 have been fulfilled. Here I follow up in turn on each aspect of the commitments made, in order to comprehensively review the extent to which any progress has been made.

First, I turn to the UNWTO/UN Women Action Plan, as outlined in Box 2.1 above. For points 1–3, the 'multi-stakeholder taskforce' was never established; the second edition of the Global Report on Women in Tourism was commissioned in 2018; and the Gender and Tourism Portal does not exist. In terms of Point 4 – build international awareness about opportunities for women in tourism – little has been done in this area since 2012. Finally, for Point 5 – call upon UNWTO members to take vigorous steps to support gender mainstreaming in national development processes, so as to achieve women's equality in the tourism sector – guidelines on gender mainstreaming for National Tourism Administrations were produced. However, the guidelines were never approved or published by UNWTO.

As such, this aspect remains unfinished, and UNWTO has not taken any steps to encourage members to advance in this area.

Second, it is useful to review the recommendations from the Global Report 2010, to see which of these have been implemented. The recommendations were presented in two different areas – by theme and by stakeholder, as set out in Boxes 2.2 and 2.3. In terms of the thematic recommendations – on Employment, Entrepreneurship, Education, Leadership and Community – it is difficult to assess whether any of these recommendations have been addressed. Likewise, with the stakeholder recommendations – addressed to the private sector; public sector including tourism policy-makers; and international organizations and civil society. As no mechanism was put in place for monitoring and evaluating the implementation of the recommendations, no information is available on whether these have been taken forward by any of the actors targeted. Moreover, as set out above, the report committed to re-evaluating the indicators at least every 3 years in order to assess how effective policy actions are in improving the situation of women in tourism. As such, the failure to commission further Global Reports has led to two key challenges for gender equality in tourism. First, there is no updated information on women in tourism beyond that included in the Global Report 2010, meaning that stakeholders are not able to access recent information or analysis. Second, there has been no pressure or momentum to implement the recommendations, as there has been no organization leading and monitoring progress across the application of the recommendations. It is hoped that the publishing of the second Global Report will be able to address these issues in a positive manner.

As such, there has been little activity on gender equality in UNWTO since 2012. The brochure 'Tourism and the Sustainable Development Goals'[7] – published in September 2015 – includes two sentences on Goal 5 in the United Nations World Tourism Organization, but this cannot be considered substantive work or evidence of organizational commitment. The most recent UNWTO initiative that at least includes gender issues is the Discussion Paper on the occasion of the International Year of Sustainable Tourism for Development 2017 (www.tourism4development2017.org/wp-content/uploads/2017/05/070417_iy2017-discussion-paper.pdf). This was produced by the International Relations department – not the Ethics and Social Dimensions of Tourism Programme that developed all the initiatives presented above. UNWTO invited comments on the Discussion Paper, and the following analysis is an excerpt from the comment presented by Equality in Tourism, an independent, non-profit women's organization dedicated to ensuring women have an equal voice in and share of the benefits from tourism globally, of which the author and several other authors in this book are directors and associates. It is useful to see how gender is framed in this paper in order to understand UNWTO's latest positioning on the issues. Tourism is hailed for its role in 'empowering women and youth', quoting statistics from both the UNWTO Global Report on Women in Tourism 2010 and the 2013 ILO paper on women's employment in tourism. Building on this, the paper argues that 'enhancing the opportunities for women and young people requires positive and purposeful action by tourism businesses, supported by governments, trade bodies and the voluntary sector'. A number of priorities for action are identified:

- Gender analysis and monitoring of employment conditions, especially in terms of the wages offered to women and men in the tourism sector.
- Setting and reporting on targets; tailored recruitment policies.
- Tailored training and capacity building for women and youth.
- Positive social benefit and support packages (including maternity conditions).
- Codes of good practice.
- Well-directed communication.

However, as argued in the Equality in Tourism comment, there are no measures put in place in the paper to demonstrate how these actions will be funded or monitored. In particular, there is no discussion of how these are to be funded, and what resources – both financial and human – will be put in place for this. Second, the paper fails to engage with the literature and contemporary debates on women, gender and tourism. The sources on which it draws – predominantly the Global Report on Women in Tourism 2010 – are long out of date. It employs a very basic understanding and analysis of gender issues and as such does not offer much to discussions of how tourism can contribute to SDG5. It is hoped that UNWTO will respond substantively to the Equality in Tourism comment, and it will be possible to re-open a dialogue on the role of UNWTO in promoting gender equality in the tourism industry.

Based on this quick review of UNWTO activity since 2012, we can conclude that there has been little or no activity in terms of gender equality in the institution. Three main reasons can be put forward for this. First, it is important to highlight that during the period 2007–2012 there was a dedicated budget for gender equality activities in UNWTO, resulting from the Memorandum of Understanding (MOU) with UN Women, which committed both organizations to funding a range of activities. Among other aspects, this budget funded the first Global Report, the development of the WITEP and the support of a gender adviser working as a consultant for UNWTO (the author of this chapter). However, since 2012 there has been no budget available for gender equality activities. As such, the commissioning of the second and third Global Reports, the development of WITEP and the publishing of the Gender Mainstreaming Guidelines have not been implemented. Moreover, since 2012 there has been no gender adviser working with UNWTO, and as such there has been no specialist knowledge or expertise on which to draw. Second, the MOU with UN Women – although effectively still valid – has not been renewed or revisited. Indeed, after the publishing of the Global Report, UN Women did not commit to any further activities or funding. This was important for UNWTO because UN Women had acted as an external pressure to be active and to take gender equality seriously. Without this pressure, it was difficult for actors within the Ethics and Social Dimensions Programme to argue the case for continued funding.

Finally, and related to the previous point, there has been no commitment to gender equality from UNWTO senior management. While gender issues were mentioned in a number of speeches and core documents, in reality there has been no substantive support from the secretary-general or programme directors for gender equality to be a priority issue for UNWTO. Indeed, there were many cases of resistance to this issue – both implicit and explicit – from a range of actors in UNWTO. This included questioning the validity of the issue; suggesting this was a waste of money; and arguing that women were already equal in tourism. These three factors – lack of funding, lack of support from UN Women and resistance to gender equality throughout UNWTO – served to undermine the progress made up to 2012. As a consequence, the review of UNWTO activities in this area from 2012 is – to put it mildly – disappointing. Nevertheless, the election of a new Secretary-General and the commissioning of a second Global Report give rise to cautious optimism that gender equality can be put firmly on the agenda of tourism policy and practice. Given this disappointing performance, we now go on to explore what can be done to address some of these shortcomings.

Conclusions and Ways Forward

What can we learn from this review of gender equality policy in UNWTO? Two key conclusions can be drawn. First, gender equality policy is a serious issue for the tourism industry. The Global Report on Women in Tourism 2010 offered a preliminary baseline for tourism NGOs and women's organizations to provide evidence of gender inequality in the tourism sector. This report was available to use as a tool for organizations to claim the need to address these inequalities. It became a tool for gender and tourism scholars, and inspired some countries to commission national reports on this area, as in the case of Mexico in 2011. Moreover, the existence of a report published by two UN agencies added credibility to those

working to increase gender equality and women's rights and empowerment in different areas of the sector. While the first report was somewhat flawed – both in its approach and analysis – nevertheless it was a useful tool for advocacy. However, the long delay of a follow-up report meant that those concerned with these issues did not have access to updated and relevant information. Initiatives such as WITEP, the Gender and Tourism Portal and the Gender Mainstreaming Guidelines have a strong potential to effect meaningful change for women in the tourism sector. However, in their current state they cannot be accessed or used by other organizations wishing to take these ideas forward and can be considered wasted potential for increasing gender equality in tourism.

Second, this analysis of UNWTO initiatives shows the absolute necessity of dedicating specialist resources, knowledge and expertise to gender equality. During the period 2007–2012, as we have seen, a number of activities and products were developed, in collaboration with specialists in the field of gender and tourism. However, the lack of funding between 2012 and 2018 meant that little progress was made on gender issues in UNWTO between these years. Lack of funding can be explained by a general resistance to taking gender equality seriously in UNWTO, expressed both implicitly and explicitly. This is also compounded by UN Women's lack of interest in tourism as a serious thematic issue for their work on gender equality and women's empowerment. More than 20 years of feminist work on gender mainstreaming in international organizations has taught us that gender equality does not happen by accident (see, for example, Daly, 2005; Walby, 2005). It requires funding, research, knowledge and senior management commitment. The example of gender equality activity in UNWTO is a clear illustration of what happens when high-level senior management support for an issue is withdrawn, delayed, withheld or denied.

Following this critique, it is useful to offer some concrete action points for moving this agenda forward. First, organizations concerned with gender equality in the tourism industry need to engage more substantively with UNWTO, as the key institution for tourism policy and practice worldwide. This involves increasing the pressure on UNWTO senior management to take gender equality seriously, and to dedicate resources and expertise to this topic. Second, further research and analysis need to be conducted to explore why the tourism industry has remained stubbornly resistant to incorporating demands for gender equality – especially compared with other sectors and industries. Even heavily male-dominated sectors such as mining[8] and energy[9] have developed guidelines and good practices for gender mainstreaming. As such, it is important to explore the factors that keep the tourism industry out of reach of pressure for increased gender equality. Finally, we need to hold the tourism industry, UN Women and UNWTO to account for the lack of gender equality initiatives across the sector. Collective action is required here to draw up proposals for monitoring and evaluating progress in this area, with a focus on encouraging the relevant organizations – both public and private sector – to meet their international comments to gender equality and women's empowerment, under SDG5 and other legal frameworks. Existing initiatives have laid the groundwork for a future agenda in gender equality in the tourism industry. It is up to us as researchers, activists and practitioners to increase the pressure and gather momentum to move the issue forward, with the overall aim of promoting transformative change for women in tourism.

Notes

[1] Address by Francesco Frangialli, Secretary-General of UNWTO, to the fifty-eighth Session of the United Nations General Assembly, New York, 7 November 2003, www.unwto.org/newsroom/speeches/2003/disc_sg_ag_nu_7nov03_A4.pdf.

[2] www2.unwto.org/en/news/2011-11-03/unwto-and-un-women-commit-further-ongoing-collaboration.

[3] http://ethics.unwto.org/content/women-tourism-empowerment-programme-witep.

[4] http://ethics.unwto.org/en/content/tourism-and-gender-portal.

[5] http://ethics.unwto.org/en/event/regional-seminar-responsible-tourism-opportunities-women-and-youth-nigeria-june-2012.

[6] http://ethics.unwto.org/en/event/regional-seminar-responsible-tourism-opportunities-women-and-youth-nigeria-june-2012.

[7] www.e-unwto.org/doi/pdf/10.18111/9789284417254.

[8] www.globalminingstandards.org/women-mining-steps-strategies-best-practices-gender-diversity.

[9] www.undp.org/content/dam/undp/library/gender/Gender%20and%20Environment/PB3_Africa_Gender-and-Energy.pdf.

References

Cole, S. (2016) A gendered political ecology of tourism and water. In: Mostafanezhad, M., Norum, R., Shelton, E. and Thompson, A. (eds) *Political Ecology of Tourism: Community, Power and the Environment*. Routledge, New York and London.

Daly, M. (2005) Gender mainstreaming in theory and practice. *Social Politics: International Studies in Gender, State and Society* 12(3), 433–450.

Ferguson, L. (2010) Interrogating 'gender' in development policy and practice: the World Bank, tourism and microenterprise in Honduras. *International Feminist Journal of Politics* 12(1), 3–24.

Ferguson, L. (2011) Promoting gender equality and empowering women? Tourism and the third Millennium Development Goal. *Current Issues in Tourism* 14(3), 235–249.

Ferguson, L. and Moreno, D. (2016) Gender expertise and the private sector. In: Bustelo, M. and Forest, M. (eds) *The Politics of Feminist Knowledge Transfer: A Critical Reflection on Gender Training and Gender Expertise*. Palgrave Macmillan, Basingstoke, UK.

Hafner-Burton, E.M. and Pollack, M.A. (2002) Mainstreaming gender in global governance. *European Journal of International Relations* 8(3), 339–373.

International Labour Organization (ILO) (2013) *International Perspectives on Women and Work in Hotels, Catering and Tourism*. ILO, Geneva.

UNWTO/UN Women (2011) *Global Report on Women in Tourism 2010*. Madrid: UNWTO.

Vizcaino-Suárez, L., Serrano Barquín, R., Cruz Jiménez, G. and Pastor Alfonso, M. (2014) El género en la investigación y las políticas turísticas en México. Asociación Española de Expertos Científicos en Turismo (AECIT), Castellón, Mexico.

Walby, S. (2005) Gender mainstreaming: productive tensions in theory and practice. *Social Politics* 12(3), 321–343.

Nukul's Story

Nukul Jorlopo

Fig. S2. Nukul with buffalo.

This country does not always feel like my home. My home is the jungle.

I, Nukul Jorlopo, am from the Karen hilltribe of Thailand. Though my ancestors settled here long before the Thai people, my tribe are treated like outsiders and made to feel like they do not belong. When I speak Thai, they know I am from the hilltribe because I do not speak right. I feel I am lower than Thai people, especially Thai men. We are farmers and perceived as poor, uneducated and dirty by the dominant culture in Thailand. So most Karen women stay in their village where life makes sense and where they are not subjected to racism and discrimination. But while the work of a farmer takes care of the family's land, it does not earn any income. So many Karen people venture to the city to find work. I was scared to go to the city. I'm scared of being lied to, taken advantage of or trafficked.

Four years ago an American social business entrepreneur, Alexa Pham, opened the Chai Lai Orchid, an ecolodge and empowerment programme for women at risk of human trafficking. In Thailand, the most at risk are women of ethnic minorities, like me. I became pregnant with my son when I was at university and had to stop my studies. I was struggling alone to support my son and help my parents. I had little hope. Two years ago, I joined the Chai Lai Orchid family women's programme at Chai Lai Orchid, called Daughters Rising. It trains women in hospitality, provides English classes and empowerment workshops in everything from internet safety to kickboxing, as well as providing a full salary and free housing. Women in surrounding villages can work close to home, rather than stepping into the vulnerability that comes with moving to the city.

Since joining Chai Lai Orchid, I have become a manager and then, a social business entrepreneur, myself, opening the first indigenous women-run tour company in Thailand – Chai Lai Sisters. Now I provide many jobs and income for my village and I am treated with respect.

Now I have met so many people and I want to travel to different countries. Now I know how to use the internet and if I don't know something I can learn, I can teach myself. I feel proud of myself and proud of my culture. I don't get so anxious about going to the city. I am not scared to be myself.

I believe tourism can confront patriarchy by making women aware of their own power. Power is realized through providing opportunities to learn, to work and to be in community with other women who lift one another up – women find this at the Chai Lai Orchid.

http://explore@chailaiorchid.com

3 Feminist Perspectives in the Development of Action Plans for Tourism

Daniela Moreno Alarcón*

Equality in Tourism, Complutense University of Madrid, Madrid, Spain

Introduction

Over the past few years there has been a boom in the idea of 'doing something' for women in tourism but not so much in reducing gender inequality and ending women's disempowerment. Therefore, at a global level there are insufficient practical actions (strategies, plans, programmes or projects) that prioritize sustainable tourism development based on gender equality and women's empowerment. The development of specific national tourism action plans from a gender perspective is one of the main challenges in the work for enhancing sustainable and responsible tourism development. To date, a few governments are working in official ways on tourism from a gender perspective, and a few countries are pathfinders on gender and tourism and are creating tourism action plans or strategies from a gender perspective. Nevertheless, there is plenty of work to do in order to plan and manage tourism from a gender perspective, especially when it comes to feminist criteria.

Drawing on my experience as a consultant and academic on gender and tourism, my aim here is to explain the importance of tourism action plans from a gender perspective, as well as draw out the implications thereof for discussions of sustainable tourism. I begin by presenting the tension that exists with the gender perspective from a feminist approach and the consequence that this may have in a correct understanding of the real meaning and purpose of a gender perspective. In order to comprehend the real purpose of a gender action plan, this chapter stresses the urgent need for understanding that gender equality needs a feminist approach in order to conduct a good gender analysis. According to Lagarde (1996, p. 13) 'gender analysis is the synthesis between the theory of a gender perspective and the so-called gender perspective derived from the feminist conception of the world and of life'.[1] Valcárcel (2008) sees in feminism a way of living, a political instrument that dissects what happens in a given reality. However, good gender analyses are achieved on the basis of a feminist policy because 'if there is a bad gender practice, a good feminist policy must correct it'[2] (Valcárcel, 2008, p. 219).

The second part of the chapter provides a reflection on the tourism sector's engagement from a gender perspective, concerning the development of tourism action plans, using two experiences I had the opportunity to work on, one in Nicaragua and the other

* E-mail: daniela@equalityintourism.org

in Cape Verde. In the concluding section, I highlight some of the elements for consideration in developing tourism action plans from a gender perspective.

Making Gender Analysis a Reality through a Practical Tool: An Action Plan

What does gender equality mean? This is the first question to ask when developing an action plan. Frequently gender analyses have been developed under the shadow of three perspectives. First, like 'a question of women only' or '*mujerío*', which means a cluster of women. This approach tends to emphasize the differences between women and men and/or to promote the 'discourse of excellence' that emphasizes the superiority of women in the framework of patriarchal codes. For example, girls are more mature than boys (and then these boys get more money for the same work); women are the best caregivers; women have a lot of 'commitment' to their work because they work at full capacity (for less money); or since she had the baby she is now an efficient worker because she does the same work in less time (for less money due to the part-time contract). The second approach could be termed a 'partial' gender perspective, which recognizes that women do have struggles, but in general this perspective never says clearly why women face a wide variety of limitations. Third, we have the ideal scenario, which is a gender analysis from a feminist perspective that aims to transform and improve any development model by identifying the causes of discrimination against women in order to reduce gender gaps.

Gender equality without feminism is confined to reproducing and making invisible the gaps between men and women. This also draws, for example, on the fact that having more or only women in a specific initiative does not guarantee gender equality if the symbolic and normative codes promoted by patriarchy are not analysed as the main challenges for reducing poverty in developed and developing countries. Consequently, this is not simply a matter of 'giving

more space to women'. Rather, it is about transforming gender relations and women's lives. At its core, after all, gender inequality is not a random, unfortunate occurrence – it is a systematic problem. A gender perspective, guided by a feminist thinking, must articulate the normative consequences that come from patriarchy because this is the only way to transform something that seems to be immovable.

According to Hunt and Lateef (2006) a gender action plan is a framework for ensuring women's participation in programmes and projects, and also it is a roadmap to translate gender mainstreaming into concrete actions. The literature about gender mainstreaming has argued the importance of deepening its meaning to strengthen its impact on the lives of women and to remodel gender relations. Daly (2005), with her research about gender mainstreaming in theory and practice in eight countries, considers that gender mainstreaming has been better developed as a policy rather than as a concept. Clisby (2005) remarks on the importance of ensuring gender mainstreaming (and avoiding male-streaming) when providing capacity building. This is to ensure positive action for women, as you cannot make assumptions about women's capabilities and their relations with the community as these could in fact reinforce the discrimination from the outset.

Walby (2005) discusses why gender mainstreaming, a powerful feminist strategy, has not had the expected results. She argues that it is necessary to address the tension between 'gender equality' and the 'mainstream', and to mainstream it with other complex inequalities such as ethnicity, class, sexual orientations and age. She also discusses the implications of gender mainstreaming interventions done by transnational development organizations, which sometimes clash with local elements such as poverty priorities or feminist cultural issues. This is especially important in tourism development given the transnational nature of both gender and tourism.

The coordinators of two rural women's empowerment organizations explained to me that they were concerned because feminism is absent from international non-governmental organizations' (INGO) funding strategies. The INGOs give money without providing the necessary information and tools for the empowerment to be sustainable. When the funding finishes the projects end. These INGOs are not interested in international frameworks particularly around the Agenda 2030. They no longer believe in these agendas as they never see the results – instead they build their own gender mainstreaming and empowerment strategies, which are sometimes more powerful in terms of results and concrete actions.

International tourism development – through international organizations, INGOs and the private sector – do not foster gender mainstreaming in terms of political will or budget. Furthermore, international gender organizations have given little consideration to international tourism development; this is the reason we need feminists on board (Moreno, 2017a). This is very important because it is the starting point to negotiate resources and support from the stakeholders for developing and implementing an action plan. The process of developing a gender action plan also requires us to:

1) See the 'feminist taboos' such as the 'quick and ready answers to the debate on gender mainstreaming or gender equality and technocratic v/s participatory' (Lombardo *et al.*, 2010, p. 113); or
2) 'the interpretation of processes of bending and stretching in mainly negative terms, or
3) the tendency to look for negative effects that reinforce patriarchy first'. (Lombardo *et al.*, 2010, p. 114).

In general terms, it means to be open to critical reflection on the role of feminist training, academic and practical feminist thinking and gender mainstreaming in itself. For a better clarification and based on my experience as a consultant, Box 3.1 shows the main points that should be considered in the developing of an action plan.

With all these elements, the process of developing a gender action plan turns into an improvement of women's and men's lives due to its impact on specific topics

---

> **Box 3.1.** Gender action plan: my key points.
>
> - In case of hesitation always believe in women, unless the accumulated data prove otherwise.
> - Ask about the main resistances towards gender equality. Be aware that the word 'feminism' and/or 'gender violence' are not allowed in many places.
> - Understand in a deep way how reproductive work affects the participation of women in the labour market, but also in their entire quality of life.
> - Analyse the causes and implications of the feminization of poverty.
> - Analyse, with the help of local women/feminist organizations, their priorities as well as the meaning of women's rights or feminism.
> - In the countries with a tendency to socialism it is very important to be aware that the class dispute does not always match with the gender dispute.
> - Work together with an ally to develop the plan but also for promoting 'sororidad,' which means the solidarity between women deprived because of patriarchy.

---

such as working conditions, health, security, violence or the environment. However, mostly it reveals the real will from institutions, governments or people in general, to fight against poverty reduction in a broad and responsible way. In accordance with Hunt and Undurraga (2009), to place gender mainstreaming from a feminist approach at the core of any action plan should facilitate the process of having a feminist political transformatory agenda. According to Lee-Gosselin *et al.* (2013), this should not be limited to a technical agenda, but should also address cultural dimensions or managing cultural/social change.

Tourism Action Plans from a Gender Perspective

Tourism from a gender perspective has been one of the missing parts of sustainable tourism development (Moreno, 2017c). Is it actually possible to achieve sustainable tourism if gender relations are not being considered? Is it responsible to promote sustainable tourism for development without considering gender-based violence, working conditions from a gender perspective or environmental impacts without knowing how they affect women and men in different ways? What about human trafficking and sexual exploitation related to tourism? There are so many issues to cover, all of which are immensely important subjects for enabling tourism to be a sector committed to sustainability for development.

It is not clear why it has taken so long for gender equality to be given serious consideration by tourism development. The United Nations declared 2017 as the International Year of Sustainable Tourism for Development (y2017). In this framework and responding to the World Tourism Organization (UNWTO) Discussion Paper on the occasion of the y2017, the organization Equality in Tourism recommended the following actions to be taken by UNWTO in order to address the gaps in its work on gender equality (Box 3.2).

The right question to understand tourism from a gender perspective should not be based simply and only on where women are in tourism. It should be about what is happening with women related to tourism (not

only with the ones that work in the sector) and why it happens. As a consequence, the efforts should be focused not only on tourism from a gender perspective and on how gender should be understood in tourism, but on how tourism should be interpreted in gender theory and practice (Moreno, 2017a). Only in this way, will tourism be an ally – theoretically and practically – of women's human condition by helping to end gender inequality and the disempowerment of women – both of which are the main causes of non-compliance with sustainable development and human rights (Moreno, 2017b).

Examples from the field

Having established a broad explanation of a gender action plan as well as the main objectives that tourism from a gender perspective should have, I now set out two examples of practice. Here I present two cases, one from Nicaragua and the other from Cape Verde, to highlight the main differences between the two countries. In general terms, both countries are worried about women's and gender issues in tourism, which allowed the creation of an action plan on gender and tourism. However, the results of each are different due to contexts, political will, budgets and the resistances associated with gender and feminist work. Table 3.1 provides a brief description of each.

In both cases the writing of the action plan is very good because they use the main tools and legal framework related to gender equality. But there are limitations, particularly in the Nicaraguan case, even though this country had a bigger donor and budget than Cape Verde. They also had the opportunity to implement the action plan in a large community-based tourism project at the national level. In Cape Verde, the situation was different. Here they only had the budget to create an action plan and then to use it as a political tool in order to look for more opportunities for its implementation. The other limitation was the political context. In Nicaragua the tensions between government and gender/feminist organizations are increasing

---

Box 3.2. A gender perspective in UNWTO.

- Establish a dedicated budget for gender equality and Sustainable Development Goal 5 (SDG5) within UNWTO to ensure that necessary actions and programmes can be carried out. This should be done in collaboration with specialists in gender and tourism in order to ensure that UNWTO work matches international norms and standards on gender equality. This is in line with the UN System-wide Action Plan on Gender Equality and the Empowerment of Women (UN-SWAP).
- Update the Global Report on Women in Tourism 2010. This was originally intended to be a triennial report. As such, it was expected that this report would have been updated in 2013 and 2016.
- Review the literature and best practices on gender equality in tourism and update the Discussion Paper accordingly, drawing on the available expertise and knowledge in the field.

Source: Equality in Tourism (2017, p. 4)

Table 3.1. Cases – action plan on gender and tourism (AP).

Nicaragua	Cape Verde
The gender and tourism AP was finalized in 2014. It was financed by an Agency of International Cooperation and coordinated by the national tourist authorities. Its aim is to counteract gender inequalities in the tourism sector and tourism institutions through the institutionalization and mainstreaming of gender practices and promotion of affirmative action for individual and collective empowerment, and to make visible and recognize the productive work of women. Its specific objectives mention the need for changing the institutional mindset and creating a Gender Unit located in the National Tourist Institution.	In 2015 the UN Women country office commissioned the development of an AP. The main objective was to incorporate tourism in the country's National Gender Plan as they see tourism as a main sector for the country, as well as an opportunity to underline the importance of gender equality in the country.

due to the conservative environment, which is reaching a scale that is constraining women's human rights (abortion is not allowed and sexual violence is an endemic problem). In contrast, in Cape Verde (abortion has been allowed since 1987) the coordination between the government and women/feminist organizations is polite and they have continuing good relations (currently one of the main gender experts has become the Minister of Health and Social Affairs).

The most controversial issue was the methodology. Both countries conducted a participative methodology that gave a voice to the local people, but the main difference was the kind of people who were allowed to participate. In Nicaragua, women's organizations (including academia or the people from the UN) were not invited to participate. In an informal conversation with the coordinator of the main Master's degree in gender studies in Nicaragua I was told that in the beginning their participation was guaranteed, but at the end the government made it difficult for them. This showed a total lack of consideration for the academic world and highlighted a clear resistance that the government had when someone tried to reach gender equality in tourism from a critical point of view.

In Cape Verde the context was more realistic with the needs of people in general. Here it was possible to conduct a participative methodology with private, public and civil organizations, and in all cases women's organizations were invited. It was also possible to work together with UN Women and with the Gender Equality Institute when gathering information and writing the action plan. A key stakeholder meeting included all linked ministries and organizations. This is a clear example of the political will that is necessary to reach sustainable tourism.

Regarding endorsement of the action plan: in Cape Verde, political will ensured the action plan was endorsed when presented at events for public, private and civil society organizations, and a second phase was set up. In Nicaragua, due to the resistance, the action plan was literally put in the drawer because it was never approved at the highest level of the government. This meant that the strategy was rejected because of 'conservative' political issues. This fact affected the entire national and international working group, mostly because they never imagined that the government could consider gender as a threat. In relation to this, one of the managers of the funding institution told me:

Look, Daniela, I'm going to be honest with you. Our Tourist Institution (name changed) does not want to launch the gender technical assistance strategy we are planning for next year because it could have an impact at the political level. For me gender equality could be complex, but it is not something so terrible. It's such a nice and interesting subject but I never imagined it could be so delicate because I've always seen it in rural initiatives. I see that it can work, but suddenly the director is very scared because of political interference so we have to drop the gender technical assistance. I never imagined it would reach that level. All these people are good, but this happens. How can it be so difficult to raise it at the political level?[3]

Nowadays, the action plan in Nicaragua has stopped and the project and budget are finished, none of the actions have been carried out, except some training which may or may not have been conducted according to the action plan. In Cape Verde the situation is different. They have created the gender and tourism unit, and in 2018, the training for this unit will start.

Lessons learnt from the field

The two cases presented tell us that developing a tourism action plan from a gender perspective is very demanding work. This happens not only because there are no mature examples of good practice of what to do or not to do, but also principally because this tool is neither a tourism action plan nor a gender action plan. A tourism plan from a gender perspective requires a deep understanding of both areas to measure the ways, the dialogue and the expertise in order to find connections between these two worlds. Therefore, it is necessary to promote gender awareness in 'tourism contexts', and on the other hand, to boost tourist awareness in 'gender contexts'. For more clarification, Box 3.3 shows some gender and tourism starting questions.

In general terms, the objectives of a tourism action plan from a gender perspective should be the following:

- Enhance gender perspective at the core of the planning and management of tourism.
- Advance the implementation of the National Gender Plan.
- Bring into practice the gender and tourism thinking that has been developed during the past 20 years.
- Analyse tourism from a gender perspective as well as the entire gender relations of the country.

Box 3.3. Key starting questions for a tourism action plan from a gender perspective.

- What kinds of opportunities are there for a gender perspective of tourism within the current and future local policies related to tourist employability and sustainable tourism development?
- What historical resistances on gender issues are there in the country that could affect sustainable tourism development?
- How could the public sector, private sector, civil society and international organizations work both separately and together on this issue?
- Are there potential budgets to address tourism from a gender perspective?
- What kinds of work have social movements done in tourism related to working conditions, environment, women's rights, etc.?

- Create a space for sharing between institutions to promote tourism from a gender perspective.
- Reduce the gaps between the increasing 'tourism mainstreaming' and the lack of consideration of gender mainstreaming. This is important to increase the sustainability of tourism development.

It is also important to be aware of resistance to gender equality because the essence of developing a plan is the ability to identify (and solve) these causes of resistance as they appear in the process. By doing this, you create the activities and set the goals. Table 3.2 illustrates the most common challenges that emerge during the process of developing a tourism plan from a gender perspective. It does so by further developing the classification proposed by Women in Development Europe (WIDE), in the framework of the current context of gender and tourism.

These types of resistance are also a breeding ground for the 'retrospective nature of gender analysis' (Ferguson and Moreno, 2015). This means that a gender perspective is addressed only to 'tick a box' and not as a strategy. In this case gender and tourism is understood as a showcase of women's projects and not as a tool to transform the bad praxis of tourism in terms of gender equality and women's empowerment.

Table 3.2. Types of resistance.

Resistance	Common phrase	Positive forward actions to achieve an action plan
Denial: Here gender equality is not a concern, therefore, discrimination against women in tourism doesn't exist.	'Tourism does not strengthen roles and stereotypes because it is a new activity.'	Brief with data and examples from theory and fieldwork on gender and tourism at international and local levels. An initial good strategy based on responsible tourism will be needed.
'The problem of women': Speeches mostly made by men. This is only lip service, and this person makes a lot of effort to showing awareness of 'women's situation', which is actually lacking. There is not any feminist content or even a real concern about the patriarchy in the lives of women and men. Any feminist could detect this situation.	'Tourism opens the doors to women.'	Search for campaigns or empirical studies that show how gender equality improves the sustainability of tourism. It is also important to consider a more participative approach for showing the gaps between men and women in tourism. Give a lot of examples.
Talking about women: Recognizes the importance of taking action, but on a very small (almost invisible) scale. Focused exclusively on the participation of women in the frame of the exclusive interests of the organization/person. Recognizes the problem in a rhetorical way: too much talking and not enough action.	'We incorporate gender in tourism.'	It is important to give the message that gender perspective goes beyond one's own interests and can improve many organizations and the lives of many people. Make a clear distinction between the results that impact on women and the ones that impact on gender equality.
Recommend women/gender research: This is okay, if it doesn't delay the process that will allow a real change for women. The real problem comes when this is done to delay a solution and erase the problem from the picture.	'Tourism is an engine for gender equality.'	Research on gender and tourism doesn't mean postponing a solution because research is the initial step and a great justification to do something quickly. Spread the results of the research that would also promote an agenda on gender and tourism.
The gender person[4]: Having a gender and tourism expert as part of any process is elementary. The problem appears when she/he has to deal with personal resistances and responsibilities, which delay the overall work.	'Gender is too difficult or, on the contrary, is too easy for me so I don't see the need to participate in the work promoted by the gender expert.'	Every person is responsible for the gender and tourism results. It is very important to give space for an organization/project to debate in order to know the resistances.
Putting women in front: Resolve the 'gender problem' by inviting a lot of women to participate in a committee, meeting, event, etc.	'Tourism empowers women. In my organization we believe in women.'	'Women in tourism' is not gender in tourism. Women's/feminist/gender and tourism organizations should work together not only to know how many women are working in tourism, but also to understand if their work is valued by the labour market. We need here women connected with the gender reality and with the disempowerment of women.

Conclusions

In this chapter, I have explored the implications of the importance of developing tourism action plans from a gender perspective and the importance of the feminist lens in this process. The chapter also showed the importance of political will and healthy political environment in developing and implementing an action plan on gender and tourism. One of the main issues is the ability to deal with the resistance that comes from different sectors, especially from the tourism sector: even if they highlight the words gender or women, the panorama may change when it comes to concrete work.

It is also important to point out that gender analysis in tourism should not be considered as a type of tourism. I say this because when the process begins, there is a tendency to position 'gender tourism', which makes it difficult to deliver the message of gender mainstreaming. By identifying gender tourism as such, this can be construed as 'tourism of inequality' – because gender itself implies unequal power relations between women and men. This fact is understood as a bad praxis because even when the word gender is highlighted, it does not promote the benefits of the sustainable development of tourism. On the contrary, it is a way of affirming the inconsistencies that exist when it comes to raising the sustainability of tourism, and that is why there is a huge gap between what is written, approved and done.

It is necessary for all countries to work with tourism from a gender perspective. For this to happen, it is also important that international tourism organizations such as UNWTO clearly support integrating gender equality in tourism (see Chapter 2 by Lucy Ferguson, this volume). This requires working in collaboration with those organizations that are working on tourism from a gender perspective. It is time for social movements, particularly feminist and women's organizations to engage with tourism because tourism will influence women's lives in many multidimensional ways.

Notes

[1] Translated from the original version: 'el análisis de género es la síntesis entre la teoría de género y la llamada perspectiva de género derivada de la concepción feminist del mundo y de la vida'.
[2] Translated from the orginal version: 'si hay una mala práctica de género, una buena política, feminista, debe corregirla'.
[3] Translated from the original version: 'Mira Daniela yo te voy a ser sincera. El instituto de turismo quería botar la asistencia técnica en género que tenemos prevista para el próximo año porque podría tener una incidencia a nivel político. Para mí el género puede ser complejo pero no es algo tan terrible. Es un tema tan bonito e interesante pero nunca me imaginé que pudiera ser tan delicado porque siempre lo vi en iniciativas rurales. Yo veo que se puede trabajar pero de repente viene la directora muy asustada porque hay que botar la asistencia técnica por el tema de incidencia política. Nunca imaginé que llegara a ese nivel. Toda esta gente es buena, pero ocurre esto. ¿Cómo puede ser tan difícil plantearlo a nivel político?'
[4] To read more about this please see Ferguson, L. (2015) 'This is our gender person': the messy business of working as a gender expert in international development. *International Feminist Journal of Politics* 17(3), 380–397.

References

Clisby, S. (2005) Gender mainstreaming or just more male-streaming? *Gender and Development* 13(2), 23–35.

Daly, M. (2005) Gender mainstreaming in theory and practice. *Social Politics: International Studies in Gender, State and Society* 12(3), 433–450.

Equality in Tourism (2017) UNWTO Discussion Paper on the occasion of the International Year of Sustainable Tourism for Development 2017: Equality in Tourism comment. Equality in Tourism, London. Available at:

http://equalityintourism.org/wp-content/uploads/2017/07/Equality-in-Tourism-response-to-UNWTO-IY17-paper.pdf (accessed 26 February 2018).

Ferguson, L. and Moreno, D. (2015) Gender and sustainable tourism: reflections on theory and practice. *Journal of Sustainable Tourism*, 23(3), 401–416.

Hunt, J. and Lateef, S. (2006) Making gender mainstreaming a reality: using gender action plans. Available at: https://www.researchgate.net/publication/261135535_Making_Gender_Mainstreaming_a_Reality_Using_Gender_Action_Plans (accessed 21 May 2017).

Hunt, A. and Undurraga, R. (2009) From rhetoric to reality: a critical analysis of the National Action Plan for the Achievement of Gender Equality in Kosovo. *Studies in Ethnicity and Nationalism* 9(1), 49–69.

Lagarde, M. (1996) *Género y feminismo. Desarrollo humano y democracia*. Horas y Horas, Madrid.

Lee-Gosselin, H., Briere, S. and Ann, H. (2013) Resistances to gender mainstreaming in organizations: toward a new approach. *Gender in Management: An International Journal*, 28(8), 468–485.

Lombardo, E., Meier, P. and Verloo, M. (2010) Discursive dynamics in gender equality politics: what about 'feminist taboos'? *European Journal of Women's Studies* 17(2), 105–123.

Moreno, D. (2017a) Tourism and gender: an essential approach in the context of sustainable and responsible tourism development. Unpublished PhD thesis. University Complutense of Madrid, Spain.

Moreno, D. (2017b) ODS, Turismo y Género: fundamentos y recomendaciones para la educación y sensibilización. CIC Batá and Equality in Tourism. Available at: www.cicbata.org/sites/default/files/ODS%20Turismo%20y%20Genero.pdf (accessed 12 March 2018).

Moreno, D. (2017c) The role of gender equality towards achieving sustainable tourism – interview with Daniela Moreno Alarcón from Equality in Tourism. Available at: https://www.travindy.com/2017/05/gender-equality-to-achieve-real-sustainable-tourism-interview-with-daniela-moreno-alarcon-from-equality-in-tourism (accessed 26 February 2018).

Valcárcel, A. (2008) Feminismo en el mundo global. Universitat de Valencia/Cátedra/Instituto de la Mujer, Valencia and Madrid.

Walby, S. (2005) Gender mainstreaming: productive tensions in theory and practice. *Social Politics: International Studies in Gender, State and Society* 12(3), 321–343.

Women in Development Europe (WIDE) (1996) Algunos pasos hacia delante. Boletín WIDE, Brussels.

Neusa's Story

Neusa Gonçalves

My name is Neusa Gonçalves; I'm 43 years old, from Sal Island, Cape Verde.

I worked as a tour guide from 1997 until the year 2000, when there was still only one travel agency in the town of Santa Maria. In April 2000 I travelled to the Azores with 22 other young people working on a passenger ship travelling between the islands. After 6 months, I moved to the island of Madeira, playing soccer for the Madeira National team until 2005 when I returned to Cape Verde.

I tried to start a mini market but went bankrupt at the time of the global economic crisis. In 2012 I returned to tour guide work as a freelancer. In 2013 I started up on my own, selling island excursions. I registered my company, Kryol Operator, in 2014 and got my professional driving licence a year later. Now I have three salespeople working for me. At the beginning, as a business led by women, there was a constant struggle with men.

Tourism is very important for us because it is the main engine of the economy in Cape Verde. It generates jobs, and almost all services on the island are linked to it. On the island of Sal the majority of manpower is in the hotels and people migrate here from all the islands in search of work.

KRYOL OPERATOR

Touristic activities company
With professional guides and drivers

Fig. S3a. Neusa Gonçalves.

Kryol specializes in trying to reach the poor people in the country. For example, we go to the poorest part of the island in Terra Boa and support the neediest children. With the help of my company, through the bank, I have invested in my own car to make the excursions and I hope in the near future to have a fleet of cars for excursions and transfers.

It is very important to have women in tourism in Cape Verde because our society is still very sexist and there are many poor single mothers. Women getting jobs or becoming entrepreneurs bring a lot of economic and social balance to the area.

Fig. S3b. Neusa Gonçalves.

4 'An Uneasy Truth?': Female Tourism Managers and Organizational Gender Equality Measures in Portugal

Fiona Eva Bakas,[1,*] Carlos Costa,[2] Marília Durão,[2] Inês Carvalho[3] and Zélia Breda[2]

[1]Centre for Social Studies, Coimbra University, Coimbra, Portugal; [2]Aveiro University, Aveiro, Portugal; [3]Universidade Europeia, Lisbon, Portugal

Introduction

Whilst two-thirds of the world's tourism workforce is female, female tourism workers continue to saturate low hierarchical levels and are paid less than their male counterparts (Baum, 2013; Eurostat, 2015). According to recent research using a feminist economics lens, one of the reasons for the low number of female managers in tourism is the ways in which gender roles connecting femininity to primary responsibility for caring mould tourism workers' perceived abilities (Cuadrado *et al.*, 2015). Increased attention to how stereotyped gender roles, as an 'invisible hand', can influence tourism labour discourse (Costa *et al.*, 2017) encourages a deeper investigation into how gender roles influence tourism labour. Since equality is largely accepted as an important goal to work towards, there is an increased interest in the ways in which workplaces can become more gender balanced.

Common gender equality measures implemented by companies include work–life balance practices and performance-related pay policies (Kato and Kodama, 2015). However, in the absence of hard sanctions in workplace gender equality regulations, few workplaces have such measures in place yet. More specifically, limited research has been conducted on what gender equality measures exist within tourism companies, whose responsibility it is to implement them and what are the roles of *female* tourism managers in creating work environments characterized by greater gender equality. This study represents an intriguing state-of-art investigation into the gendered intricacies surrounding gender equality measures in tourism workplaces.

Definition of Case Study Area

The data that support this investigation are part of the results of a wider, innovative and unique two-phased research project on gender issues in the tourism sector that was conducted in Portugal over a 6-year period, from 2009 to 2015. The findings presented in this study refer to the second phase, concerning both male and female top-level tourism managers from both private sector and public tourism organizations, with the primary aim of understanding how gender influences tourism labour. The whole Portuguese national territory (mainland and islands) is

* E-mail: fiona.bakas@ua.pt

represented. Questionnaires and focus groups were conducted in the Portuguese language and during the analysis phase, the questionnaire and the focus group transcripts were translated into English. Transcripts were edited for clarity and coherence by a native English speaker researcher.

Two methods were used to co-construct knowledge in this chapter: online questionnaires and focus groups. For the online questionnaires, a database of tourism businesses was created to represent all tourism subsectors as defined by the Tourism Satellite Account, by merging existing databases from different official bodies. A proportionate stratified sampling with a minimum of three subjects per stratum was applied, based on two criteria: region (location) and type of tourism activity. Invitations to complete the online questionnaire were sent to the targeted managers from September 2013 to March 2015 and 401 valid questionnaires were collected, which fulfilled the sample size criteria.

Focus groups had an average duration of 3 h each and took place over 5 months, between November 2013 and March 2014. Seventy-nine tourism managers participated in them. Focus group narratives reveal tourism leaders' positionality in relation to aspects of managerial discourse that are related to organizational gender equality measures. Participants reflect the socially constructed images of maleness and femaleness through discursive moves, the expression of norms, the use of language and affirmation of values. Participants' names appear as a number in brackets – for example *(P66-male)* – to protect the anonymity of participants. Focus groups discussed: external bodies' role in promoting gender equality in organizations; measures taken by the company to promote gender equality within its organization; and awareness of gender equality issues within their organization. Through these questions, focus groups created interpretations of what they perceived as 'gender equality policies'.

Thematic analysis was used for a systematic examination of the collected data, using a mix of deductive and inductive approaches in the iterative process. In order to conduct thematic analysis, the literature surrounding gender equality in tourism labour needs to be critically analysed, which is done in the next sections. This begins with a brief introduction to the history of gender equality measure implementation in tourism labour, followed by an analysis of various aspects of gender equality implementation that arose during the empirical research. The analysis sections focus on who was perceived as responsible for implementation of gender equality measures (the company or the state); the types of gender equality measures in place in Portuguese tourism organizations; and the role of female managers in implementing gender equality measures.

History of Gender Equality Measures in Tourism Labour

According to research participants, gender equality measures within tourism companies are a recent development, only being implemented within the past decade. As one tourism manager said: 'only recently, 6 or 7 years ago did we decide to address these issues in an autonomous manner' *(P42-male)*. However, gender equality-specific policies are still very much in their infancy, partly because of the lack of recognition of economic value in increasing gender equality at work. As one participant said: 'Human resources are usually under the responsibility of those who are in charge of the finance department and don't look at these issues specifically … It seems to me that most companies don't have policies that protect women' *(P19-female)*. Other participants expressed how the whole idea of social responsibility within companies, under which they perceived the subject of increasing gender equality to fall, is purely a marketing ploy and hence not taken seriously. As one participant said of gender equality policies: 'this is like social marketing, which is not intended to be social, but to look like the company is doing something for society' *(P27-female)*. However, other participants did see the financial benefits of introducing gender equality measures, highlighting how these could actually boost productivity. As one participant said of the implementation of gender equality policies within companies: 'it serves to prove that you don't lose money, on the contrary it can boost productivity' *(P44-male)*.

One of the reasons why more gender equality policies are introduced, according to some participants, is related to changes in family structure. In fact, whilst in 2010 women in the Organisation for Economic Co-operation and Development (OECD) member-countries spent at least *twice* the amount of time on caring as men did (Veerle, 2011), recent research shows that today men are more central within the family and more involved in housework than they used to be 10 years ago (Goldscheider *et al.*, 2015). Simultaneously, the number of women who work has also increased, with 4.3% more women working on average in the OECD than there were 10 years ago (OECD, 2017). Increasing divorce rates may explain this phenomenon as it means that men are having to act as single parents, thus taking on more childcare responsibilities than they had as a married parent. A participant mentions how, since getting divorced, her male business partner took on childcare responsibilities and so everyone in the company adjusted their schedules for him to be able to pick up his son from school. As she said: 'He had a fixed time to get him and we adjusted our meetings to fit everyone's agenda' *(P79)*. This quote suggests that a change in family structures, which has repercussions on the gendered distribution of childcare arrangements, can influence the gender equality measures adopted by tourism companies.

Recent years have seen divorce rates in Portugal rise dramatically, from 30.0% in 2003 to 70.4% in 2013 (Pordata, 2017). When men divorce and have children from their marriage they often take on more childcare responsibilities than during their marriage, since they spend more time alone with their children. This may affect the importance attached to having workplace policies on flexibility regarding childcare. When male workers start to have caring responsibilities, the invisibility of this caring labour (Federici, 2012) comes to light. Consequently, in the future, the discourse of a tourism worker having caring responsibilities may become progressively normalized.

Many participants pointed out that the number and type of gender equality measures that a company can apply depended on company *size*. For example, the provision of a 24-h nursery for tourism employees was found to be part of the Portuguese national airline company's policy. But as one participant remarked: 'It is easy for a big company to create the conditions for a better work–family balance. A company of 1700 workers can manage things more objectively. A small hotel of 15 employees, if three of them are at home with parental leave, it is difficult to organize work shifts' (P56-male). Since the European Union (EU) service industry is made up of 99.8% of companies with under ten employees (European Commission, 2013a), the significance of this observation in the implementation of gender equality measures within tourism companies is obvious. However, not all gender equality measures require massive investments, and as one participant stated: 'sometimes it is easier for companies and for the public administration to give better working conditions than to increase remuneration' *(P27-female)*. Looking at small and medium-sized enterprises (SMEs) in the US that implement policies that aid social and environmental goals, it is evident that social equality measures that aim at offering equal opportunities for men and women are feasible to implement, and simultaneously do not threaten the profitability of the company (Arend, 2014). In the Portuguese context, where the 2010 macroeconomic crisis had serious negative consequences, creating gender equality may have a significant impact, as this also helps promote social and economic resilience, as seen in recent research on tourism SMEs in Greece (Bakas, 2017).

Who is Responsible for Implementing Gender Equality Measures in Tourism Companies?

Whilst many participants feel that measures to increase the provision of equal opportunities for both men and women are the company's responsibility, some tourism managers in the focus groups do not agree. One manager illustrates this opinion particularly well by saying that: 'it's not the company that should adjust to the workers' needs, it is the employees that should adjust to the company's needs' *(P72-male)*. Another participant illustrates how a tourism employee is often expected to have no responsibilities outside their work, as also discussed in research into the connection between flexibility and 'ideal tourism worker' discourse (Costa *et al.*, 2017). Some tourism managers view these caring tasks as an impediment and the worker as less than ideal, rather than think that maybe they should try and accommodate their employees' needs. One male manager says: 'It's impossible for me to have someone in a travel agency that comes to me and says "now I am leaving because I have to take my son to school". If they have that kind of attitude they're not suitable to work in tourism or in any other area' *(P54)*. This opinion illustrates the contemporary clash between an increased push to accumulate accentuated by capitalist policies, and the ongoing need to reproduce as a species. Whilst the participant does not mention the sex of the employee he refers to, it is often women who are in the middle of this dyadic separation of economic worlds. Indeed, this example of an employer's inconsiderate attitude towards women who work in tourism, who often also have caring responsibilities, also illustrates the devaluation of feminized labour like childcare. This devaluation of caring work means that paid, productive labour is assumed to be of superior value and importance to caring tasks (England, 2010; Federici, 2012).

For the majority of tourism managers who participated in the focus groups, the state's role in helping to create gender equality policies in tourism labour was considered as crucial. Indeed, welfare and the EU are perceived by focus group participants as having a strong effect on promoting gender equality in tourism. Participants position institutions such as the EU and the state to be significant in increasing organizational gender equality as they have implemented

the following: (i) a quota system; (ii) state provision of childcare facilities; and (iii) definition of a parental leave period.

Quotas and gender equality in tourism companies

The quota instrument is characterized as a positive tool to increase the number of women in decision-making positions, by establishing a fixed percentage or number for the representation of a specific category of persons (EC, 2015).

At the time this chapter was written, the Portuguese parliament passed a law that mandates public and listed companies to hire a certain percentage of women for their supervisory and corporate boards. Since the empirical study was carried out 3 years ago, it was not possible to collect the subjects' opinion on quotas in tourism organizations (as they did not exist). At the time the focus groups took place, there were only quotas to step up women's participation in politics. However, what follows is an interesting pre-appraisal of how quotas in tourism organizations were perceived by the tourism managers. Various focus group participants questioned the competence of women placed in such 'quota positions'. As one tourism manager said: 'I think the quota system is ridiculous. If I were a woman I would think: "will I be included in this list just because I am a woman or because I'm capable/competent?"'*(P48-female)*. However, recent research shows that quotas backed by legislation are one of the most significant ways of affecting change as they are more effective than soft company initiatives, and help ensure that society and firms reflect diverse ideas and talents (Perrons and Lacey, 2015). Recent empirical research into the Portuguese tourism industry shows that women working in tourism often face gendered constraints such as 'old boys' networks and masculinized economic discourses. These constraints impede working women's progress, education and training, making it hard for women to rise to management positions without quotas (Carvalho, 2017).

As one participant points out, although quotas have a somewhat tainted reputation, they are a very useful organizational gender equality measure. He said: 'the idea I have about the quotas is that although they are not a positive way of achieving global inclusion of women, they turned out to be a way to do it, to ensure their inclusion' *(P8-male)*. Whilst there is no evidence of a *spontaneous* reduction of gender inequality, quotas can help ensure that constant progress is made towards gender equality in tourism labour (EC, 2013b).

Welfare state and gender equality in tourism companies

The state of gender equality measures in tourism labour has significantly improved in the past 30 years. As one participant said: 'It was in 1976 that we got equality for women, but it was only on paper' *(P39-female)*. Indeed, various participants pointed to how current political agendas are now positively influencing the implementation of gender equality measures in tourism organizations. As one participant said: 'the growing concern of equal opportunities and gender mainstreaming in the political agenda has been encouraging companies and organizations to also define support measures' *(P75-female)*. Similarly, another participant suggested that: 'the political agenda is also contributing to the implementation of these measures' *(P15-female)*.

Focus group participants said that the welfare state has a significant role in implementing gender equality measures within tourism labour. In many cases, the state offers childcare facilities close to employees' workplaces, provides activities for workers' children in the summer, allows new parents to have more flexible working hours, encourages new forms of teleworking and optimizes parental leave systems. One participant highlighted how in Faro (Algarve, Portugal), which receives the highest number of tourists per annum in Portugal, the municipality has a central role in providing work–family reconciliation measures for tourism employees in the form of holiday camps for tourism employees' children. As he says: 'In already existing buildings and facilities that are under the municipality's management, they created holiday camps for the employees' children' *(P66)*.

Some participants say that the state should play a more significant role in increasing gender equality at work. As one participant pointed out: 'the issues of childcare and old peoples' homes are pushed as the companies' responsibility when the state does not have enough resources, although this should be the state's responsibility' *(P54-male)*. The role of the welfare state in Europe is well-established, but neoliberal political directions that aim at drawing the responsibility for citizen well-being away from the state and towards private institutions are on the rise. Another participant drew attention to the way in which state policies are important in encouraging tourism companies to implement gender equality policies, by saying that: 'the state has an important role not only in configuring the access to opportunities, but also in defining and implementing policies that allow for a better compatibility of professional responsibilities and personal life' *(P56-male)*.

State initiatives in the form of legislation relating to maternity leave are perceived by many participants as an important form of gender equality measures. One participant said: 'We deal very well with the issue of motherhood ... if a pregnant lady at reception has to be replaced, the company does not see it as a great cost. The Social Security is the entity that supports motherhood' *(P78-male)*. Yet, Portugal has one of the shortest maternity leaves in Europe, with new mothers only being given 6 weeks' paid leave, compared to the OECD average of 17.7 weeks (OECD – Social Policy Division, 2017). However, it is noteworthy that participants explicitly refer to the maternal leave, while not addressing paternal leave in their discourses. In fact, in the Portuguese context, new fathers rarely make use of their paternal leave. This is despite Portugal having a relatively high level of paternity leave, with new fathers being able to take 5 weeks' paid paternity leave (3 days of which are compulsory), compared to the OECD average of 1 week. This shows how traditional gender roles within the family are still deep-seated in the Portuguese society. One focus group participant stresses the low number of men who take advantage of paternity leave by saying that: 'There was only one case of a man that shared the leave with his wife' *(P2-female)*.

Types of Gender Equality Measures in Tourism Businesses

Drawing on past literature, one of the possible reasons why male workers do not want to take parental leave relates to the stereotyped roles of masculinity in neoclassical economic discourse, according to which workers should operate as rational economic beings, unencumbered from any exterior obligations (such as parenting duties). Even in states with strong welfare provision such as Sweden, worker discourses are based on the male breadwinner model (Eriksen *et al.*, 2013). However, recent research, such as that on female tourism entrepreneurs in Greece, shows that tourism workers are increasingly challenging stereotypical gender roles (Bakas, 2014).

According to focus group participants, various gender equality measures are being adopted by tourism companies. These policies are largely related to work–family balance and helping employees in childcare arrangements. As one participant said: 'Companies are […] offering day care centres, schools or allowing people to work from home' *(P76-male)*. A participant narrated how the tourism company he works at offers childcare for tourism employees during the peak season. He said: 'They offered children's activities in key periods, namely July and August, so the parents who didn't have vacations in these months could have alternatives to leave their children' *(P61)*. Another measure that a Portuguese tourism company is implementing in order to increase gender equality is the creation of a nursery that operates 24 h a day, 365 days a year. As one participant remarked, this was

very important to tourism workers and a 'precious help' because it allowed them to have peace of mind regarding childcare. Another participant said that their company provided 'reduced working hours for those who have children under 12 years old' *(P34-female)*. Other measures included not scheduling work tasks at inconvenient times and offering a 10% discount to employees at certain kindergartens.

Figure 4.1, based on questionnaire data, paints a slightly different picture regarding what are the most frequent measures adopted by tourism companies in Portugal to promote gender equality. Although focus group participants spoke mainly about work–life balance measures as being the most important measures to implement in order to achieve increased gender equality at work, according to the questionnaire data, very few tourism organizations actually have such measures in place. Only 3.7% of tourism companies had childcare equipment and only 8.2% had protocols with family support services. Besides, most of the measures adopted hardly go beyond the law.

Female Managers' Role in Implementing Gender Equality Measures

Looking more closely at the percentages of managers who said that they had work–life balance policies in place as a measure to increase gender equality, some gendered differences are observed. It can be seen that a higher proportion of female managers than male managers mention that their companies have implemented actions related to work and family life harmony, namely:

- specific measures (e.g. information and adequate training) to reintegrate workers who have interrupted their careers for family reasons (15.3% female versus 9.4% male managers);
- protocols with family support services (10.8% female versus 6.6% male managers); or
- their own childcare facilities (5.7% female versus 2.5% male managers).

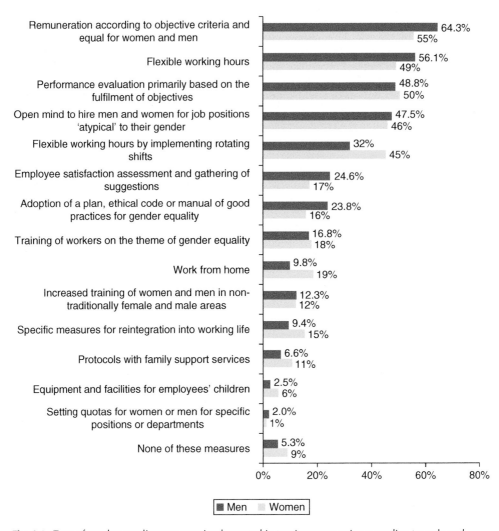

Fig. 4.1. Type of gender equality measures implemented in tourism companies according to male and female managers (questionnaire data).

This may indicate that female managers are more aware of work and family balance constraints and so are more aware of the gender equality measures that are in place. It is also interesting that the proportion of male tourism managers (4.5%) with absolutely no knowledge of any of these measures existing in their companies is three times that of female tourism managers (1.3%).

Performing an analysis of the questionnaire data relating to the *number* of gender equality measures implemented, we find that each tourism company has implemented an average of four gender equality measures

each (M = 3.95, SE = 0.124). Looking more closely at the number of adopted measures, a gendered difference in the number of gender equality measures implemented in tourism companies is observed. Our results show that female managers said that their companies had more gender equality measures (M = 4.13, SE = 0.210) than male managers did (M = 3.84, SE = 0.152). These differences were found to be statistically significant after a *t*-test was carried out ($t(362) = 1.138$, $P = 0.256$). This could be because female managers are more *aware* of the existing gender equality measures or because female managers help *implement* more gender equality measures; however, further research would need to be conducted to ascertain this.

The position of female managers also plays a role, with a higher number of gender equality measures being implemented in companies where women occupy *top* management positions. The relationship between the number of measures taken to promote gender equality and the representativeness of women in top-level management positions is found to be statistically significant, using a Mann–Whitney U test ($U = 10,036$; $W = 33,256$; $P < 0.001$). So, the higher women's representativeness in top-level management positions is, the higher the number of gender equality measures implemented. In more detail, 3.79 gender equality measures are implemented in tourism companies with *only men* in top-level management positions; 3.97 gender equality measures are implemented in tourism companies in which top-level boards have *equal proportions* of men and women; and 4.77 gender equality measures are implemented in companies in which top-level management positions are occupied *exclusively by women*.

Conclusion

Both quantitative and qualitative data indicate that the manager's gender plays a significant role in both the type and number of gender equality measures that are implemented within a tourism organization. Regarding the *type* of measures, those related to work and family life reconciliation are more frequently reported by female managers. We find that it is more frequently the case that female managers promote: (i) specific measures to reintegrate workers who interrupted their career for family reasons; (ii) protocols with family support services; and (iii) company childcare facilities. Furthermore, looking at the *number* of adopted measures according to the gender of the respondents, results show that the companies where participating female managers work have more measures than the companies managed by male managers, with these differences being statistically significant.

Whilst our quantitative data point to a connection between the presence of women in top-level management positions and the implementation of gender equality measures, qualitative data illustrate how gendered structures in society oppress women, such as the perception that maternity leave is a gender equality measure, rather than a human right and essential to the continuation of the human species. This finding highlights how the perception of what constitutes a gender equality measure needs to be better defined, if real progress in gender equality at work is to be achieved. In some cases, research participants refer to measures that are merely the result of compliance with the law, as also observed by Carvalho (2017).

The success of gender equality measures implemented by tourism companies is highly dependent on the cultural context that moulds employees' gender roles. One participant points this out by highlighting how, even though there is adequate provision of private childcare services in areas with high tourism activity, 'it will always be required of women to leave work at 6pm to take care of their children' (*P61-male*). This demonstrates the way in which gender roles connected to femininity continue to dictate primary responsibility for childcare, despite the changing face of labour demands on women. This happens partly because the dominance of male norms has changed much less in 'the personal' than in the job world (England, 2010, p. 155). Indeed England (2010) notes that 'changes in the gender system are uneven' (p. 161), affecting the lives of some people more than others, which should be taken into consideration when formulating and implementing measures aimed at increasing equality in the opportunities available to men and women within the tourism labour market. One way of integrating this concept into policies would be to attempt to 'de-gender' normative obligations to care, based on the idea that if women cared less, the economic disadvantages to them would be fewer than if they did care (Folbre, 2012).

Whilst SMEs are vital to the tourism industry (Hjalager, 2007), this study illustrates that they have specificities such as having limited margins to offer their employees childcare allowances and limited numbers of employees to allow for work flexibility. These specificities need to be taken into consideration when creating policies that aim at increasing gender equality within tourism labour. Further research on the creation of gender equality policies that could be implemented in tourism SMEs at a minimal cost could greatly benefit the promotion of gender equality measures at the tourism organizational level. New measures should not construct women workers and mothers as the work/family problem to be 'fixed', as this leaves women even more rushed and pressed for time, as seen in research in Australia (Pocock *et al.*, 2013). Some examples of gender equality measures that could be adapted for use within tourism companies, are suggested by Perrons and Lacey (2015): (i) allowing for jobs to be available on a part-time basis without adverse career impacts; (ii) encourage policies that eradicate the long hours culture and expectation of presenteeism; and (iii) introduce individual, earmarked, non-transferable rights to paid leave, to encourage the idea that men as well as women should have time to care without penalties. Another way to achieve gender equality would be to give department managers bonuses depending on the number of men who took flexible hours. A report done by Equality in Tourism on Unilever found that this was quite radical

and very successful (Barnett, 2014). The more men in a department persuaded to do the school run at one end of the day or the other, the more normal it became and so snowballed.

Another interesting observation this study makes is that as family structures change, due to soaring divorce rates, this has an influence on the responsibilization of men to complete caring tasks, which in turn seems to alert tourism managers to the need to have gender equality measures in place. Investigating along these lines, that is, investigating the effect of changing family structures on the implementation of gender equality measures, could provide fruitful insight into the role of gender in tourism labour.

Acknowledgements

This chapter results from a research project on gender issues in the tourism sector, which is entitled 'Does gender equality have a say in the boost of innovative forms of economic growth? Reviving the economy through networks and internationalisation in the tourism sector' (PTDC/CS-SOC/119524/2010). The authors would like to acknowledge the support provided by the Portuguese Foundation for Science and Technology, as well as the co-financing of the EU through the National Strategic Reference Framework, European Regional Development Fund and the Operational Program for Competitiveness Factors.

References

Arend, R. (2014) Social and environmental performance at SMEs: considering motivations, capabilities, and instrumentalism. *Journal of Business Ethics* 125(4), 541–561.

Bakas, F.E. (2014) Tourism, female entrepreneurs and gender: crafting economic realities in rural Greece, PhD thesis, Otago University, New Zealand. Available at: http://hdl.handle.net/10523/5381 (accessed 8 June 2018).

Bakas, F.E. (2017) Community resilience through entrepreneurship: the role of gender. *Journal of Enterprising Communities: People and Places in the Global Economy* 11(1), 61–77.

Barnett, T. (2014) Enlightenment from Unilever Food Solutions, Equality in Tourism. Available at: http://equalityintourism.org/enlightenment-from-unilever-food-solutions (accessed 26 February 2018).

Baum, T. (2013) *International Perspectives on Women and Work in Hotels, Catering and Tourism.* International Labour Organization, Geneva.

Costa, C., Bakas, F.E., Breda, Z., Durão, M., Carvalho, I. and Caçador, S. (2017) Gender, flexibility and the 'ideal tourism worker'. *Annals of Tourism Research* 64, 64–75.

Cuadrado, I., García-Ael, C. and Molero, F. (2015) Gender-typing of leadership: evaluations of real and ideal managers. *Scandinavian Journal of Psychology* 56(2), 236–244.

England, P. (2010) The gender revolution: uneven and stalled. *Gender and Society* 24(2), 149–166.

Eriksen, M.J. *et al.* (2013) *Gender and Well-Being: The Role of Institutions*. Ashgate Publishing, Farnham, UK.

European Commission (EC) (2013a) Annual report on European SMEs 2012/2013. Available at: https://www. researchgate.net/profile/Deborah_Cox/publication/259174567_A_RECOVERY_ON_THE_HORIZON_ Annual_Report_on_European_SMEs_201213/links/0046352a1c259e4936000000/A-RECOVERY- ON-THE-HORIZON-Annual-Report-on-European-SMEs-2012-13.pdf (accessed 12 March 2018).

European Commission (EC) (2013b) She figures 2012: gender in research and innovation. Luxembourg, EC. Available at: http://ec.europa.eu/research/science-society/document_library/pdf_06/she-figures-2012_en.pdf (accessed 26 February 2018).

European Commission (EC) (2015) The European Union explained: Europe 2020: Europe's growth strategy, pp. 1–12. Available at: www.renatosoru.eu/wp-content/uploads/2015/02/Europe-2020.pdf (accessed 12 March 2018).

Eurostat (2015) Statistics explained. Gender pay gap statistics. Available at: http://ec.europa.eu/eurostat/statistics- explained/index.php/Gender_pay_gap_statistics (accessed 26 February 2018).

Federici, S. (2012) *Revolution at Point Zero: Housework, Reproduction, and Feminist Struggle*. PM Press, London.

Folbre, N. (2012) Should women care less? Intrinsic motivation and gender inequality. *British Journal of Industrial Relations* 50(4), 597–619.

Goldscheider, F., Bernhardt, E. and Lappegård, T. (2015) The gender revolution: a framework for understanding changing family and demographic behavior. *Population and Development Review* 41(2), 207–239.

Hjalager, A.M. (2007) Stages in the economic globalization of tourism. *Annals of Tourism Research* 34(2), 437–457.

Kato, T. and Kodama, N. (2015) Work-life balance practices, performance-related pay, and gender equality in the workplace: evidence from Japan. IZA Discussion Paper No. 9379.

Organisation for Economic Co-operation and Development (OECD) (2017) Employment : Time spent in paid and unpaid work, by sex. Available at: http://stats.oecd.org/index.aspx?queryid=54757 (accessed 26 February 2018).

Organisation for Economic Co-operation and Development (OECD) – Social Policy Division (2017) Key characteristics of parental leave systems. Available at: https://www.oecd.org/els/soc/PF2_1_Parental_leave_ systems.pdf (accessed 26 February 2018).

Perrons, D. and Lacey, N. (2015) *Confronting Gender Inequality: Findings from the LSE Commission on Gender, Equality and Power*. Gender Institute, LSE, London.

Pocock, B., Charlesworth, S. and Chapman, J. (2013) Work-family and work-life pressures in Australia: advancing gender equality in 'good times'? *International Journal of Sociology and Social Policy* 33(9/10), 594–612.

Pordata (2017) Number of divorces per 100 marriages – Portugal. Available at: www.pordata.pt/en/Portugal/ Number+of+divorces+per+100+marriages-531 (accessed 26 February 2018).

Veerle, M. (2011) Cooking, caring and volunteering: unpaid work around the world, OECD social, employment and migration, Working Paper No. 116. OECD, Paris.

Perrine's Story: Social Entrepreneurship in Vienna (Austria)

Perrine Schober

Fig. S4. Perrine with students on a tour.

I often wonder if my passion for tourism derives from my character or from my experiences growing up. My mother is French, my father is Austrian and they met in Canada. So I grew up hearing, understanding and speaking three different languages. My mother worked for an international organization, which meant that when she organized dinner parties, the room was filled with different skin colours, languages, accents and traditional clothes. To be surrounded by different nationalities and cultures was an utterly normal thing for me. I guess that this international environment nurtured my curiosity for foreign countries and their diverse traditions. At the age of 15 I absolutely wanted to speak Spanish enabling me to interact with an even larger community.

I started working in the tourism industry at 18. After graduating from high school, I spent my summer working for an international language school in Spain. I guess this was when my character evolved, and I understood that I loved working with tourists and trying to make their experience unique. This is when my service-oriented mind and my hosting skills grew exponentially. From then on, I always worked in tourism companies. From marketing and sales, as a receptionist or waitress, in catering and in strategy development for consulting companies (Europraxis – Tourism and Leisure) or development aid organizations (SNV and the World Tourism Organization (UNWTO)).

My passion for the tourism industry lies in the ultimate desire to give people an amazing experience. And I see it as an honour that they are trusting in me to make it unique.

Two years ago, I decided to unite my business skills and my passion for social development. I am not rich, so it had to be a self-financed business model. I founded SHADES TOURS, a social business that employs homeless people to become alternative tour guides, offering unique tour experiences, where they highlight the socio-political system of the most liveable city on earth, Vienna. Today SHADES TOURS is 2 years old, has welcomed over 7000 people on its educational tours and has seven employees, of which three made it out of homelessness after working for 6 months with us. The special aspect of SHADES TOURS is that we provide information on the social welfare system, and this information helps society to better engage and interact with homeless people. And the fact that homeless people themselves are providing the information is not an act of charity. Homeless people are the best human resources for explaining these issues with a high degree of authenticity, which results in empathy. We also run team-building events for companies, cooking in soup kitchens.

After 2 years, SHADES TOURS is financially sustainable, creating a small and yet unique impact on our society.

The funniest thing about its success is that it is surprising, especially to me. As you can imagine, most people were very sceptical about this business model: 'This will not work', 'Could be interesting, but no-one will be willing to pay for it', 'Perrine, you better go back to look for a 9 to 5 job with a real pay cheque at the end of the month', 'Perrine, you are 32 you should rather think of having a family and get babies' – these were the most common comment I got when I tried to pitch my business idea. And I understand that, I really do! Especially when it comes to self-employment, Austrians are very sceptical and not very empowering. In addition I had come up with such an innovative approach, that it did not make sense to most of my contacts.

Now 3 years after the creation of SHADES TOURS, the mindset of people towards this project has changed, but it was far from being easy – it was very hard work. For the first 2 years I worked 85 h per week, juggling the recruiting and training of the guides, searching for the first clients to fill up the first tours. In addition to that hard work came the big emotional stress of ensuring my own financial survival, the sometimes painful empathy for homeless people, the stress of whether my employees would endure the situation, etc. This situation of course affected my psychological and physiological condition. I worked hard, and when at home, I found it difficult to switch off. It directly affected my relationship to the point that I could not recover it anymore.

The lack of time meant that I had to juggle my priorities. I had different roles: a friend, a girlfriend, a daughter and a sister on the one side, and an entrepreneur, a human resources department, a marketing and sales manager, an accountant and a web administrator, on the other side. I hardly found time to keep in touch with my friends and my social life, and constantly heard my parents asking me if another job wouldn't be better for my financial security. Now they have stopped arguing with me and the nicest comment from my mother was when one of her neighbours approached her with an article featuring SHADES TOURS, and she told me that she felt embarrassed. I thought that she felt embarrassed as I was in the newspaper: 'No, I am embarrassed that I didn't support you earlier, and I am sorry for that!'

5 Tourism as Empowerment: Women Artisan's Experiences in Central Mexico

Paola Vizcaino Suárez*

Facultad de Turismo y Gastronomía, Universidad Autónoma del Estado de México, Mexico

Introduction

In the past decade, feminist scholars in Mexico have added to the research on gender and tourism by focusing on the impacts of tourism development in host communities and discrimination patterns in tourism employment. A handful of these studies have examined tourism's potential to promote gender equality and women's empowerment (e.g. Fernández and Martínez, 2010; Díaz-Carrión, 2012; Mendoza and Chapulín, 2015). The subfield has advanced the critical analysis of gender and work, exploring: (i) how the meanings of masculinity and femininity circumscribe the ways in which women get involved in tourism; and (ii) how the continuous interaction with tourism processes may contribute to the modification of gender definitions (Swain, 1995), opening up productive and social opportunities for women.

This chapter seeks to contribute to the debate on tourism as empowerment, through the exploration of the life stories of two urban mestiza women who work as producers and vendors of handicraft pottery catering to domestic and international visitors in the 'Magical Town' of Metepec, in central Mexico. As discussed in Chapter 1, the

feminist approach to empowerment includes 'power to' and 'power from within' and involves 'undoing negative social constructions, so that people come to see themselves as having the capacity and the right to act and influence decisions' (Rowlands, 1997, p. 14). The women in the case study assess local gender roles in a patriarchal society and challenge the entrenched belief that only men can be artisans or lead a pottery workshop. The analysis of the broader socio-economic context in which the research participants live and work facilitates the understanding of structures, policies and gender–power relations that enable or limit women's agency (Kabeer, 1999).

The data for the life stories come from the ethnographic research conducted for my PhD thesis, in which Delfina and Edna were key respondents (the names have been changed to maintain confidentiality). A variety of methods consistent with a feminist interpretive methodology were employed, including formal and informal interviews, participant observation and document analysis during 9 months of fieldwork in 2014 and 2015. The narratives were translated from Spanish into English. The aim is not to generalize the life stories in question but to examine the ways in

* E-mail: lvizcainosuarez@bournemouth.ac.uk

which women make sense of their gendered interactions with tourism and the possibilities for empowerment.

Gender and Tourism in the Mexican Context

Gender encompasses crucial aspects in the lives of women and men; including activities and creations, perceptions of the self, material and symbolic assets, power and sense of individual limits (Lagarde, 1996, pp. 13–14). The construction of gender roles and stereotypes in Mexico has historically characterized men as heads of household and breadwinners (conceived as productive work in the public sphere); whereas women have been assigned care and domestic chores (conceived as reproductive work in the private sphere). The ideology of *machismo* emerged from the Mexican Revolution at the beginning of the 20th century and contributed to the exaltation of virility expressed by indifference to danger, the disparagement of feminine virtues and the affirmation of authority by men from the subaltern classes (Monsiváis, 1981).

The macrostructural adjustments promoted by neoliberal policies in Latin America, the deterioration of working conditions, increased social vulnerability and poverty levels, along with profound demographic and sociocultural transformations, have modified traditional family arrangements of male breadwinners and female housewives. Through their massive incorporation into the labour market and economic contributions to their families, women have increased their presence in the productive and public realms, redefining their role in society (Carosio, 2012). However, reproductive work has been less prone to change, with women bearing the burden of care and domestic responsibilities (Arriagada, 2004).

The increased participation of women in the labour market can be observed in Mexico's tourism industry, where women represent over 57% of the total labour force and 45% of the workers in tourism-related sectors (calculated from INEGI, 2015). The tourism-related sectors include the production and sale of handicrafts and food in tourist destinations. Women also participate in the informal sector as vendors in international coastal resorts (Gámez *et al.*, 2011) and small or medium-sized cities involved in cultural tourism (Bayona, 2013). Employment opportunities in tourism are largely based on the sexual division of labour, limiting the types of jobs available for women (horizontal segregation) and relegating them to occupations with lower pay and status (vertical segregation) (SECTUR-COLMEX, 2011). Despite market limitations, tourism processes in Mexico have opened up spaces for women to redefine their identities, learn new skills, obtain financial autonomy, and establish social and business networks (Fernández and Martínez, 2010; Díaz-Carrión, 2012; Fierro *et al.*, 2014), which can support the contestation of unequal gender relations.

The 'Magical Town' of Metepec

Metepec is an internationally renowned pottery production centre in the state of Mexico, located next to the state capital of Toluca and 47 km southwest of Mexico City. The pottery tradition dates back to pre-Hispanic times and adopted new manufacturing techniques under the Spanish influence during the colonial period (Schneider, 2001). Until the 1960s, pottery production in Metepec focused on ritual and utilitarian purposes that satisfied the demand of local families. Production has shifted in the past 50 years to decorative and aesthetic purposes, to satisfy the growing demand of tourism markets (McAllister, 2001; Hernández and Zafra, 2005) (Fig. 5.1).

The preservation of traditions and festivities in its historical quarters gained Metepec a coveted place in the national 'Magical Towns' programme in 2012. The programme has increased municipal, state and federal funding for tourism infrastructure and promotion. The main infrastructure project for the period 2014–2015 was the rehabilitation of the handicrafts market, built in the late 1990s with the purpose of providing a space for artisan families to sell their production directly to the public.

Fig. 5.1. Pottery shops at the Metepec Handicrafts Market.

In both Metepec's pottery workshops and wider community, dominant gender norms and ideologies assign different activities, spaces and value to the work performed by women and men. Power imbalances are also evident in community organizations where leadership positions continue to be predominantly occupied by men. Despite being at the margins of local power systems, the two life stories illustrate how women negotiate gender roles and define strategies to take advantage of tourism transformations with the resources available to them.

Women Artisans' Experiences in Metepec

Negotiating gender, work and identity

In Metepec's patrilineal system, the social status as artisan is ascribed to the male heads of household (Schneider, 2001). This is consistent with patrilineal traditions in other pottery towns in central Mexico (Moctezuma, 2012). Artisans in Metepec rationalize the sexual division of labour within the family workshops due to the physical demands of some tasks involved in pottery production. Men undertake processes that require more physical strength (preparing the clay mix, sculpting large objects, firing), while women specialize in tasks that require dexterity (sculpting smaller objects or 'miniature', painting or decorating the finished pieces).

Delfina (50) has worked as a producer of decorative handicrafts for 30 years, yet finds it difficult to recognize herself as an artisan:

> When you asked me if I was an artisan, I answered that I am not, because my parents weren't artisans, my family didn't have that tradition ... so in this market ... people point at you and say: 'You are not an artisan'. You may do all the creative work, but you are not considered an artisan.

Edna (35) more readily embraces her identity as artisan, perhaps because she's younger and she did not grow up in Metepec. She got involved with handicraft pottery through her marriage to an artisan assistant 15 years ago. Edna enjoyed observing her now ex-husband's work and started practising the painting and sculpting techniques on her own:

> Nobody transmitted the knowledge to me, I didn't inherit it… But I had to adapt and I learned to make all the process. From the beginning: from mixing the clay, sculpting it, drying it, firing it and then painting it, until obtaining my own customers… Yes, I consider myself an artisan.

Edna's account shows how women can contest gender norms through agency. But women's agency does not always manifest as contestation, it can take the form of more subtle negotiations (Kabeer, 1999). In my research, married women were more likely to express support for the sexual division of labour in pottery production, if this meant avoiding activities they didn't enjoy. Delfina's description of the 'heavy work' required to prepare the clay mix illustrates this point:

> It is heavy work, because you see, they bring you a big block of clay, it can weigh up to 5 kg, it depends. You have to grind that block of clay with a stone roller that may weigh some 70–80 kg. So for a woman – and yes, there are women who do this work – for a woman, it is heavy work because you lay down some two or three wheelbarrows of clay and you have to crush the clay with the roller over 100 times, until you obtain a thin sand or powder… This work is done by my husband. I know how to do it, but since it is heavy work, I avoid doing it.
> I take the prepared mix from my husband to sculpt my objects.

Unlike 50 years ago, artisans do not have to collect clay from the nearby hills, nor carry big blocks that require heavy lifting, nor pulverize those blocks into the dust required for the clay mix. Even though male artisans continue to perform some of these activities, there are several alternatives to the clay preparation process that are readily adopted by women who lead their own workshops, like Edna:

> Since I don't even have room to store big clay blocks, I buy sacks of ground clay. They previously grind, clean and sieve the clay. So I simply add water and *plumilla* [a kind of reed flower found in the few remaining wetlands of Metepec] to make the mix.

The alternatives to the physically demanding processes traditionally deemed as men's work, have opened opportunities for Edna and other women to start their own handicraft pottery production. This has contributed to women challenging the belief that pottery production is reserved for men. Another perception that women are beginning to challenge is that of men being the primary breadwinners (Lagarde, 2004), as exemplified in Delfina's reflection:

> There is still the belief that men are the breadwinners. I mean, it is losing strength because nowadays we all participate in the production, but we still think that it is the men who do the heavy work.

Gender inequalities within the private realm are most persistent when it comes to the distribution of housework, as confirmed by research on social change and continuity in the context of Latin American families (Arriagada, 2004). Delfina explains:

> Men usually do not do much housework. Maybe they heat up coffee or milk in the morning, but the real housework … no, no… We are still under *machismo*. In my case, my husband does *help* me a little [emphasis mine]. He deals with the yard and garden. He knows those are his tasks. While he is cleaning the yard, I prepare breakfast and put the clothes in the washer. Then we both take our youngest daughter to school.

While married women like Delfina undertake negotiations with partners to attempt a more equitable distribution of housework, women heads of household have to develop strategies to organize productive and reproductive work on their own (Rojas, 2016). Edna's experience illustrates this case. She separated from her husband a couple of years ago and has become the primary supporter for her children (aged 15 and 8), intertwining both types of work at home:

> I work based on times. For example, I wake up at 6:00 am, help the kids get prepared for school. Come back home at 8:00 am and if I have orders, I get that work done, if not, I have time to clean up, make food and all. But then I pick up the kids from school, I feed them and then sit for another while to work [on handicrafts]. I check the kids' homework, make sure they have everything ready. I work more at night, from 10:00 pm to 1:00 am, more or less, depending on the orders. There are days when work decreases. Other days, I have work in excess.

To cope with the periods of 'work in excess', Edna has incorporated women in her immediate social circle to help her with production, and in turn provides an opportunity for these women to gain an income. This is consistent with the notion of women strengthening links through the recognition of each other (Lagarde, 2004):

> Three other women work in my workshop. I don't know if it's because of the difficulties I faced to start my workshop, I have offered other women the opportunity to work. For example, my neighbour has diabetes and it's difficult for her to find a job, because she gets sick, or she needs to go to the doctor ... so ... she helps me. I give her paint [to decorate handicrafts], she takes it to her apartment and she works there. My mother, since she became a widow, also helps me to paint and make small objects. And my 15-year-old daughter helps me decorate handicrafts.

Even though individual women are negotiating their identity as artisans and gaining confidence in their productive capacities, their efforts are not always recognized by the larger community. There are cultural and institutional barriers that continue to limit women's advancement (Deere and León, 2002). This is illustrated in Delfina's account:

> Local authorities usually promote the work of male artisans. Pottery artwork is usually commissioned from men from well-known families. Competitions are won by the same male artisans ... I know a lot of women artisans who do excellent work but have little recognition because they don't have a well-known family name or because

they don't have influence in the local government. So they start to fall behind.

There is a marked hierarchy within the artisan community in Metepec. Members of families who contributed to the internationalization of local pottery through the creation of monumental 'Trees of life' hold a higher status, participate in international competitions and export their work abroad as signature artists (F. Pagés, Metepec, 2015, personal communication). Delfina provides an example of how local politics works in the handicrafts market:

> Here in the market we have five strong men. They go everywhere to demand aid and they exchange favours with the local officials. 'Here, you become the godfather of my child', or 'I will organize a meal for you'. So those five men are always working [the system].

Very few actors gain from these type of arrangements, whereas a broad group of artisans who lack political networks (usually younger, poorer, female or from a different town) end up being excluded from key decision-making processes and other productive opportunities (e.g. training programmes, access to aid and credit, or participation in sale exhibits). Women producers feel particularly relegated due to gender discrimination, as exemplified by Edna's reflection:

> If you do not belong to one of those [well-known] families, you are not taken seriously. Often times, they make you feel unwelcome and that you have nothing to do there... Maybe they thought that my husband was the one who worked with clay and not me ... they couldn't believe that I did all the work – from preparing the clay to firing the objects. They are not used for women to do that.

The situation for women artisans improved with the introduction of gender-aware policies in the two administrations led by female mayors during the periods 2009–2012 and 2012–2015. For the first time in decades, an open call was made for women to register in the municipal artisan census, where members receive information on public aid, training and competitions. A newly appointed young female official was assigned the responsibility of following up on the needs of women artisans, as Edna recalls:

> Before, it was the male municipal officials from the Handicrafts Promotion area that did not let me show my work or anything. But the new female official made sure women producers could register in the census, just as men always have. Currently, I am in the census and I have an ID. Now I can prove that I'm an artisan too [laughs].

Taking advantage of tourism transformations

Despite being at the margins of the local power system, Delfina and Edna have taken advantage of the material and symbolic transformations brought about by tourism development in Metepec. One of the material transformations that had the most impact on artisan families was the creation of commercial tourist places like the handicrafts market, where over 50 families sell their pottery directly to visitors, tourists and wholesalers. The market has changed women's daily routines and provided a new space for productive work and socializing. Positive changes in women's lives (e.g. increased self-esteem and strengthening of social networks) have also been documented in community-based tourism projects; whereas negative changes refer to increased workload and less free time (Rodríguez and Acevedo, 2015). Before the creation of the market, women worked at home mostly on domestic and caring responsibilities as well as activities related to handicrafts production or other sources of income. Delfina recalls:

> I used to paint and sculpt at home. Well, I had my time to be with my children, but I also did other things. I sold gold, shoes, clothes ... depending on the season. But even then, I did my housework. When the market started, then we had to divide our time and come here. But I think most women used to work at home before the market.

For Delfina, working an 8-h shift every day has meant family disunion, because women no longer spend most of the time with their children. But the market has opened new sources of income for women, as Delfina explains:

> We can sell in the market and then my husband sells at the workshop, so not only my husband brings in money, there's another source of income.

In contrast, Edna continues to work from home and does not sell directly to tourists, but the demand for her handicrafts significantly depends on the tourist market: 'I don't sell directly to tourists, but I take my work to six shops in the handicrafts market'. Edna appreciates the flexibility of working from home at her own pace and not having to open a handicrafts shop during fixed hours:

> I'm always working, even on weekends, so when I have some free time I like going to family reunions and social events ... and yes, we like to go out a lot, since we are from Tenancingo [a nearby town] ... we like to go there and rest a bit. If I had a shop, I would have to stay every weekend, which is when most visitors come.

Both women have obtained financial autonomy through their work as producers of handicraft pottery, and tourism has contributed to opening new markets for their work. This is consistent with the experience of female artisans in other parts of the country (Rojas-Serrano et al., 2010; Fierro et al., 2014). Despite the literature's emphasis on women's economic empowerment (Tucker and Boonabaana, 2012), the experiences of women in Metepec show an appreciation for psychological empowerment. Some of the symbolic transformations brought about by tourism development stem from women socializing with people outside their family networks (other artisans, tourists, local authorities). This has contributed to the redefinition of women's identities and, in some cases, the recognition of their work by outsiders. For example, Delfina expressed experiencing a sense of personal growth through her interactions with visitors in the handicrafts market:

> I have met a lot of people from whom I have learned a lot ... one grows as a person. You grow in the sense that you are not only at home watching soap operas. You are in a

business, serving people, meeting people, doing what you like and making money, what else can you ask for?

Edna values the community recognition she has obtained from participating in handicraft competitions. She won her first award a few years ago at the *Quimera* Cultural Festival in Metepec, which receives thousands of visitors annually in October:

> I felt a great emotion, like receiving ... I don't know ... like when I finished High School ... that is, another accomplishment. It is like saying: 'I was able to do it'. Because when you receive the award, they call you *maestra*. And there is a huge change in how people see you.

Women are also weighing the positive and negative aspects of Metepec's incorporation into the 'Magical Towns' programme, as illustrated in Delfina's account:

> I think it's great that we are a Magical Town. This is attracting more visitors, mainly from other parts of the country... There are people who come saying: 'We came because we heard Metepec is a Magical Town and it looks really nice'. But something negative is that we are being forced to pay more taxes.

Defining power and empowerment

Throughout our conversations, Delfina and Edna reflected on personal, family and institutional barriers they have encountered as women artisans in Metepec. They were able to articulate ways in which they had overcome some of those barriers through what feminists understand as 'power for' and 'power from within' (Rowlands, 1997). The interconnections between tourism and culture have opened spaces for negotiating power (Serrano-Barquín, 2008) through a process of learning and creating, as evidenced in the participants' narratives.

Edna defines 'power for' as the capacity to create handicraft pottery, from beginning to end. The 'power from within' is her perseverance to support her family after separating from her husband and provide work for other women in a vulnerable situation. These definitions are illustrated in her account:

> The first challenge was to demonstrate that I could do the work. To confront the men, because I tell you that men – I don't know if it's because of the physical strength required to knead the clay or to carry large objects – they think a woman is not enough for that. But yes, they questioned how I could do it: 'How could she? How?' The first challenge was that. And then, as a woman, to demonstrate myself that I could support my family, my children... Another challenge was to have people help me [with production] and being able to pay them. Because, that isn't easy. I mean, it is easy to say: 'Yes, come help me and I will see how much I can give you'. No, a fair salary for their work. And then, the recognition that I obtain as a woman, by demonstrating I can do all the production process.

Delfina also defines 'power for' as her capacity to create handicraft pottery. The 'power from within' refers to overcoming her fears and gaining self-confidence:

> Look, I have an economy, not a very good economy, but I have my income. I have a family, which is not always supportive of my work, but I have one. In my work, I have done what I've wanted. When it comes to meeting people, I think I have a treasure there. I know a lot of people: very humble, middle class and rich people... Before, I used to have a lot of fear, but I have read a lot, that fear limits you and makes you useless. So now, with that fear, I give myself strength ... and I take a step forward. Being here in the market for 17 years has opened a lot of doors. I have learned many things.

As for their plans for the future, Delfina wants to continue working in the market and becoming more active in community organizations, while Edna wants to have a bigger workshop in a central location, where she can work, exhibit her handicrafts and sell to the public.

Conclusion

The cases presented highlight how tourism can open productive and socializing opportunities for women, contributing to their economic and psychological empowerment. The life stories illustrate how women engage in negotiations to redefine gender, work and identity, challenging the entrenched belief that only men can be artisans or lead pottery workshops. Women's interactions with people beyond their family networks (e.g. tourists, other artisans and local authorities) have generated spaces for the recognition of their work as producers and vendors of handicraft pottery, increasing their self-esteem and sense of accomplishment.

The stories also show how women experience politics in everyday life (Lagarde, 2004). The family level is crucial for negotiating changes towards more equitable gender relations and redistribution of care and domestic work traditionally assigned to women. But broader social and institutional support is required to produce transformations at the community level. Despite women's individual efforts, the work of male artisans continues to be placed in higher esteem, and the leadership positions within the artisan community continue to be occupied by men. There is a dynamic of exclusion around women's participation in decision-making processes, which is reinforced by the lack of institutionalization of gender-sensitive policies at the local level. The efforts started by the two female mayors have stalled under a new male-dominated administration.

Furthermore, despite legal and policy frameworks that call for the promotion of gender equality and women's empowerment in Mexico's tourism planning, these goals have not been implemented in existing programmes (Vizcaino Suárez *et al.*, 2014), such as the national 'Magical Towns Programme'. To transform regulative ideals into tangible efforts, it is necessary to bring women's voices to the forefront of national and local policy debates. Tourism research with a gender perspective can contribute to identifying pathways for empowerment from individual and everyday standpoints (Bergareche and Vargas, 2010). Policy can focus on supporting what women are already doing to produce change in their lives, and advance strategies to dismantle the structural barriers that limit women's agency and exclude them from decision-making processes. Policy should also contribute to provide public alternatives to private arrangements for care and domestic work, since women continue to carry the burden of these responsibilities on top of their income-generating activities in tourism and other sectors.

References

Arriagada, I. (2004) Transformaciones sociales y demográficas de las familias latinoamericanas. *Papeles de población* 10(40), 71–95.

Bayona, E. (2013) Textiles para turistas: tejedoras y comerciantes en los Altos de Chiapas. *PASOS. Revista de Turismo y Patrimonio Cultural* 11(2), 371–386.

Bergareche, A. and Vargas, E. (2010) Nuevos desafíos, renovadas miradas: algunas propuestas al debate sobre género, desarrollo y turismo en el Pacífico mexicano. *México y la Cuenca del Pacífico* 13(37), 75–102.

Carosio, A. (2012) Presentación. In: Carosio, A. (ed.) *Feminismo y cambio social en América Latina y el Caribe*, 1st edn. CLACSO, Buenos Aires, Argentina, pp. 9–17.

Deere, D.C. and León, M. (2002) *Género, propiedad y empoderamiento: tierra, Estado y mercado en América Latina*. Universidad Nacional Autónoma de México – FLACSO, Mexico City, Mexico.

Díaz-Carrión, I.A. (2012) Turismo de aventura y participación de las mujeres en Jalcomulco. *PASOS. Revista de Turismo y Patrimonio Cultural* 10(5), 531–542.

Fernández Aldecua, M.J. and Martínez Barón, L.A. (2010). Participación de las mujeres en las empresas turísticas privadas y comunitarias de Bahías de Huatulco, México. ¿Hacia un cambio en el rol de género?. *Cuadernos de Turismo* 26, 129–151.

Fierro Reyes, I.G., García de Fuentes, A. and Marín Guardado, G. (2014) Turismo de hacienda, trabajo femenino y transformaciones locales: el caso de los talleres artesanales de la Fundación Haciendas del Mundo Maya. *Península* 9(1), 105–125.

Gámez, A.E., Ivanova, A. and Wilson, T.D. (2011) Género y comercio informal en destinos turísticos. El caso de las vendedoras de playa en Los Cabos, Baja California Sur, México. *TURyDES: Revista Turismo y Desarrollo Local* 4(9), 1–31.

Hernández, J. and Zafra, G. (2005) *Artesanas y artesanos: creación, innovación y tradición en la producción de artesanías*. Plaza y Valdés, Mexico City, Mexico.

INEGI (2015) *Encuesta Nacional de Ocupación y Empleo*. Available at: www.inegi.org.mx/est/contenidos/Proyectos/encuestas/hogares/regulares/enoe/ (accessed 10 October 2016).

Kabeer, N. (1999) Resources, agency, achievements: reflections on the measurement of women's empowerment. *Development and Change* 30(3), 435–464.

Lagarde, M. (1996) *Género y feminismo. Desarrollo humano y democracia*. Horas y Horas, Madrid, Spain.

Lagarde, M. (2004) Vías para el empoderamiento de las mujeres. Available at: www.femeval.es/proyectos/ProyectosAnteriores/Sinnovaciontecnologia/Documents/ACCION3_cuaderno1.pdf (accessed 10 May 2017).

McAllister, L. (2001) Suave misticismo del barro. *Artes de México* 30, 47–53.

Mendoza Ontiveros, M.M. and Chapulín Carrillo, J. (2015) Turismo, trabajo femenino y empoderamiento de las mujeres en Bahías de Huatulco, Oaxaca, México. *Estudios y Perspectivas en Turismo* 24(2), 316–335.

Moctezuma Yano, P. (2012) Familia patriarcal y trabajo artesano: una forma organizativa laboral sustentada en el parentesco. *Revista de estudios de género: La Ventana* 4(36), 134–177.

Monsiváis, C. (1981). ¿Pero hubo alguna vez once mil machos? *Fem* 5(18), 9–20.

Rodríguez, G. and Acevedo, A. (2015) Cambios en la vida cotidiana de las mujeres a través de la incorporación al trabajo turístico en la Reserva de la Biosfera de la Mariposa Monarca. *El Periplo Sustentable* [Online] 29.

Rojas, O.L. (2016). Mujeres, hombres y vida familiar en México. Persistencia de la inequidad de género anclada en la desigualdad social. *Revista Interdisciplinaria de Estudios de Género* 2(3), 73–101.

Rojas-Serrano, C., Martínez Corona, B., Ocampo Fletes, I. and Cruz Rodríguez, J.A. (2010). Artesanas mixtecas, estrategias de reproducción y cambio. *Revista de estudios de género: La Ventana* 4(31), 101–138.

Rowlands, J. (1997) *Questioning Empowerment: Working with Women in Honduras*. Oxfam, Oxford, UK.

Schneider, L. (2001) Tradición y fantasía del barro. *Artes de México* 30, 30–45.

SECTUR-COLMEX (2011) *Análisis Económico del Mercado Laboral en el Sector Turístico: Hacia una Política Pública para la Igualdad entre Mujeres y Hombres*. SECTUR, El Colegio de México, Mexico City, Mexico.

Serrano-Barquín, R. (2008) Hacia un modelo teórico-metodológico para el análisis del desarrollo, la sostenibilidad y el turismo. *Economía, sociedad y territorio* 8(26), 313–355.

Swain, M.B. (1995) Gender in tourism. *Annals of Tourism Research* 22(2), 247–266.

Tucker, H. and Boonabaana, B. (2012) A critical analysis of tourism, gender and poverty reduction. *Journal of Sustainable Tourism* 20(3), 437–455.

Vizcaino-Suárez, L.P., Serrano-Barquín, R., Cruz-Jiménez, G. and Pastor-Alfonso, M.J. (2014) *El género en la investigación y las políticas turísticas en México*. Available at: www.aecit.org/el-genero-en-la-investigacion-y-las-politicas-turisticas-en-mexic/congress-papers/67 (accessed 15 May 2017).

María's Story: Between My Home and My Job

María Isabel

Fig. S5. María Isabel.

My name is María Isabel, I'm 39 years old. I live in Puná, an island in the Gulf of Guayaquil, Ecuador. I've been working in tourism for 14 years now. When I first got married I hadn't finished school, and my husband was very traditional. He didn't think I needed to study anymore, or to have any business outside of the home. He's a fisherman, but he also did the occasional tour when the odd visitor came. I started going with him on these tours. At the beginning I was very quiet with the visitors. I was there just to keep my husband company while he showed people around. But I began to get interested in tourism. I realized tourism had a lot of potential in my community and that I wanted to get involved.

I asked my husband to let me finish school and, after a long struggle he accepted, as long as I found somebody to take care of our little girls. I also attended every single training course in tourism – the Tourism Ministry came, the municipal government, universities and non-governmental organizations (NGOs), the provincial government, you name it. I took advantage of all the courses, workshops and training sessions they offered us. My family was always there to help me with the girls. My mum, my dad, my brothers and sisters, they all helped so I could finish school and study tourism. I know I'm very lucky since I come from a very close-knit family. In my community not all women have a family to help with their children and that means they can do little else other than staying at home. By attending every single meeting I got a reputation among the authorities – they could see that I wasn't just enthusiastic but also reliable. If an organization wanted to arrange something, a training course, a tour for other authorities, a farm trip, they would call me first because they knew I'd organize the others.

More tourists started to come and my husband and I started working together, as partners. I was happy for him to keep the earnings from our work in tourism. But he really couldn't understand why I wanted to give our tourists more than the other tour operators in the community. If everybody in the village was charging the same for the tours, I'd give my tourists a free coconut, an extra ride, something. We disagreed about this but I was completely convinced about what I was doing. I wanted to give them the best possible experience, I wanted them to come back, I wanted them to remember me and recommend my tours to their friends. The extra effort was incredibly important for me. After a while, I decided to take over the responsibility for the tours. I would invest the money; pay my husband for his services with the boat, for the coconut collection and I would keep the earnings. Of course, he wasn't entirely convinced to begin with. But some time after that, he had an emergency and he needed money. I gladly gave him everything I'd saved. He looked at me differently after that – with respect. He didn't flinch when I said I wanted to buy a bigger boat. Not a fishing boat, but a boat specifically for tourists. He trusted me all along and we did it together. Now, we have the only tourist yacht in the village.

Tourism in our community has improved a lot since we started. Now we have certified guides, some basic tourist services, a dock for the boats, we offer lifejackets and the boats themselves have been improved. Now the tourism activity has been legalized by the Tourism Ministry through our community-based tourism centre: *Subida Alta de la Isla Puná*. After all that study, I'm proud to say that I'm now a certified tour guide. But tourism has also changed our community. Before, there was more interest on our part to show tourists around, to show them how beautiful our community is, to take them to our beaches. But now it's different, we only take the tourists to see the dolphins and the birds because it's quicker. We don't bring them to our community or to spend time on our beach. That means the restaurants don't benefit, and nor do the other members of our village. It's so short-sighted. It's all about the quick money but we're not thinking about developing a kind of tourism that can benefit us all. Tourism has meant that some of us have benefited, but not others. We are no longer as united as a community as we used to be.

I've had many difficulties in my life, but for me, the worst difficulties have had to do with dealing with men who do not allow us, women, to go out in the world to pursue our dreams. There are men involved in tourism in our community, but it's mostly women. But that doesn't mean that men cannot help. They can help their partners and their relatives by encouraging them, with their ideas, and their support so they can go out to study and work. In my own home, tourism has brought me respect and admiration from my husband. Now, we're equal partners and friends. I wish my daughters could work in tourism too, because through tourism they can help their community and have the comforts I didn't have in my time. I also hope they find good husbands who really value them as women and human beings. I want them to be an example for future generations.

6 Trekking to Women's Empowerment: A Case Study of a Female-Operated Travel Company in Ladakh

Belén Martínez Caparrós*

University of the West of England, UK

Introduction

Although the importance of women's empowerment in achieving sustainable development has been increasingly recognized in the international development community, most initiatives still focus on income-generating projects for poor women. The assumption is made that economic empowerment will also bring empowerment to other aspects of their lives. Often these projects fail because they are motivated by economic growth, offering women temporary and part-time employment in traditionally female skills, which have limited markets. The question arises as to whether women would be more empowered if they had the option to leave traditionally female-dominated work roles and enter other economic sectors. Based on a feminist approach, this chapter plans to address this question through the case study of the Ladakhi Women Travel Company (LWTC). The LWTC is a travel agency based in Leh, India, owned and operated by Ladakhi women. Local guide Thinlas Chorol founded the LWTC in 2009 to give women in Ladakh the opportunity to participate in the traditionally male-dominated areas of trekking and mountain climbing. The treks are completely organized by these women who act as guides, porters and cooks as well as customer service, serving as an example that women can fulfil roles normally reserved for men. By working as trekking guides, these women are challenging gender stereotypes in Ladakh, where a woman is expected to be submissive and conform to a traditional Ladakhi notion of obedience and discipline.

Women's Empowerment, Gender Stereotypes and Tourism

The word empowerment has been used by many organizations in different ways and there is no clear consensus on the definition of the term. From the variety of interpretations, Kabeer's definition of empowerment as 'the expansion in people's ability to make strategic life choices where this ability was previously denied to them' (1999, p. 437) is especially relevant for this study because it contains two elements that help distinguish empowerment from other closely related concepts: the idea of process from a condition of disempowerment, and the concept of human agency and choice. Similarly, there is not a standard, collective approach for tracking progress in levels of empowerment

* E-mail: belen.martinez.coporos@gmail.com

either. Among the many frameworks developed to measure women's empowerment, this study makes use of Malhotra and colleagues' (2002) conceptual framework, measuring empowerment in several dimensions and at different levels, and Scheyvens' (2000) framework, which considers the social relationships within the community and an increase of self-esteem, based on beneficial tourism encounters. Both authors' understanding of empowerment and their links to women as the decision-maker are central to this study.

This study also takes on board Malhotra and colleagues' (2002) idea that different dimensions of empowerment are independent: women may be empowered in one area while not in others. Thus, it should not be assumed that if a development intervention promotes women's empowerment along a particular dimension, such as the economic, empowerment in other areas will necessarily follow. Moreover, despite gaining power by becoming economically independent, women may find themselves unable to make the changes that could bring them greater empowerment, because prevailing social norms and limiting self-beliefs restrict their ability to imagine new horizons (Cornwall, 2016). A contemporary understanding of women's empowerment, while keeping the idea that women need to be aware of their choices if they are to become decision-makers, adds the need for a change in cultural and social norms. Ultimately, empowerment is a process that challenges assumptions about the way things are and can be.

One of the economic sectors that has been depicted as beneficial to empower and help women progress is tourism due to its diverse, dynamic and flexible nature (Ateljevic, 2008). However, some scholars consider tourism a highly gendered activity that in fact reinforces traditional gender roles and unequal divisions of labour (Tucker and Boonabaana, 2012). This chapter seeks to shed some light on this discussion and specifically explore the involvement of women in a non-traditional economic activity such as mountaineering, as a contributor to women's empowerment, with attention paid to gender stereotypes.

Ladakh: A Subtle Yet Strong Patriarchy

Ladakh is a region of India located high in the western Himalayas. The landscape is barren and dry, and the climate is extreme with temperatures ranging from 30°C in the summer to −50°C in the winter (Daultrey and Gergan, 2011). The population of Ladakh has traditionally been widely dispersed in small agricultural villages (Norberg-Hodge, 2013). For centuries, Ladakhis pursued a relatively self-reliant existence, economically based on subsistence agriculture and trade with Tibet in wool, salt and dried apricots (Norberg-Hodge, 2013).

Ladakh remained almost totally isolated until 1962 when, in response to the conflict in Tibet, a road was built by the Indian Army to link the region with the rest of the country. Opened for tourism in 1974, Ladakh has witnessed a steady growth in numbers of visitors (Norberg-Hodge, 2013), resulting in the tourism industry becoming an important economic sector for Ladakh. This has led to many changes in the region, such as growth in the population of urban centres and the proliferation of travel agencies. There were 426 registered agencies in 2014, with LWTC being the only agency in the sector to be owned by a woman (Kulkarni, 2016). Tourism is generating revenue for the region and enormous employment opportunities for both skilled and unskilled workers.

My research found that Ladakhis have the general conception that women are equal to men and enjoy a relative emancipation compared to other rural parts of India. Some authors go further and describe no patriarchal structure in Ladakh (Chhewang, 2006, cited by Ladol, 2013). This idea is based on the fact that women in Ladakh play an important role in the economy and not only look after the household but also the fields and animals. Despite this general perception, some voices challenge this by describing Ladakhi society as 'a subtle yet strong patriarchy' (Ladol, 2013, p. 1). Ladol (2013) recognizes that, although the status of women is better in Ladakh compared to other parts of India, it does not mean patriarchy does not exist. Culturally, a woman is expected to be submissive and conform to a traditional Ladakhi notion of obedience and discipline. Politically, the centre of the decision-making system is male-dominated. Meetings regarding the village are held in community halls where all the families are represented by a male head of the family or other male members. Men hold the public positions and often sit separately from women at community meetings and make the decisions. In the current male-dominated political landscape, no one talks about the marginalization of women because the powerful maintain the status quo. Based on my time spent in Ladakh, I agree with Ladol in that patriarchal structures exist and are strong in Ladakh and that the general perception of the high status of women is only in comparison to other parts of India where women are more visibly oppressed.

This Research: A Feminist Qualitative Approach

This study followed a feminist approach by focusing on gender differences and how they relate to the elements of social organization. By using this approach, this researcher is committed to making women's voices more audible and explore women's empowerment through ordinary talk (Maguire, 2001). The primary means of data collection in this research was semi-structured interviews that explored individual experiences, opinions and feelings (Hesse-Biber, 2013). I travelled to Ladakh in September 2016 to conduct face-to-face interviews, carry out research observation and make field notes. The participants were all trekking guides currently working in the LWTC (see p. 67 for Thinlas, the founder's story). The demographic profile of respondents was similar: the majority were young (under 30) and single. Only two of the participants were married and had children. Participants had been working at the LWTC for between 2 and 8 years, and they came from villages around Ladakh where there are few employment opportunities. In total, I conducted 11 audio-recorded interviews (between 40 and 60 min each) in English,

which meant no translator was necessary, and therefore interviews were conducted without anyone else present. The interviews were transcribed and coded in order to identify patterns, from which I deciphered themes.

Themes from the Interviews

This section shows the main themes identified during the interviews. Naturalized transcriptions have been employed that used minimal editing in order to stay true to the actual speech (Oliver *et al.*, 2005). To meet ethical standards and keep anonymity of participants, pseudonyms have been used.

Expanded awareness

During the interviews, many examples of high self-esteem and self-confidence were found, showing that the women recognize their own power and motivate themselves into action. There was a sense of pride about breaking gender stereotypes and gaining new skills, which demonstrated high self-confidence. 'I am proud. Before, there were no women doing this. I am proud I am one of them now. I like that there are opportunities to learn English and to meet different kind of people' (*Prisha*).

When asked about the learning of particular skills, all participants stressed learning English as their biggest achievement and, with it, the ability to communicate with foreigners and learn about other cultures. However, interviewees showed a westernized view of the outside world (Sadler, 2013), probably because most tourists who visit Ladakh are from western countries. They seemed to see everywhere outside India as 'the west', where English is the only spoken language. For example, this was seen during Myra's interview: 'In modern times English is very important because if you go to another country, everyone speaks English. English is a major subject.' While English seemed to be the most valued skill developed, it is linked to gaining knowledge of other cultures. The women seemed excited about the awareness of other cultures and the relative confidence of the western women: 'all foreigners have confidence, maybe better than us, better than Ladakhi people' (*Prisha*).

Interestingly, this newly gained awareness also allowed them to reflect with pride on aspects of their own culture, such as the importance of family: 'I think I am fortunate because in other countries they are not living together with the parents. After 18 years old they are going to separate. In Ladakh many families are joined families. So I feel proud of myself and I feel happy with my family, how we are still together, sharing and caring. It makes me feel proud of my culture and my country' (*Anika*).

In general, it is shown how by interacting with tourists, there is an increased ability to interact outside the known environment, the home, and these women felt they were exposed to realities they have not met before.

Social norms remain unchallenged in the private sphere

Traditionally, the vision of the public sphere as masculine and the private sphere, or family life, as feminine has been deeply embedded in the social understanding of roles attributed to men and women (UNDP, 2013). In this traditional view, men are considered to have a greater role in the public sphere as well as enjoy more freedom of choice, while women tend to be responsible for the household and childcare, often seen as supportive tasks, where their ways of expression and action are limited (UNDP, 2013). Women play an important role, but face persistent structural constraints (UN Women Watch, 2012).

The interviews show how participants feel strong and able to challenge stereotypes in the public sphere. Riya described during the interview how 'traditionally people said that trekking guide was a male job but I never saw it like this. Every people can do everything.' Contrary to this, when private or family matters were discussed, social norms seem to remain unchallenged, as Anika exemplified:

'I cook at home because in Ladakh mostly women cook. Some who are lucky, her husband cooks [laughing]. But my husband doesn't cook, so I have to cook alone.' This is an example of how housework is believed to be women's responsibility and this assignment is so deeply institutionalized in household rules and practices that it appears non-negotiable.

Despite challenging feminine roles in the working environment, the idea that women are socially and culturally expected to conduct household chores was still widely shared among respondents: 'When I am here [in Leh], I do everything and my brothers don't do anything. I think they think that it's the sister that needs to do it. I agree with them, but it's not right' (*Aditi*). In their study, Keizer and Komter (2015) found that, in general, women ascribe the responsibility for the housework to themselves. Participants in this research seemed to assume this responsibility, which was a recurrent topic throughout all the interviews. Similarly, other studies suggest that improvements in women's labour market opportunities do not translate into an improvement of intra-household outcomes in their favour (Badola *et al.*, 2014). Instead, the inclusion of women into the labour market appears to only increase the burden they must bear, inducing them to increase their effort in work and decrease their leisure time (Chen *et al.*, 2007).

Additionally, some participants highlighted that, when staying at homestays,[1] they are expected to help in the house: 'They are also happy that we are there and they want more women to go there because we help them in the homestay cooking and shopping. Boys don't do that' (*Kyra*). Consequently, they are also expected to perform the role of domestic helper when working. These implicit expectations of women as the helper and cook are strong, as they are based on automatic or habitual responses (Rudman and Kilianski, 2000). Keizer and Komter (2015) argue that perceptions and observations of reality can be influenced in such a way that they prevent people from experiencing situations as negative so that they acquiesce. Participants did not seem to consider any option other than helping, and even seemed happy to do it, as by assuming their expected role they felt accepted. This is an example of how traditional gender roles become internalized and can be used by patriarchal societies to maintain the existing task division in the household.

Another extension of this traditional gender role is seen in the care of family members. Some participants explained how they would look for a female family member to look after their child or siblings when they have to go on a trek. 'When I go on a trek, I take him [my son] to the village so he can stay with my parents. If I have to go suddenly, I have to leave him with his auntie' (*Anika*). Interestingly, they would not even consider leaving them with the father. We can see here that the role of women as primary carers is deeply embedded in the society. The assumption that women are responsible for looking after family members is also seen during Zara's interview, when she recognizes she has not even considered how the person taking care of her child feels: 'She doesn't say if she is not happy. (…) I have never thought about it.' These are examples of how these women have internalized the female role as the carer. This illustrates how patriarchal structures are maintained and reproduced by being internalized not only by the dominant group who benefits from it, but also by those that occupy a minority status within it. The internalization of schemas that make up patriarchal structures becomes the mechanism by which it is legitimized and reproduced, becoming guidelines for people's behaviours (Gallagher, 2007).

Interestingly, findings in this case study contradict Kabeer's (2005) research from the South Asian context. Kabeer suggests that the renegotiation of power relations, particularly within the family, is often about changes in informal decision-making, with women opting for private forms of empowerment, which retain intact the public image, and honour, of the traditional decision-maker but which nevertheless increase women's 'backstage' influence in the decision-making process (Kabeer, 1999). On the contrary, participants in this research demonstrated higher levels of confidence in the public sphere but maintained traditional roles at a familial level. This could be due to a lack of freedom from domination by the family (Schuler *et al.*, 2010) highlighting the importance of the family unit (Acharya and Bennett, 1981). Sen (1997) shows the impact of internalized oppression when women believe that their health and well-being are less important than other family members'. Examples of this domination by family were heard during the interviews and all interviewees agreed they would stop working as a trekking guide if their prospective husband would not accept it. Riya, for example, explained: 'If my husband or the family don't accept my job, I think I will need to stop'.

In this case study, the power to challenge stereotypes in the public sphere by working as trekking guides does not correspond with challenging stereotypes in the private sphere, where participants carry the housework responsibility and childcare with a sense of it being non-negotiable.

The shadow of sexual assault

Despite being strong in challenging stereotypes in the public sphere, one of the common themes reflected throughout all the interviews was vulnerability and insecurity. All participants reported feeling insecure when working as trekking guides and choosing to work at a female-only agency made them feel more secure. Zara described it during the interview:

> I know I wouldn't be working as a trekking guide if it wasn't for this company. Other agencies would not employ me as a woman. This company is also better for women working because everyone is female: porters, guides… Some women can be scared of working in another company because of porters and guides being males. This company is good because all are female and this is good for the guide and good for the porter.

The insecurity they feel is not a surprise as violence against women is considered a 'global health problem of epidemic proportions' by the World Health Organization (2013). In India, sexual violence against women has reached alarming proportions. The latest National Crime Records Bureau data show that 34,651 women were raped in 2015 in India (NCRB, 2016). Despite no cases of violence being reported during any of the interviews, vulnerability and insecurity were constant themes, showing the fear they felt while working as trekking guides. Myra explained:

> I like this company because it is only women. This is why I've chosen this company. I like working with women because it is more comfortable than working with only men. Like working with porters. When we go to trek with other companies, they only offer male porters. Here only female. This is why I like it. One time I did the Nubra Valley trekking with male guide, male porter, male cook... All staff was male. First I thought I could do that. But later I came to know that it was a bit uncomfortable and danger with only men.

For Sharma and Bazilli (2014), this feeling of insecurity is a consequence of the patriarchy where men are placed above women, often resulting in the oppression and exploitation of women. Similarly, Bradley (2006) states that domestic violence is seen as a way for men to sustain inequalities against women and to reinforce women's subordination. Patriarchal norms are embedded in Indian culture and frequently accepted by women, as seen in this case study, where women assume they must change their behaviour to remain safe.

Wesely and Gaarder (2004) highlight that women have not been encouraged to be comfortable in public space but instead have learned that the private, domestic realm is their domain. A woman in a public arena may feel vulnerable to unpredictable invasions of her physical self, ranging on a continuum from objectification to violent crime. These unpredictable invasions cumulatively contribute to women's fear in public spaces and their fear of rape in their everyday life: what Ferraro called the 'shadow of sexual assault' (1996, p. 667).

Interestingly, participants seemed to agree that it is women's responsibility to avoid situations of risk. This can be seen during Aisha's interview:

> It really depends on women and how they behave. If we [women] behave ourselves there is no danger. Actually in our society in Ladakh it is believed that it is not good one woman working with a man. People gossip and talk bad. But I think we should behave ourselves, then we can do anything as men.

This idea of women being in control of their own safety is in line with Stanko's argument (2013, p. 73) that 'women learn, often at a very early age, that their sexuality is not their own and that maleness can at any point intrude into it'. Isha explained in her interview how when men are not present, she is not scared: 'No problem because there are always female as our clients'. This links to the general presumption that women are the gatekeepers of male desire (Tolman, 1991), which has justified men's limited accountability for aggressive, harassing and criminal sexual conduct. This was also seen during the research, as participants did not blame men, but often justified men's actions by the consumption of alcohol. Prisha exemplified this:

> I wouldn't work for another trekking agency because they are mainly men like helper, porter, cook. During the nights men drink alcohol and smoke and I don't like that. I wouldn't feel safe. Men mostly drink alcohol and when they are drunk they don't know what they do.

This self-assumed responsibility supports the idea that women think they should be able to prevent violence against them by changing their own behaviour. In India, this is supported by the terminology used in legislation and media when describing safety and protection of women (Livne, 2015). The law effectively perpetuates gender hierarchy by focusing on women taking measures to protect themselves by remaining inside the house, dressing conservatively and travelling with male escorts, instead of recommending practices that protect women's independence and livelihood. The campaign about violence against women is dominated by patriarchal understandings of safety and violence (Dutta and Sircar, 2013). The patriarchy indirectly blames women for the violation of women's safety, reflected in Myra's belief that 'if woman keeps distance with men, men will respect the woman'.

One of the inhibitors of women's empowerment is the fact that women feel insecure in the shadow of sexual assault, which leads them to feel uncomfortable in public spaces. The interviewees demonstrate how women absorb the patriarchal message that they are responsible for the violation of women's safety. It is clear that changing the patriarchal norms that support violence against women is central to achieving gender equality and women's empowerment.

Decision-making within limited options

Considering empowerment involves the expansion in people's ability to make strategic life choices (Kabeer, 1999), it was essential to discuss with participants their ability to make decisions in different areas of their life. Therefore, an important question during the interviews concerned what they did with their salary. Participants gave diverse answers, but all of them stated they had independently made that decision. For instance, Meera explained: 'I pay for the house. My brother and sister are studying, so I pay for everything. I decided it.' This independence in controlling economic resources shows a high level of economic empowerment. However, the decisions they make are from a relatively limited list of options. Chopra and Müller (2016) broaden the concept of decision-making to encompass not just whether women are free to make a choice between options, but to how many options there are and whether women are confined in their choices by internal and external expectations. Based on this concept, I challenge the idea that participants demonstrated a high level of agency because of their demonstrated lack of vision of other choices in regards to spending their income. Additionally, when they were asked about other possibilities of gaining income apart from their current role, most of them appeared shocked and were unable to think of any. This was common for any question related to possibilities or options in the future, whether related to income, personal development or overcoming difficulties. Very few participants answered

these questions, with responses ranging from 'looking for another job' (*Myra*) to 'staying at home. My husband would need to get enough money' (*Anika*). Although Rowlands (1997) suggests that this could be due to the lack of employment opportunities in the area, I maintain that their level of agency is not as high as one may initially assume based on the lack of vision of other options.

An important area of decision-making is the political sphere. In Ladakh, one of the direct ways to participate in politics is by attending the village meetings where decisions about the village are made. When asked about attending these meetings, all participants said they go sometimes but do not usually participate. As Mendelberg and Karpowitz (2016) highlight, political intervention is an important aspect of equality and empowerment. The village councils make decisions that govern every aspect of life, but women are vastly underrepresented in them. In this research, women do not seem to be unrepresented in numbers, but in level of participation:

> Usually these meetings are with more women than men because men are working outside the village. If there is an important decision, then men would come to the meeting. (*Riya*)

Some scholars argue that the involvement of women in political processes is the way to initiate an empowering change at the individual level (Johnson, 1992, cited by Rowlands, 1997). Therefore, organizing women to achieve power in politics will influence the social fabric and achieve individual empowerment.

By analysing the different levels of participants' decision-making, it is clear empowerment is more than simply opening up access to decision-making. It includes having a variety of options and being able to envision new options. It must also include the processes that lead people to perceive themselves as able and entitled to occupy that decision-making space (Rowlands, 1997).

Conclusion

Implications from the findings are not intended to be generalized but can provide insight in dealing with gender issues, particularly in situations that begin to challenge traditional gender roles such as women joining male-dominated environments. The complexity of empowerment is highlighted in this research. The women in this case study are negotiating their role between their public and private lives, allowing them to keep their cultural representation of being 'good women'.[2] By working in the mountaineering sector, they are achieving financial independence and learning about other cultures, improving their ability to communicate with others and bringing some self-efficacy. These women are still not prepared to profoundly challenge many of the socio-cultural norms and expectations imposed upon them, causing them to carry a double burden of domestic and work responsibilities, even in their working environment.

Results have shown how vulnerability plays a significant role in these women's lives and restricts their choices, demonstrating that violence against women is a major inhibitor of women's empowerment (Barnett et al., 2005). Examples of insecurity and the belief that they should change their own behaviour to prevent violence against them were dominant during the interviews. Mitchell rightly states that violence against women 'destroys the potential of girls and women in developing countries and prevents them from pulling themselves out of poverty' (DfID, 2012, p. 2). If violence against women is the most widespread form of abuse worldwide, the question remains: how can women become more empowered if they do not feel secure? As women feel more confident to challenge the social norms that subtly condone violence against women, this will allow women and girls to be more active in the public sphere, and therefore to feel more empowered. As ActionAid UK states, 'empowering women is both the means and the end' (Moosa, 2012).

There was a high agency of decision-making in these women shown through the independence in controlling their economic resources, which in turn shows a high level of economic empowerment although showing a lack of vision on other options. However, their participation in the village councils seems to be extremely low, which shows how unrepresented and unheard they are in the decision-making structures. These women have not yet gained the necessary confidence to insist on their voices being heard in the political sphere.

The above findings demonstrate that projects focusing only on economic empowerment ignore other vital aspects of women's empowerment, allowing social and patriarchal norms to go unchallenged and continue to limit women's lives. Effective gender equality initiatives need to go beyond economic empowerment and ask 'what is meaningful empowerment?' Effective empowerment is not only the increased choices, but that these choices can go against patriarchal norms or women's status, changing ideologies. This is the kind of process that can create lasting change for multiple generations. Non-governmental organizations (NGOs) and governments working on women's empowerment should plan their efforts thinking about the kind of empowering methodologies that engage critical consciousness, question norms that were taken for granted and, in doing so, make a vital contribution to shifting power relations.

The case study drawn upon in this research, underscores the importance of working at the level of individual consciousness to expand women's sense of their own possibilities and critical recognition of the societal dimensions of the obstacles they currently face. Freeing women from these constraints and unlocking their potential should be considered a priority in future initiatives.

Acknowledgements

I would like to thank the Developing Areas Research Group (DARG) for honouring me with the DARG travel bursary award to conduct my fieldwork in Ladakh. I would also like to thank my interviewees and everyone who gave up their time for interviews and support.

Notes

[1] Homestay is a form of accommodation where visitors stay in a house of a local of the place to which they are travelling. It allows visitors to experience the local community and culture of the place they're visiting.
[2] A 'good woman' is a respectable woman in the community living within the cultural expectations (Boonabaana, 2014).

References

Acharya, M. and Bennett, L. (1981) Rural women of Nepal: an aggregate analysis and summary of 8 village studies. *The Status of Women in Nepal. Volume II, Part 9: Field Studies.* Centre for Economic Development and Administration, Tribhuvan University, Kathmandu, Nepal.

Ateljevic, I. (2008) *Women Empowerment through Tourism.* Wageningen University, Wageningen, The Netherlands.

Badola, R., Ogra, M. and Barthwal, S. (2014) Ecodevelopment, gender, and empowerment: perspectives from India's protected area communities. In: Oberhauser, A.M. and Johnston-Anumonwo, I. (eds) *Global Perspectives on Gender and Space: Engaging Feminism and Development.* Routledge, New York, pp. 200–223.

Barnett, O., Miller-Perrin, C.L. and Perrin, R.D. (2005) *Family Violence Across the Lifespan: An Introduction* [online], 2nd edn. SAGE, Thousand Oaks, California.

Boonabaana, B. (2014) Negotiating gender and tourism work: women's lived experiences in Uganda. *Tourism and Hospitality Research* 14(1–2), 27. DOI: 10.1177/1467358414529578.

Bradley, T. (2006) *Challenging the NGOs: Women, Religion, and Western Dialogues in India,* 10th edn. I.B. Tauris, London.

Chen, N., Conconi, P. and Perroni, C. (2007) Women's earning power and the 'double burden' of market and household work. Available at: https://ssrn.com/abstract=1135507 (accessed 27 June 2017).

Chopra, D. and Müller, C. (2016) Connecting perspectives on women's empowerment. *IDS Bulletin* 47(1A).

Cornwall, A. (2016) Women's empowerment: what works? *Journal of International Development* 28(3), 342–359. DOI: 10.1002/jid.3210.

Daultrey, S. and Gergan, R. (2011) Living with change: adaptation and innovation in Ladakh. *Climate Adaptation.* Available at: www.ourplanet.com/climate-adaptation/Daultrey_Gergan.pdf (accessed 20 July 2017).

Department for International Development (DfID) (2012) *Britain Combats Domestic Violence and Trafficking Across Developing World.* Available at: https://www.gov.uk/government/news/international-womens-day-uk-tackles-violence-against-women (accessed 27 June 2017).

Dutta, D. and Sircar, O. (2013) India's winter of discontent: some feminist dilemmas in the wake of a rape. *Feminist Studies* 39(1), 293–306.

Ferraro, K.F. (1996) Women's fear of victimization: shadow of sexual assault? *Social Forces* 75(2), 667–690. DOI: 10.1093/sf/75.2.667.

Gallagher, S.K. (2007) Agency, resources, and identity: lower-income women's experiences in Damascus. *Gender and Society* 21(2), 227–249. DOI: 10.1177/0891243206296990.

Hesse-Biber, S. (2013) *Feminist Research Practice: A Primer* [online], 2nd edn. SAGE, Los Angeles, California. DOI: 9781412984270.

Kabeer, N. (1999) Resources, agency, achievements: reflections on the measurement of women's empowerment. *Development and Change* 30(3), 435–464. DOI: 10.1088/0022-3727/41/12/125502.

Kabeer, N. (2005) Is microfinance a 'magic bullet' for women's empowerment? *Economic and Political Weekly* 40(44–45), 4709–4718.

Keizer, R. and Komter, A. (2015) Are 'equals' happier than 'less equals'? A couple analysis of similarity and well-being. *Journal of Marriage and Family* 77(4), 954–967. DOI: 10.1111/jomf.12194.

Kulkarni, N. (2016) Ladakh's first and only all-women travel company and the woman who started it all. *The Better India,* January, p.23.

Ladol, C. (2013) A subtle yet strong patriarchy. *Contemporary Ladakh.* Institute of Peace and Public Studies (237).

Livne, E. (2015) *Violence Against Women in India: Origins, Perpetuation and Reform.* Carnegie Mellon University. Available at:fwww.cmu.edu/hss/globalstudies/images/livne-gs-capstone-paper.pdf (accessed 1 April 2017).

Maguire, P. (2001) Uneven ground: Feminisms and action research. In: Reason, P. and Bradbury, H. (eds) *Handbook of Action Research: Participative Inquiry and Practice* [online]. SAGE, London, pp. 59–69.

Malhotra, A., Schüler, S.R. and Boender, C. (2002) *Measuring Women's Empowerment as a Variable in International Development*. World Bank Publications, Washington, DC. DOI: 10.1002/jid.3050.

Mendelberg, T. and Karpowitz, C.F. (2016) Women's authority in political decision-making groups. *The Leadership Quarterly* 27(3), 487–503. DOI: 10.1016/j.leaqua.2015.11.005.

Moosa, Z. (2012) A theory of change for tackling violence against women and girls. Available at: https://www.actionaid.org.uk/sites/default/files/doc_lib/theory_of_change_on_vawg.pdf (accessed 8 April 2017).

National Crime Records Bureau (NCRB) (2016) *Crime in India – 2015*. Chapter 5 Crime Against Women. National Crime Records Bureau, New Delhi.

Norberg-Hodge, H. (2013) *Ancient Futures: Learning from Ladakh*. Random House, London.

Oliver, D.G., Serovich, J.M. and Mason, T.L. (2005) Constraints and opportunities with interview transcription: towards reflection in qualitative research. *Social Forces* 84(2), 1273–1289. DOI: 10.1353/sof.2006.0023.

Rowlands, J. (1997) *Questioning Empowerment: Working with Women in Honduras*. Oxfam, Oxford. DOI:10.3362/9780855988364.

Rudman, L.A. and Kilianski, S.E. (2000) Implicit and explicit attitudes toward female authority. *Personality and Social Psychology Bulletin* 26(11), 1315–1328. DOI: 10.1177/0146167204271710.

Sadler, M. (2013) 2020 Vision. *Itnow* 55(1), 22–23.

Scheyvens, R. (2000) Promoting women's empowerment through involvement in ecotourism: experiences from the third world. *Journal of Sustainable Tourism* [online] 8(3), 232–249. DOI: 10.1080/09669580008667360.

Schuler, S.R., Islam, F. and Rottach, E. (2010) Women's empowerment revisited: a case study from Bangladesh. *Development in Practice* 20(7), 840–854. DOI: 10.1080/09614524.2010.508108.

Sen, G. (1997) Empowerment as an approach to poverty. Background Paper to the Human Development Report. Report number: Working Paper Series 97.07. UNDP, New York.

Sharma, R. and Bazilli, S. (2014) Violence against women: what's law got to do with it? A reflection on gang rape in India. *International Journal for Crime* 3(3), 4–21. DOI: 10.5204/ijcjsd.v3i3.155.

Stanko, E.A. (2013) *Intimate Intrusions: Women's Experience of Male Violence*. Routledge, Abingdon, UK.

Tolman, D.L. (1991) Adolescent girls, women and sexuality: discerning dilemmas of desire. *Women and Therapy* [online] 11(3/4), 55. DOI: 10.1300/J015V11N03_04.

Tucker, H. and Boonabaana, B. (2012) A critical analysis of tourism, gender and poverty reduction. *Journal of Sustainable Tourism* 20(3), 437–455. DOI: 10.1080/09669582.2011.622769.

UN Women Watch (2012) Facts and figures: rural women and the Millennium Development Goals. Available at:www.un.org/womenwatch/feature/ruralwomen/facts-figures.html (accessed 15 September 2017).

United Nations Devopment Programme (UNDP) (2013) *Public Perceptions on Gender Equality in Politics and Business*. UNDP Georgia, Tbilisi, Georgia.

Wesely, J.K. and Gaarder, E. (2004) The gendered 'nature' of the urban outdoors: women negotiating fear of violence. *Gender and Society* 18(5), 645–663. DOI: 10.1177/0891243204268127.

World Health Organization (WHO) (2013) Violence against women: a 'global health problem of epidemic proportions'. Available at: www.who.int/mediacentre/news/releases/2013/violence_against_women_20130620/en (accessed 1 April 2017).

Thinlas' Story

Thinlas Chorol

Fig. S6. Thinlas.

Thinlas had to break several barriers when she decided to become a mountaineering guide in Ladakh, a place whose rugged terrain demands extreme physical endurance for trekking. This is her story.

My Journey

I was born in 1981 in Takmachik, a remote village in western Ladakh. My mother died when I was just a baby. I used to go up the mountain with my father and his herds of goats and sheep. This is how my love for mountains grew up in me.

It was while at college that I began trekking with foreign volunteers when a woman told me she wanted a female guide after unwanted sexual advances from her male guide. I felt it was natural for me to walk in the mountains so went with her. I was then mistaken for a foreigner during this trip. Locals assumed I was a tourist and were trying to talk to me in English as they could not, in their wildest imagination, guess that a Ladakhi woman could be a trekking guide. But the trip was a great experience and I decided to attend mountaineering courses to gain some professional skills, and began looking for work as a mountaineering guide.

Local agencies offered me only cultural work, taking tourists around monasteries. Despite my trekking competence, many travel companies refused to hire me as a guide, solely because I was a woman. Most men, on the other hand, were hired as trekking guides even without any professional training or knowledge of trekking routes or awareness of environmental impact. I was repeatedly told that a Ladakhi woman going into the mountains with a group of foreigners would be frowned upon by society. I persevered, got some qualifications and, after a few years as a freelance, in 2009 I set up my own agency, the Ladakhi Women's Travel Company (LWTC). The LWTC has the distinction of being Ladakh's first and only travel company completely owned and operated by women. We are just one agency, whereas there are several hundred that are male-owned.

Now I am training more local women to become female guides. I am proud that I am able to create job opportunities for Ladakhi women and to create an option for female tourists who prefer trekking with female guides. Local women join as interns and later they become porters and finally guides. Unfortunately, this process needs to be done regularly as many leave: some get other jobs, some get married and some find the job too difficult.

Gender Inequality

At the beginning people thought women couldn't do this and the trekking agency was not going to last long. But things have changed in Ladakh and now people have started accepting women as guides. A big change is that now other agencies are interested in hiring our professional guides as more clients are asking for female guides.

In 2012 I co-founded the Ladakhi Women's Welfare Network (LWWN). This group aims to help women in different ways, to empower and educate them on their legal rights and to build confidence in them. In a few short years, this group has given a voice to women and girls who were not being heard. LWWN is currently planning a women's shelter and a very ambitious learning centre, which will focus on social justice issues for women.

The Challenges

The main challenge for LWTC is the seasonal nature of our work, with the season being barely 4 months from June to September. This is the main reason behind my last project, the Ladakhi Women's Café, which opened in 2016. This is a little café situated in Leh selling local food. The idea of the café is that women will be able to work during the off-season period, getting a stable income through the year, becoming more independent and confident.

My Vision

Women should think for themselves and not depend on their families. If they believe in themselves, they can achieve what they want. Women should not listen to what society is saying. They should listen to their own ability to work. Then, definitively, they will succeed if they work hard.

My vision for LWTC is to see trekking guides spread their wings across the globe and, in turn, inspire many others to actualize their dreams.

7 Women and Tourism in the Township: Tourism for Empowerment?

Meghan Muldoon*

University of Waterloo, Waterloo, Canada

Introduction

In South Africa, the term 'township' is used to refer to generally underdeveloped and underserviced residential areas, which, up until the end of the 20th century, were the only urban areas non-white citizens were permitted to reside in. Created as spaces of racial, economic, and geographic segregation and oppression during the period of apartheid, townships continue to be characterized by impoverished housing, poor sanitation and inadequate infrastructure. In this chapter I present some of the photographs and stories that were shared with me by the members of a women's empowerment organization as part of a larger PhotoVoice study of the hosts' gaze in township tourism.

In 2016 I undertook my PhD research in three township communities surrounding the city of Cape Town, South Africa. Guided by a feminist postcolonial theoretical framework, I was motivated to learn about how residents of the townships perceive the foreign tourists who tour their communities, and in particular how they use their own hosts' gaze to negotiate, reinforce or resist the gendered, racialized and economically privileged tourists' gazes that are cast upon them. A PhotoVoice methodology was used, in which research participants were given digital cameras and asked to take photographs of what tourism *is like* in the township and what tourism *should be like*. A total of 14 cameras were distributed to participants and I conducted a number of unstructured group and individual interviews over a period of several months. In the course of this research, I encountered the women of Indawo Yethu[1] and six of their members agreed to participate and take photographs.

Indawo Yethu was founded in 2008 when an American tourist to Khayelitsha Township chose to purchase and donate the building that now houses the centre. Ongoing project funding is provided by Manyano,[2] a township tour operator that redirects its profits from tourism back into community programming. The centre is also supported by the tourists who come to visit Indawo Yethu and purchase the handicrafts that are produced and sold by the women. Much more than a stop on the tourists' circuit, however, Indawo Yethu has become a fulcrum for women's engagement and empowerment in the community. Through Indawo Yethu, women come together to learn new skills, build a community garden, offer after-school programming to marginalized children and provide a hot lunch daily for anyone in need.

* E-mail: mmuldoon@uwaterloo.ca

Indawo Yethu is a space where women can come together and create employment for themselves, whilst also strengthening their community. As they go about their daily work, the centre plays host to frequent groups of tourists who arrive in big white vans with cameras at the ready. Rather than see these incursions as invasive, the women welcome the tourists and are eager to talk about the work that they are doing. I conceptualized this research with a view of township tours as exploitative and voyeuristic, but over time I began to appreciate the ways in which the women's perspectives differed from my own. The women at Indawo Yethu told me that they value the tours as opportunities to support their livelihoods and share their stories with the people who come to learn about their lives. Their experiences of oppression and invisibility in the highly racialized society of South Africa have meant that they feel a sense of pride in having the tourists wish to come and see the places where they live.

While the women shared overwhelmingly positive accounts regarding their experiences with the tourists, their photographs and stories also demonstrated an understanding of how the tourists' conceptualizations of who they are as people operate within a truncated framework that does not extend beyond their perceptions of the community and its residents as impoverished and victimized, a tourists' gaze that the women are gently trying to subvert in their exchanges with the tourists. The differences between my own initial, western-informed perspective of how women would perceive the tourists and the views that they shared with me support the use of a feminist postcolonial framework through which to examine issues related to female tourism hosts in a township in South Africa.

In this chapter, I present a brief overview of feminist postcolonial theory, PhotoVoice methodology, the contexts of apartheid and the townships, and the photographs and narratives that the women of Indawo Yethu chose to share with me. Viewed through the lens of feminist postcolonialism, the positive support for the presence of tourists in the townships, as well as the understated messages of resistance to the tourists' gaze, speak to the insidious nature of the effects of colonialism in the lives of these women as well as the resilience of those who continue to resist its implications in their everyday lives.

Feminist Postcolonial Theory

In tourism studies, feminist postcolonial theory is taken up in order to expose the (neo)colonial nature of much of tourism practice and how people and places are Othered and gendered in tourism spaces (Aitchison, 2001). Much work has been dedicated to examining how images and representations in tourism invariably depict non-western Others as 'mysterious, backward, sensual, deviant, peripheral' (Santos and Caton, 2008, p. 192) in a manner that is highly reminiscent of colonial ways of knowing (Cohen, 1995; Buzinde et al., 2006; Echtner and Prasad, 2003). Mowforth and Munt (2003) refer to the 'subservience' that is inherent in tourism in the developing world (p. 44), Cole and Eriksson (2010) talk of the 'master-servant relationship' that is reminiscent of colonial times (p. 110) and Higgins-Desbiolles (2010) decries the 'exploitative nature' of some forms of tourism (p. 195).

Feminist postcolonial theory represents an effort to counteract the homogenizing tendencies of both feminist and postcolonial theories (Lewis and Mills, 2003). Many developing world scholars, including Spivak (1988), Mohanty (2003) and Trinh (1989), have protested the tendency of feminist meta-narratives to represent all women as universally oppressed, which acts to erase or homogenize the experiences of women in the global south. Mohanty (2003) has argued that this essentializing tendency leads to a single construction of 'an average Third World woman', who is invariably oppressed, uneducated, religious, powerless, poor and victimized (p. 53). Feminist postcolonialism strives to name and shed light on the ways in which white, western perspectives are constructed as normative in a binary that both silences and makes secondary the experiences of the southern Other.

South African feminist scholarship emerged during the period of the 1970s and 1980s, which saw opposition to both apartheid and colonialism more broadly by those living under colonial rule as well as from supporters in the global north (Morrell, 2016). South African feminism was informed by western feminism, but also emerged along its own path, embedded within the social complexity and political aspirations of the times (Morell, 2016). In her 2007 book, Raewyn Connell coined the term 'Southern Theory' in order to challenge the hegemonic status of knowledge produced in the global north and centre knowledge produced under colonial rule and its attendant inequalities (Morrell, 2016). She stated that the 'theoretical frameworks developed in the metropole become embedded in the intellectual work of the periphery, not by the exercise of direct control, but by the way the whole economy of knowledge is organized' (Connell, 2007, p. 524). In being guided by the perspectives of the township residents, this research represents an effort to continue in the feminist postcolonial intention of decentring northern perspectives and sharing a research space within which voices of people from the global south may be prioritized.

PhotoVoice Methodology

PhotoVoice is a participatory methodology developed by Wang et al. (1996) in their work with rural women in China. Founded in theories of emancipatory education, feminisms and documentary photography (Wang et al., 1996, p. 1391), PhotoVoice has three primary objectives:

1. To provide women with a tool to record and share issues of importance to them from their own perspectives.
2. To learn collectively about significant issues in their lives.
3. To have a means of sharing these issues of importance with policy-makers and other stakeholders. (Wang et al., 1996, p. 1391)

This participatory methodology provides a visual representation that can be discussed,

explored and analysed (Wang and Redwood-Jones, 2001). In addition, and unlike traditional interviews, PhotoVoice allows participants to reflect on how they construct and reconstruct their narratives as they engage repeatedly with the photographs over a period of time (Ryzdik et al., 2012; Oliffe and Bottorf, 2007). Finally, for researchers working in a community that is not their own, PhotoVoice creates opportunities to follow avenues of conversation that may not have presented themselves via traditional interviewing techniques, due to the interviewer's lack of insider knowledge (Wang and Burris, 1997). As a white, western woman who self-identified as a researcher/tourist while in South Africa, I employed PhotoVoice to engage township residents in a fun and creative outlet through which to share their perspectives, as well as to decentre my own voice and allow participants to lead the conversations in ways that were meaningful for them.

Before going any further into the details of the study, it is important that we pause here and reflect on South Africa's historical context and why I felt a study of tourism in the townships was warranted.

The Legacies of Apartheid for Black South African Women

South Africa's history is fraught with colonial abuses, violence, racial segregation, international censure and civil strife. As other African states found their ways to independence throughout the latter half of the 20th century, South Africa's white ruling minority rigidly enforced its apartheid policies of racial segregation and oppression. Black women have often been the most marginalized by the abuses of apartheid (McEwan, 2003; Moorosi, 2009), resulting in their disproportionate vulnerability to poverty, violence, limited education and lack of voice in public affairs (McEwan, 2003; SAHO, 2017). Unequal gendered lives in South Africa are embedded within a complex multitude of pre-, during, and post-apartheid factors, and continue to dominate in many black women's lives despite strong constitutional and public policy emphases on gender equity (Coombes, 2011). Women's subordinate roles in South African public life can be demonstrated through their experiences with the Truth and Reconciliation Commission (TRC), which was mandated to only examine *gross* abuses of a political nature, and thus failed to acknowledge the daily structural abuses that black women were exposed to under apartheid (Coombes, 2011; McEwan, 2003). When women were given an opportunity to have their voices heard in women-only hearings during the Commission, these events received very little attention in the media, presumably because violence against women is so commonplace that it does not merit being reported on (Goldblatt and Meintjies, 1998; McEwan, 2003). Finally, when women *did* speak at the TRC, they often spoke of abuses that were inflicted upon their male relatives or other acquaintances, and rarely centred their own stories of violence and trauma (Coombes, 2011; McEwan, 2003). While violence, the Bantu Education system and hegemonic masculinities all contribute to the marginalization of black women in South Africa, the physical and psychological erasure of black women's bodies from the public sphere through the enforcement of the Group Areas Act also played a role in the continued subordination of women in South Africa.

Townships as Spaces of Racial Segregation

In 1950, the apartheid government enacted the Group Areas Act, which mandated that white and non-white South Africans live separately. Desirable urban areas were declared 'whites only', and thousands of black families were forcibly relocated to the townships on the outskirts of cities. Despite apartheid having been abolished in the early 1990s, unofficial racial segregation in South Africa continues to dominate in the places where people live, and townships remain almost exclusively black spaces:[3] black spaces that remain characterized by entrenched poverty, woefully inadequate housing, illegal electrical connections and

violence. Townships are not homogenous or one-dimensional communities; however, in the collective imaginary they exist primarily as spaces of marginalization and poverty. The question then becomes, why have they become such a large attraction for international tourists?

Tourism in the Townships

Township tourism, as a localized form of 'slum tourism', has become a highly popular mainstream tourism activity in South Africa, and is often featured on lists of 'must do!' tourist activities. As is to be expected, a tour that brings the wealthiest people in the world – tourists – to gaze at the living conditions of some of the world's poorest has drawn its share of critique. Characterized as being an amalgamation of 'misery and leisure, suffering and fun' (Freire-Madeiros, 2013), critics claim that slum tourism is exploitative, voyeuristic and 'poverty porn' (Frenzel, 2012; Scheyvens, 2011). Supporters, on the other hand, argue that tourism to slum areas makes visible marginalized communities, brings tourism dollars directly into the places where poor people live, celebrates cultural heritage and empowers local people to take pride in their communities (Freire-Madeiros, 2013; Frenzel, 2012; Frenzel *et al.*, 2012; Manfred, 2010; Scheyvens, 2011). While there has been much debate in the media and academic circles regarding the good and bad of township tourism, for me what was missing were the voices of local people who play host to these tourists.

Indawo Yethu

Khayelitsha Township ('new home' in isiXhosa) was founded in 1984 and has become one of the largest and fastest growing townships in South Africa, with an estimated 400,000 residents (Frith, 2011). In the spring of 2016, I participated in a tour of Khayelitsha, met the women at Indawo Yethu and invited them to participate in my research involving hosts' perspectives of township tourism. Six women agreed that they would like to participate, and I returned to give each of them a digital camera and some training, and returned again 6 weeks later to conduct a group interview in which each woman was invited to choose two photographs and describe why she chose to take those particular photos in relation to tourism. I returned an additional three times in order to allow each of the women to speak in as much detail as they wished about their photographs.

To my surprise (dismay?), overwhelmingly the stories that they told about their encounters with tourism were positive. These included occasions where tourists made donations that improved people's lives, opportunities to share stories and break down racialized barriers, as well as opportunities to show the tourists that African women are strong and resilient. I also found that the women took dozens photos of their normal everyday lives. Initially, I was afraid that the majority of the photographs they took had nothing to do with tourism at all, and that they would be of no use to my study. I later came to realize that the women were showing me – the tourist – the parts of their lives that they want the tourists to know about, and that the tourists are either not being shown or are choosing to overlook. What follows is what I came to understand about the women's perceptions of tourism in Khayelitsha.

The Things That Tourists Bring

What became immediately apparent to me as I interviewed the participants was that many of the women's stories were about tourists helping people. Tourists are known to be people with means and mobility, and every single person that I spoke with had a story about tourists' generosity. Unbeknownst to me, this may have contributed to the ladies' willingness to speak with me in the first place. One of the very first statements made in the group interview, and spoken in isiXhosa,[4] was:

> Yes it is something great to take photos so that you can assist us ... My aim is for the tourists who came here, came with the aim

of what we do here so that she can assist us when she go back home ... Because she said, when she go back home she will see how she can assist us when she gets there in her country ... Yes it is something great to take photos so that you can assist us.

My heart sank when I first read this, and I worried that I had not been explicit enough in explaining either my objectives for this project, or my inability to support them financially going forward. However, it seems there is an implicit expectation that tourists will often reciprocate with donations once they have been welcomed by the local people they are there to meet.

Support for this belief immediately followed, as this same woman described the first photo she chose to share:

> *Nozi:* ... this guy ... came here at Indawo Yethu to see what is happening inside Indawo Yethu and he has a vision to help Indawo Yethu.
>
> ...
>
> *Meghan:* And what does he hope to help with?
>
> ...
>
> *Nozi:* He didn't specify what he is going to help with, but he will see what he can do ... it is something nice to take the photos so that you as a tourist you can help us ... and he thinks okay I can help then it's very interesting to me because we are here and we need help, whatever help to come.

Whether or not this tourist had expressed his intention to support Indawo Yethu and the women once he returned home, stories of people receiving support from tourists once they have returned home abound, so these assumptions are founded in a real hope. One woman, who has a job in a leadership position at Indawo Yethu, arranged a photo in which another lady was sitting outside, doing beadwork:

> I didn't have any job by that time and I was doing like she is doing now in front of my house and now I'm here at Indawo Yethu because of the tourists... If it was not because of the tourist that built this building maybe I was not going to have a shelter now to come every day and do the beadwork and have this opportunity to have a job ... So

I think the tourists can help us. *When I look at the tourists I always think okay they can change our lives* [my emphasis].

Another woman took a photo of what appeared to be a car parked under a sheet of zinc siding held up by four poles:

> The tourist talked with them about what are their needs ... So they come up with an idea of getting some shops which sell second-hand vacuums ... and also buy some zinc to make the shelter so that they can put their cars under this roof ... so as to get some sort of income generation. So that's why I took this picture.

The tourists have also been known to bring gifts with them when they arrive. Manyano encourages the tourists to 'Pack for a Cause', and suggests that unused books are always appreciated by children. Others arrive with food or money, knowing that it will always be welcome:

> Those tourists that they brought food for them, they brought plastic bags.

> First of all, these books that you are looking at are the books donated by the fine people from overseas. Which are the tourists. When they are coming here they brought

something for the children, as they see that we are working with the children.

In addition to bringing gifts, monetary donations and helping people establish sustainable livelihoods, the tourists are understood to also bring learning opportunities and the chance to have new experiences. This was often referenced in relation to my own presence in the township:

> What I was thinking here, Andiswa is focusing on her camera and it's because of the tourists ... Because if Meghan didn't come here at Indawo Yethu and think okay I can work with those women then Andiswa would not be having that camera and be a person to take photos. *For you guys to come here and think okay I can help then it makes a difference to us* ... Yes because we learn new things not focusing on one thing so we get to know other things [my emphasis].

One of the women took a photograph of her neighbour cooking sheep entrails at her home (Fig. 7.1). Her explanation demonstrates her understanding that having access to tourists has the potential to help sustain a person's livelihood in ways that they would likely be unable to attain on their own:

Fig. 7.1. A woman cooking sheep entrails at her home in the township.

> Okay this lady first of all is not working ...
> And she believes the women can do on
> their own, not going out there look for a job.
> And she thought the tourists can also help
> the women like her ... so maybe the tourists
> can come and see.

Her understanding of how tourists' spending could support this woman financially completely belies the fact that tourists have little independent mobility while on tour in the township, nor are they likely to wish to sample such exotic fare.

Though there is some suggestion, as with the lady cooking above, that unequal access to tourists may create some jealousy or resentment amongst neighbours, there is no question that many tourists' donations have had the intended benefit. Although many of these encounters with tourists speak to broader issues of dependency and paternalism, at the face-to-face level it is impossible to deny that these gifts are having tangible positive long-term impacts on people's livelihoods.

Regaining Power Through Tourism Encounters

It bears recalling that the deeply oppressive and centuries-old relationship between blacks and whites in South Africa only came to a legal end in 1994. While whites and blacks today have the same rights under the law, South Africa is still in many ways a deeply segregated society. The women that I spoke with at Indawo Yethu see tourism as having a hand in helping to change some of that and helping to 'polish the wounds of the past'. For them, tourism is playing a role in bringing people together to learn about one another and establish a shared humanity:

> ... it's helping us to close that gap between
> black and white. We're all human beings
> and there's no black there's no white ...
> I think it's helping to have tourists to come
> and work with us, share ideas.

> We are lucky. The people who come from
> other places ... They are not, no you are
> blacks, I am white. No, no, no, no they say
> 'hi how are you' and then we make friends
> and that's why I like it here.

This emphasis on a shared humanity goes beyond the value in establishing friendships with people from afar, as has been noted elsewhere (c.f. Cole, 2007). There is a depth of meaning associated with predominantly white outsiders coming into what has been euphemistically referred to as a 'previously disadvantaged environment' and casting value on both the space and its residents. People spoke about younger township residents learning not to be afraid to speak to white people and older people feeling empowered to share their stories. South Africa's history of blacks as third class citizens has added a layer of meaning to the tourist encounter in the township that would not necessarily be understood or presumed by the tourists.

Black Women as Strong Women

The women at Indawo Yethu expressed to me that through their encounters with the tourists they are able to show the tourists that they are strong, that they are able to create livelihoods for themselves, and to work towards bettering their community. My sense is that this desire is based in part in their own awareness that the tourist gaze that is cast upon them is often one in which they are conceptualized as victims. I have this belief in part due to how forcefully some of the women communicated this to me – again, the tourist:

> Yes, they see the women who are very
> strong. A strong women, yes!

> Here, I am taking this to show the people
> are not working, they do not stay saying I'm
> not working. They do something. The
> others they go to ask and buy, and go to sell
> it for other people. You see? ... *She's a
> shark this one.* The shark is not a victim
> like this, she's a shark. [my emphasis]

This is not something I had anticipated learning, and will require additional study to better understand, however it is significant to me that these women's desire to be perceived as strong and empowered is founded in their understanding of how they are cast as victims in the tourists' gaze.

Truncated Tours and Disempowering Tourism

One thing that I completely failed to anticipate when conceptualizing this research was how much time the women and I would spend together talking about the mundane, everyday details of life in the township. The women took photos of fruit and vegetable stands, furniture shops, parks (Fig. 7.2), butcheries, graduation ceremonies, public art, birthday parties, children playing and so on. At first I was dismayed at how few of the photographs were actually related to tourism, until I came to understand that these other photos represented a significant portion of their lives that they wished for the tourists to know about. As was explained to me by two women:

> V: Okay I took this photo there by our community park and I just want to show the tourists that we also have beautiful places like this. So if you want to go and chill then you can go there and relax, do whatever you want to do there, enjoy yourself. That was it.

> M: Okay, and do you think, when the tourists come here, do they get to see places like this? ... Or do they only see the shacks?

> B: No they don't go to places like this. They are only interested in shacks, yeah.

Another woman also expressed her feeling that the tourists were only interested in seeing the shacks:

> Some they want to see our shacks, how the people look like in these shacks, how do the people live in these shacks.

That the women chose to focus so much of their photographic gazes on the parts of the township that the tourists choose not to see indicates that, despite their increased visibility and interaction with outsiders via tourism, they continue to feel that significant aspects

Fig. 7.2. Children at a playground in the township.

THE WOMEN OF TOWNSHIP
TOURISM

The women that worked with me on
this project shared many more
photographs and stories than could
be included in this brief chapter.
To see more of the images they
captured narrating their lives in the
township, please visit the website
that has been created to showcase
their efforts:

www.womenoftownshiptourism.com

Fig. 7.3. The women of Township Tourism.

of their lives are being obscured. This lack of empowerment in being able to share their lived realities with the tourists is reflected in their awareness of the tourist gaze that is cast upon them. The ladies that I spoke with understood that they were held in the tourists' gaze as 'poor women' with little ability to effect change in their own lives. When given the opportunity, the women from Indawo Yethu hotly protested their characterization as victims, and yet the very nature of their encounters with most visitors 'on tour' does not allow them to present a more holistic representation of their lived realities (Mohanty, 2003). While the visitors who come as part of the tour have only a finite amount of time to interact with the women as handicraft artisans and community caretakers, their more lengthy engagement with me allowed them to speak of themselves as strong leaders in the community and as change-makers for improving lives in the township.[5] This emphasis in their conversations with me is contrasted with their inability to bring these aspects of their lives to the fore in their truncated encounters with the other tourists.

Conclusion

Whilst township and other forms of 'slum' tourism have been celebrated as empowering for local residents, in that they allow people to share their stories, celebrate local culture and heritage, and create incomes and livelihoods (Manfred, 2010; Scheyvens, 2011; Freire-Madeiros, 2013; Frenzel, 2012; Frenzel et al., 2012). This form of tourism also has the potential to pigeonhole stakeholders into roles that represent only a small fragment of their lived realities. If empowerment is understood to be both 'a condition and a process' (Timothy, 2007, p. 2007), the women of Indawo Yethu have been left out of the process of tourism delivery in their community, and thus have little power to influence how their lives are perceived by the tourists.

The women spoke with me at length about how the tourists are doing good in the community through their gifts and spending, and also impressed upon me the empowering and humanizing element that tourism brings in providing visibility and a sense of pride to people who continue to feel the effects of centuries of racially motivated oppression and hatred. The engagement in a shared humanity through tourists choosing to come and learn about and celebrate the lives of women and men living in the townships was valued just as highly as the monetary and tangible benefits that accrued to them as a result of tourists' largesse. However, lack of involvement in the delivery of the tours has left them little able to inform what it is that the tourists are able to come to know about their lives and their community. When the tourists arrive in the townships expecting to see poverty – and while this is an ever-present aspect of the lives of the women that I spoke with – the women resisted this imposed and truncated gaze through their insistence that tourists understand the ways in which they are strong, while at once having little ability to reframe the overarching narrative of the township tour.

The women who worked with me on this project shared many more photographs and stories than could be included in this brief chapter. To see more of the images they captured narrating their lives in the township, please visit the website that has been created to showcase their efforts: www.womenoftownshiptourism.com.

Notes

[1] Indawo Yethu, meaning 'our place' in isiXhosa, is the fictionalized name I have chosen for this women's empowerment organization in order to protect the anonymity of the centre and its members who did not play a part in this research.

[2] Meaning 'unity' in isiXhosa.

[3] In addition to black townships, there are also coloured townships in South Africa where the so-called coloured people of South Africa were forced to live under apartheid. I am not aware of any coloured townships hosting organized tours, and thus these were not included in this research. For simplicity's sake, in this chapter the term 'township' refers to black townships.

[4] I hired linguists from the University of Stellenbosch to help me with the translation, so that interviewees could feel free to speak in their first language if they preferred to do so.

[5] Go to www.womenoftownshiptourism.com for more stories and images of how women are effecting change in their own lives and their community.

References

Aitchison, C. (2001) Theorizing other discourses of tourism, gender and culture: can the subaltern speak (in tourism)? *Tourist Studies* 1, 133–147.

Buzinde, C., Santos, C. and Smith, S. (2006) Ethnic representations: destination imagery. *Annals of Tourism Research* 33(3), 439–458.

Cohen, E. (1995) Contemporary tourism: trends and challenges – sustainable authenticity of contrived post-modernity? In: Butler, R. and Pearce, D. (eds) *Change in Tourism: People, Places, Processes*. Routledge, New York.

Cole, S. (2007) Beyond authenticity and commodification. *Annals of Tourism Research* 34(4), 943–960.

Cole, S. and Eriksson, J. (2010) Tourism and human rights. In: Cole, S. and Morgan, N. (eds) *Tourism and Inequality: Problems and Prospects*. CAB International, Wallingford, UK, pp. 107–125.

Connell, R. (2007) *Southern Theory: The Global Dynamics of Knowledge in Social Science*. Allen & Unwin, Sydney, Australia.

Coombes, A. (2011) Witnessing history/embodying testimony: gender and memory in post-apartheid South Africa. *Journal of the Royal Anthropological Institute* 17, S92–S112.

Echtner, C. and Prasad, P. (2003) The context of third world tourism marketing. *Annals of Tourism Research* 30(3), 660–682.

Freire-Medeiros, B. (2013) *Touring Poverty*. Routledge, New York.

Frenzel, F. (2012) Beyond 'Othering': the political roots of slum tourism. In: Frenzel, F., Koens, K. and Steinbrink, M. (eds) *Slum Tourism: Power, Poverty and Ethics*. Routledge, New York, pp. 49–65.

Frenzel, F., Koens, K. and Steinbrink, M. (eds) *Slum Tourism: Power, Poverty and Ethics*. New York: Routledge.

Frith, A. (2011) *Khayelitsha*. Available at: https://census2011.adrianfrith.com/place/199038 (7 August 2017).

Higgins-Desbiolles, F. (2010) Justifying tourism: justice through tourism. In: Cole, S. and Morgan, N. (eds) *Tourism and Inequality: Problems and Prospects*. CAB International, Wallingford, UK, pp. 194–211.

Lewis, R. and Mills, S. (2003) *Feminist Postcolonial Theory: A Reader*. Edinburgh University Press, Edinburgh.

Manfred, R. (2010) Poverty tourism: theoretical reflections and empirical findings regarding an extraordinary form of tourism. *GeoJournal* 75(5), 421–442.

McEwan, C. (2003) Building a postcolonial archive? Gender, collective memory, and citizenship in post-apartheid South Africa. *Journal of Southern African Studies* 29(3), 739–757.

Mohanty, C. (2003) Under Western eyes: feminist scholarship and colonial discourses. In: Lewis, R. and Mills, S. (eds) *Feminist Postcolonial Theory*. Edinburgh University Press: Edinburgh, pp. 49–74.

Moorosi, P. (2009) Gender, skills development, and poverty reduction. *Agenda: Empowering Women for Gender Equity* 81, 110–117.

Morrell, R. (2016) Making southern theory? Gender researchers in South Africa. *Feminist Theory* 17(2), 191–209.

Mowforth, M. and Munt, I. (1998) *Tourism and Sustainability: New Tourism in the Third World*. Routledge, New York.

Oliffe, J.L. and Bottorff, J.L. (2007) Further than the eye can see? Photo-elicitation and research with men. *Qualitative Health Research* 17(6), 850–858.

Ryzdik, A., Pritchard, A., Morgan, N. and Sedgley, D. (2012) The potential of arts-based transformative research. *Annals of Tourism Research* 40, 283–305.

SAHO (2017) Contemporary issues: women's struggle, 1900–1994. South Africa History Online, 10 March 2017. Available at: www.sahistory.org.za/article/contemporary-issues-womens-struggle-1900-1994 (accessed 6 August 2017).

Santos, C. and Caton, K. (2008) Reimagining Chinatown: an analysis of tourism discourse. *Tourism Management* 29, 1002–1012.

Scheyvens, R. (2011) *Tourism and Poverty*. Routledge, New York.

Spivak, G. (1988) Can the subaltern speak? In: Nelson, C. and Grossberg, L. (eds) *Marxism and the Interpretation of Culture*. Macmillan Education, Basingstoke, UK, pp. 271–313.

Timothy, D.J. (2007) Empowerment and stakeholder participation in tourism destination communities. In: Church, A. and Coles, T. (eds) *Tourism, Power, and Space*. Routledge, New York, pp. 199–216.

Wang, C. and Burris, M.A. (1997) Photovoice: concept, methodology, and use for participatory needs assessment. *Health Education and Behaviour* 24(3), 369–387.

Wang, C., Burris, M.A. and Ping, X.Y. (1996) Chinese village women as visual anthropologists: a participatory approach to reaching policymakers. *Social Science and Medicine* 42(10), 1391–1400.

Wang, C. and Redwood-Jones, Y. (2001) Photovoice ethics: perspectives from Flint photovoice. *Health Education and Behaviour* 28(5), 560–572.

Priscilla's Story: From Waitress to Manager

Priscilla Alexander Shirima

I was born in Ngaseni Village, Tanzania, as the fifth child of Mr and Mrs Alexander Msale in 1976. My parents took good care of me until 1986, when they registered me in primary school. I studied while at the same time assisting my mother in daily home activities. I went to secondary school in Moshi and completed my level four in 1997. In the following November, my cousin, Thomas, who was doing a consultancy at the Leopard hotel, advised me to apply for a position as a waitress. This was hard because at that time I had no idea about waitressing. I thank my mother who encouraged me, she told me that nothing is impossible, just to work hard, cooperate with other waitresses and always be honest. Following the interview I was happy to be among the 16 selected applicants. So my mother allowed me to move from our village to town to start my job. After selection, we were given in-house training for 3 months.

Fig. S7. Priscilla Shirima.

I worked as waitress for 9 years, but I often tried to help out in other sectors in the hotel like store, reception and accounts. Even when I could do these jobs and helped whenever the hotel needed me to, they never paid me anything extra above my waitress salary. Then, I had the idea of increasing my education, and joined an evening programme at Ushirika College. In 2007 after a year's course, I earned a certificate of procurement. In the hotel I was shifted from the restaurant section to the store section, where I had more time to learn about the accounts. I also spent a year working in reception. In each area I taught myself and learnt on the job, but did not receive any extra salary. In 2010 I was shifted from doing the accounts in reception to keeping all the hotel accounts records, and working as the director of HR accounts for 2 years. In 2012 the hotel's director begged me to take the position of operations manager. It was not easy for me to accept but my director convinced me and insisted, 'You can do it, because you have passed through all the sections in the hotel'. So finally, I accepted the post.

My duties and responsibilities as a manager include:

- To ensure efficient performance of the 51-bedroom hotel.
- To ensure customer satisfaction.
- To supervise and manage all the hotel's finances.
- To supervise all construction in the hotel and to make all payments to constructors while the hotel was being expanded.
- To cooperate with catering to check all orders and bills, and ensure customer satisfaction.
- To cooperate with the housekeeping section to ensure the rooms are up to standard.
- To cooperate with the reception section to pass through all invoices and suggestions from clients if any.
- To receive and answer all hotel e-mails.
- To act as an HR manager – to interview and employ workers in cooperation with our accountant and FB manager.

I am an honest, experienced, hardworking, determined, respectful and decisive woman, but for all these responsibilities and qualities I only earn $320 (500,000/=) per month salary + $70 (150,000/=) house rent. I am not satisfied with my salary, as really it does not help me to meet my family requirements well. I think about getting a job in another hotel, but most people think that people with good certificates are good workers. I disagree, I have got so far with so little formal education.

During my time at the hotel I have had three children. First, I had twins, Benedict and Catherin. My director was not happy: he was only thinking about his hotel and several times asked who will handle my work when I was on maternity leave. I returned to work after only 82 days of maternity leave and the situation was the same with my second-born, Alvin. The children's father, my partner, is a good man but I have made the conscious choice to remain unmarried so I can retain control over my finances. In Tanzania, if I were married, my husband would control family finances, even if I earned more than him.

It's very hard managing my job and motherhood, I am always mindful of managing time. I wake early to prepare everything for the children before I leave for the hotel. But, as my mother said, with hard work and determination 'nothing is impossible'.

8 Journeys of Emancipation: Disrupting Poverty in Nepal

Wendy Hillman[1,*] and Kylie Radel[2]

[1]*School of Nursing, Midwifery and Social Sciences, Central Queensland University, Rockhampton, Australia;* [2]*School of Business and Law, Central Queensland University, Rockhampton, Australia*

Nepal is a nation comprising approximately 29 million people who are multi-lingual, multi-class, multi-ethnic and reside within multi-ecosystems (Worldometers, 2017, p. 304). Nepal traditionally hosts four castes, 36 sub-castes and 61 ethnic groups, together with 125 language classifications (Bhushal, 2008). While Nepali society is marked by time-honoured ideals, customs, traditions and principles, religion and traditional philosophies have continued to inspire the hegemonic patriarchy of men as dominant over women (Bhushal, 2008). For example, Table 8.1 reflects some of the main gender issues women experience in Nepal.

There is significant and widespread maltreatment of women, and there is pervasive 'social pressure to conform to heteronormative social conventions' (Boyce and Coyle, 2013, p. 6). As a result of regional and cultural superstitions, philosophies and traditions, exploitation, abuse and inequality are lived realities encountered by many Nepali women, where their societal, financial, emotional and physical positions have been disrupted and invalidated.

This chapter provides an overview of the entrepreneurial roles played by women forming grassroots organizations within the developing economy of rural and remote Nepal. Their stories demonstrate their desire for emancipation from socially constructed power roles, through the disruption of poverty. This chapter also includes some insights into the trajectory of Nepali women's social entrepreneurship. A social entrepreneur is often defined as an 'innovator' who seeks to create change by adopting and sustaining a personal mission, creating social value, pursuing new opportunities, and engaging in continuous innovation, adaptation and learning – boldly accepting risk and acting in the interests of the 'social good' (Thompson *et al.*, 2000). Commencing with some background relating to emancipation the chapter will examine, through the use of an inductive, grounded theoretical approach, two overarching categories: personal environments, processes and motivations for Nepali women entrepreneurs; and the entrepreneurship pathways experienced by Nepali women. Both these categories contain six key themes of 'changing social impressions of women/girls'; '*self-dependence*'; 'barriers are support mechanisms for entrepreneurship'; 'two-way transformations'; 'branching out'; and 'women retain control', which emerged from the data. In presenting this research, the chapter provides a starting point for those interested in a local approach to disruption of poverty for disregarded and disadvantaged women in developing economies.

---

* E-mail: w.hillman@cqu.edu.au

Table 8.1. Main gender issues in Nepal. (Adapted from: Bhushal, 2008; UNDESA, 2017; UNSD, 2017.)

Child matrimony	The legal age is 20 years without parental consent and 18 years with parental consent. However, many girls marry at much younger ages
Literacy rates	Literacy rate for adult male population is 75.58%. However, for adult female population it is 55.11% (persons 15 years and older)
Male infidelity	Many women punished for their husband's infidelities
Polygamy	Polygamy is illegal, but women are often forced to divorce their husbands, so the men can remarry
Low caste women who indulge in 'illegal' relationships with high caste men	Any children from the union may not be able to gain Nepali citizenship
Employment	12.8% of women are paid employees, while 33.7% of men are paid employees. However, nearly 71% of women are considered to hold a 'self-employment job' where any remuneration is entirely dependent on the profit derived from the goods and services produced including for their own consumption (i.e. subsistence living). A further 13% of women are unpaid staff of households belonging to other family members ('contributing family workers')
Religion and traditional philosophies	Perpetuate the hegemonic patriarchy of men as dominant over women
Male to female ratio approximately 50:50	Men constitute 49.6% of the population, and women constitute 50.4% of the population

Emancipation and Empowerment for Women in Nepal

The literature that connects female emancipation through tourism and entrepreneurship is sparse.

Ateljevic and Peeters (2009) suggest that, overall, the literature on communal advancement and female emancipation in tourism is almost certainly distanced from the emancipation literature in general. However, they argue that there is an established interconnection concerning women, emancipation, entrepreneurship and tourism, highlighting it as a practice of 'social innovation' (Ateljevic and Peeters, 2009; Thien, 2009).

Significantly, emancipation may be defined as a process through which people, groups and societies acquire control over their own existences. Emancipation and the idea of liberation from oppression have played a key role in a wide variety of fields of research and disciplines of practice. Particularly, the emancipation ideals have been deeply embedded in the development of educational theories (see, for example, Mezirow, 1977; 2000; Pascoe and Radel, 2008), and the refinement of teaching and

learning practices. In these frames, the educational process is to develop 'students to become independent and autonomous, to be able think for themselves, to make their own judgments and draw their own conclusions' (Biesta, 2012, p. 39).

Empowerment of women as process and outcome is also debated within the premise of 'community development'; specifically, for example, through ecotourism contexts (see Cole, Chapter 1, this volume; Scheyvens, 1999; 2000; Zeppel, 2006). Scheyvens (1999) devised a framework to evaluate the influences of ecotourism activities on local communities, which is made up of four dimensions of empowerment: economic, psychological, social and political. Scheyvens (1999) further clarified the symptoms of empowerment (or indeed its opposite being disempowerment), endeavouring to highlight the significance of regional communities having some influence upon, and participating in, the advantages of ecotourism schemes in their region, where ecotourism should be supported and progressed at a community level. However, regarding the wider political contexts of empowerment and its rhetoric, Giddens (1991) and Kalma (1994) both suggested that, while governments tend to focus on emancipation as a process of providing access to justice, equality and participation, this focus is potentially outdated in terms of its meaning and relevance to individuals. Emancipation and the empowerment of individuals are now connected to individuality, standards of living, personal independence and a rejection of self-seeking, materialistic practices (Vermeulen, 1996).

Women and emancipation through enterprise and tourism

It has long been recognized that the empowerment of women and the continuing pursuit of equality between women and men is essential for 'achieving political, social, economic, cultural and environmental security among all peoples' (UN Women, 1995). The Beijing Declaration and Platform for Action noted that 'equitable social development that recognizes empowering the poor, particularly women living in poverty, to utilize environmental resources sustainably is a necessary foundation for sustainable development' (UN Women, 1995). From a gender and/or feminist perspective, it has been suggested that the practices and processes of 'community' and 'participatory development' as elements of evaluation have frequently led to social orders and gender disparities remaining hidden from scrutiny (Moser and Moser, 2005). Participation in community development as a politicized domain may constitute a form of subjection and subjugation; however, the consequences are never completely controlled through these political frames (Williams, 2007).

Empowerment, then, is the process of giving women the tools to define and control their destiny, and emancipation is the outcome – the result of having or taking that control. Females are a vital component of any society and, therefore, female empowerment is constantly embedded in the problem of societal emancipation, which is, in many circumstances, highly integrated with the economic development of tourism (Beeton, 2006). Women and other disadvantaged

social sectors and castes are often prohibited from the decisions of development, with women particularly restricted to low-paid, support roles (Beeton, 2006; Thien, 2009).

There is comparatively limited literature on women's emancipation specifically through tourism, but overall, 'women's emancipation' is recurrently alluded to during debates about tourism studies (see, for example, Garcia-Ramon et al., 1995; Wilkinson and Pratiwi, 1995; Connell and Rugendyke, 2008; Ferguson, 2010; 2011). For instance, Connell and Rugendyke (2008), throughout their discussions to correlate tourism and gender, show that tourism as a task-concentrated activity facilitates a variety of examples of 'emancipation and expansion' amidst conventional work prospects for women where these occupations are correspondingly scarce and unskilled. The authors imply that tourism presents women with innovative prospects for social progress, better influence on domestic earnings (because of their participation in them) and, in certain situations, a respite from male-dominated culture (Connell and Rugendyke, 2008; Thien, 2009).

Women, entrepreneurship and tourism

The expression 'entrepreneurship' has been broadly used as an inclusive term for diverse models and commercial strategies, and for this reason it is practically unfeasible to acquire a sense of a comprehensive perception of the exact nature of entrepreneurship in a tourism-specific context (Getz et al., 2004; Weiermair et al., 2006). Consequently, entrepreneurship is researched in various types of tourism, for instance, community-based tourism initiatives (Manyara and Jones, 2007) and cultural tourism entrepreneurship (Yang and Wall, 2008).

So, this leads us to the fact that there are disparities in tourism development, and one of the techniques to appreciate the subtleties and encourage change concerning equality is from within the analysis of gender interactions (Swain, 1995). Sofield (2003) described empowerment as being a reciprocal process due to the unequal distribution of power; that is, how the 'powerless' procure power and how the 'powerful' relinquish power. The author reveals how females secure power and how tourism enables the acquiring of these influences by women. Supporting the capacity of females to express their thoughts in a profound way (voice) and to develop into the agents of their individual emancipation (agency) is essential to prevail over indoctrinated socio-cultural habituation and the gendered division of labour (Jones *et al.*, 2008; Sofield, 2003; Thien, 2009).

Methodology and Thematic Findings

The grounded theory study on which this chapter is based was conducted with seven different Nepali women's organizations that provide products or services for tourism in Nepal and are owned and run by women. As qualitative, constructivist, grounded theory researchers (Charmaz, 2000; 2002; 2006; Radel and Hillman, 2016; Hillman and Radel, 2018) in tourism, we sought to interpret the lived realities of Nepali women entrepreneurs. This positionality enables us to uncover and examine the mediated 'intersections of structures and practices' (Olesen, 2000, p. 226) that can enable an examination of the many texts and contexts using multiple lenses and from multiple 'angles of vision' (Peshkin, 2001). In this way we sought to co-create a theoretical framework for understanding the motivations, perceptions, contexts and experiences impacting on women entrepreneurs in developing nations.

The in-depth interviews and conversations were conducted largely in English. However, there were instances where the participants used Nepali terms to express their thoughts and feelings. While one of the researchers has undertaken Nepali language studies, the resulting audio recordings were transcribed by a Nepali woman working and studying for her PhD in Australia, to ensure that the lived realities were expressed appropriately in the transcripts.

Of those women interviewed, five run organizations located in Kathmandu and the other two organizations are located in Pokhara, western Nepal. However, a number of the women noted that, while their main location was either Kathmandu or Pokhara, they had managed to draw female staff and to provide services and products to many more remote locations throughout Nepal. In all cases the women were poor. Each of the women who participated was interviewed using constructivist, in-depth, open-ended techniques and, following the grounded theory principles of constant comparison (Glaser, 1969; Charmaz, 2006), data were compared with data, codes with codes and themes with themes throughout the research to develop the substantive theory (Glaser and Strauss, 1967).

Question prompts that focused on techniques for training, processes of teaching and mentoring for new staff, guidance and education for themselves and their staff, and empowerment of women generally were asked of each participant. Further, basic demographic queries relating to their age and place of birth, and a range of other topics regarding the women's own experiences of starting and growing their businesses and being empowered through the activities were also raised. All initial, open-ended, question prompts were formed through engagement with the literature on women's empowerment and female entrepreneurship in developing countries. However, following the constructivist philosophy, the discussions and interviews with the women participants were free-ranging, conversations co-created between the interviewer and participant to encourage the women to provide their own lived experiences of their entrepreneurial journeys.

Thematic analysis was then undertaken on the interview transcripts, utilizing a four-step process as identified by Radel (2010, p. 59), demonstrated in Fig. 8.1.

An open coding process, followed by more focused coding for making theoretical comparisons was undertaken. Theoretical sampling was then conducted to further refine the categories and themes, and finally integrating the codes and writing the

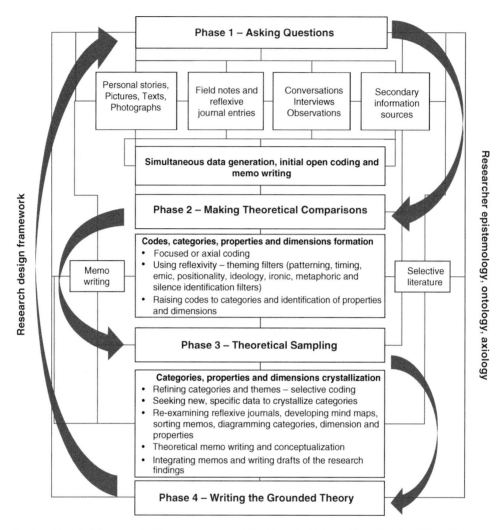

Fig. 8.1. Model of the grounded theory process used for this study. (Adapted from Radel, 2010, p. 59.)

grounded theory (Radel, 2010). As indicated by van Teijlingen *et al.* (2011, p. 304) 'a qualitative analysis usually leads to a number of key themes, each supported by one or more sub-themes'. Consequently, an inductive, interpretive approach was used to construct the grounded theory of entrepreneurial emancipation for women in tourism in Nepal that was based firmly in the data emergent categories and themes (Charmaz, 2006). The data therefore informed continued analysis and data collection through the 'discovery of theory' that subsequently 'emerges' from the data (Glaser and Strauss, 1967).

Thematic Findings

Based on the grounded theory analysis process, six key themes emerged from the data including: 'changing social impressions of women/girls'; '*self-dependence*'; 'barriers are support mechanisms for entrepreneurship'; 'two-way transformations'; 'branching out'; and 'women retain control'. These six key themes were further integrated into two main categories: (i) personal environments, processes and motivations for Nepali women entrepreneurs; and (ii) the entrepreneurship pathways experienced by Nepali women.

Figure 8.2 provides an illustration of the personal environments, processes and motivations for Nepali women in this study in relation to themes one and two.

Theme 1 – 'changing social impressions of women/girls'

All of the women began their entrepreneurial journeys from a common state of felt deprivation that manifested, nurtured and sustained their motivations to develop their own business. Participants indicated they wanted to 'be free' from social expectations; they wanted to 'change social impressions of women/girls' in Nepal. They felt that they had no control over their own lives and that decisions had been made 'on them' rather than 'for' or 'with' them. They all suffered from a lack of education, no money, limited knowledge of any work ethics or conditions outside of the home environment, lack of family support, and most of the women were from lower social castes.

> It was very hard to start because it really needs an experience. Because different countries will visit Nepal and also the money and financial things are difficult with so many different people. When I worked with other people [other companies] I did not get [understand] the money… I had to work very hard in many different companies. And then also

I learned rafting guide. I moved to rafting industry [and] I also learned kayaking. That's why I took a little bit time to start with my own business.

But regardless of their caste status, they all felt powerless and lacked choices; they lacked the capacity to consider alternatives for themselves in their own lives. As a result of these motivations and deprivation, each of the women 'dreamt' of a different future for themselves and for other women in their situation.

Theme 2 – 'self-dependence'

The second key theme that arose in their stories was, as one participant stated, that of 'self-dependence'. When we first reviewed the stories, and in particular the narrative of the participant who used this specific word to describe her situation, we thought perhaps that it was an incorrect translation of the Nepali meaning into an English word. However, on reviewing the audio tapes and continuing to practise the grounded theory process of constant comparison (Charmaz, 2006) to the data from other participants, we have revised our initial interpretation.

> Give for them [sewing] machines, weaving things and raw materials and we can give for them and make for the products for self-dependence.

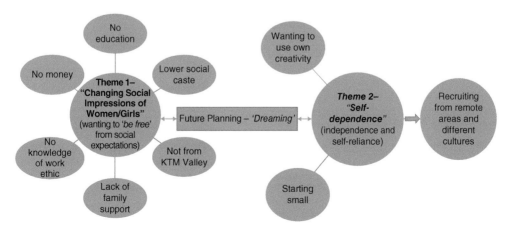

Fig. 8.2. Category 1 – Personal environments, processes and motivations for Nepali women entrepreneurs.

Indeed, 'self-dependence' for these women is quite different to independence in the traditional meaning of the term – where independence is proposed as 'freedom from the control, influence, support, aid, or the like, of others' (Dictionary.com Unabridged, 2017). 'Self-dependence' encapsulates their understanding of empowerment and the resulting emancipation when linked to entrepreneurial spirit from a gendered perspective. Independence is perhaps a measure of myself against or away from others. However, the theme of 'self-dependence' is about myself alone – not how I stand in relation to others. Another participant noted this need for 'self-dependence', as she explained how she began to think about developing her own business:

> At that time, you know ... we were staying at our relative's place. We are from outside of Kathmandu valley. We are independent, and we don't want anyone's pressure... Whatever we did we did freely... I also saw some of my friends staying in hostel and that concept raised in our mind and thought why not start a thing [start a hostel]. Then people like us from outside of Kathmandu valley don't have to search for places where to stay. For their convenience ... only for girls.

In each case, the women wanted to use their 'own creativity' and they all started very small businesses, usually without any forms or networks of support. Their focus on their own 'self-dependence' also became a reflection of the ways they developed and grew their businesses. Their own motivations and personal situations were reflected in the women staff they recruited for their enterprises – drawing from many low social castes, remote areas and different Nepali cultures, Nepali women entrepreneurs seek to support other women like themselves to achieve their own 'self-dependence'.

> Some ladies they do [training] for business, like that. They do is good [own their own business]. [We have trained over] 200 people they get to job somewhere. They do for their self-dependence.

At this stage in the entrepreneurial journey, 'self-dependence' is the driving force that moves Nepali women entrepreneurs forward through the business development process and keeps them focused on their goals and dreams.

The Entrepreneurship Pathways Experienced by Nepali Women

Returning to Fig. 8.2, the first two key themes identify the values, beliefs, attitudes and background situation of the Nepali women and their motivations for becoming an entrepreneur in Nepal. The next set of themes demonstrates the pathways to enterprise development that the women followed in their entrepreneurial journeys. Figure 8.3 provides an overview of the second category – entrepreneurial pathways experienced by Nepali women entrepreneurs. Figure 8.3 presents the entrepreneurial journey for the women from barriers, to support, to transformation and control of their own lives and journeys. This category integrates the remaining four key themes.

Theme 3 – 'barriers are support mechanisms for entrepreneurship'

The third key theme that arose from the data was the theme of 'barriers are support mechanisms for entrepreneurship'. This theme presented the juxtaposition of the relationships of support mechanisms that would ordinarily assist entrepreneurs to develop their enterprises, which were subsequently perceived more often as barriers to the success of these women.

Access to education and training at even rudimentary levels is often difficult for Nepali women, and more so for women from low castes or rural and remote locations (Bhushal, 2008; Guinee, 2014). More importantly perhaps, access to education in business practices, tourism industry requirements and hospitality service provision is almost too difficult. As noted by one of the participants in her story:

> ... for the girls who came from the Nepali school background and young girls and

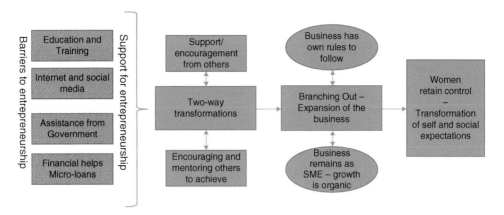

Fig. 8.3. Category 2 – the entrepreneurial journey for women in Nepal.

little education, for them it was [frightening]. They were really scared. They would say to us, 'Oh my god, we cannot understand anything, we cannot do this job!' So, we said 'Okay. This is good, okay, this can work, but how? We have to … We have to work on that.'

Building on the tensions created by the barriers of access to education for Nepali women, business owners, perhaps particularly in tourism enterprises, require a strong knowledge of and access to internet-based market access mechanisms. A natural progression for business in today's globalized world is use of, and access to the internet, and in particular, social media to attract and engage potential and previous customers. Another participant noted her struggle for business experience and her use of the internet as the mainstay of her business:

> [And you have got Facebook and a website?]
>
> Yes of course! Yes! Also, I have Twitter. I use a lot of social media now. LinkedIn [and email]. I don't have an office … I work [from] my office in [my own] rented apartment [my home], which is nearby …

With regard to more formalized forms of assistance through government development support and financial support mechanisms, the women generally also experienced little or no help. As Sofield (2003) noted, the main constituents of the empowerment process through tourism and entrepreneurship

are the government and the community. However, for these women support was not available, they 'learned on the job', started out with just themselves, their hard work and an idea. Another participant stated:

> Actually, when I started my business nobody helped me. Some tourists wanted to give me some ideas. Some of [my] Nepalese colleagues said 'I want to help … ' but only [gave] conversation … not help … Nobody helped me actually, but they just gave me small ideas.

Theme 4 – 'two-way transformations'

One of the most surprising themes to emerge from the data was the theme of 'two-way transformations'. Most of the women in their journey towards emancipation through entrepreneurship experienced a transformation of themselves. However, they also impacted equally on others in their inspiring struggles. One participant told of her journey to become a female kayaking and rafting guide in the highly male-dominated trekking and adventure tourism industry that is Nepal.

> In 2008, there also I met [a lady] in a group from Sweden and am just like talking with Inga Didi [sister]. She is already a rafting guide and I am so exiting to talk with Inga. After we talk rafting things … also and I am so happy to meet her and I asked her to … 'can you teach me like kayaking and other things also'. She also very happy to teach me … and this day we talk like rafting things and

there after tomorrow we decide to go to lake again and she hires kayak to go to lake and she is so happy that I am doing kayaking.

This finding was a surprising outcome for the participants. They had not previously had assistance from their families, most of their friends or other Nepali trekking and tourism industry staff. Yet, their drive and determination to achieve their own goals had a reciprocal emotional impact on others that would inspire them to achieve their dreams. Another participant narrated her story:

The attitudes have been changed. That is a really big impact of our programme. At the beginning, many people they don't even talk with us because they found we are the strangers. We are not doing good things for community and society. We are against the culture. You know they were thinking like that way. That's why people they don't talk even [with us] either. But now, many people come by themselves and they say, 'Oh, can you please give a seat [place] for my daughter for this training programme. She is interested like ... ' Before, even if they are interested, they cannot motivate their family, their parents like that. Now, the parents they are motivated, and they bring their children by themselves.

Theme 5 – 'branching out'

The final two themes are closely related and provide an overview of the women's business growth and maturity processes. The development of the women's businesses for all participants in this study was an organic process – following a need and filling a gap in the market more by 'feel' than by developing a strong business plan or strategic goal setting approach. The following participant began her non-governmental organization (NGO) in an attempt to provide training and resources for poor women from the mountains.

Nine years ago, I started. This is for [in] my opinion ... [to help the] women ... we really [want to fix the] problems ... we like to [lift them] up. That is important.

[Make them come out of poverty. Yes?]

Yes. First, we start with four ladies. Now we have around 200 people [that] I give for

training already. And now we have 22 people [in the business in total].

For these women, the importance of giving back and supporting their communities, to 'lift other women out of poverty' is the significant element in their entrepreneurship journeys. In reality this is the same as social entrepreneurship. The growth and progression of their entrepreneurial spirit aligns with Das (2000), and it is clear from the women's stories that they have elements of all three categories, of chance, force and creation, in their journeys. However, based on the findings from this current study, a fourth key category of women's entrepreneurship for Nepali women can be added – 'empowerment' entrepreneurship.

Theme 6 – 'women retaining control'

The final theme to emerge from this study describes the point at which the growth of the businesses is finally constrained. In each case, while the women demonstrate significant rates of growth and development for their business, there is a point at which this growth is halted due to the women's need to retain control of their business. Their personal identity is strongly integrated with their business success and their initial drive to overcome their social circumstances eventually provides the limits beyond which they cannot progress. They cannot relinquish their control over, and involvement with, every element of their business. Another participant noted when talking about their business:

[I do] Everything before and after the trekking. [Booking the] hotel in Kathmandu and lots of things. Airport to airport. Hotel, transport, everything! If they want to do rafting or sight-seeing, I take... I wanted to do [for] myself. I wanted to use my creation. I wanted to do whatever [for] my company ... I wanted to use my techniques also...

Perhaps due to their lived experiences where decisions were made on them due to their social and cultural circumstances, this translates into their desire to be the owner, manager, worker, caretaker or nurturer of every component for their business – eventually providing a natural boundary and the limits for the enterprise size and capacity. Even for participants where their business grew to include other staff or locations, there was a point at which continued growth was no longer sustainable: to retain their control over their enterprise and their destiny, the women will decide on the limits they can accept. As another participant noted:

> Then I started from smaller one, there were six or seven beds only at that time. Then after 6 months I took two floors. Then ... 14 or 15 students and then did 4 or 5 years like that. After 4–5 years I took the whole building. I am here since 14 years.
>
> [Okay ... So how many beds do you have now?]
>
> Then after I started two building. This also and another one also, around 50 students. Two to 3 years I did that and now this time, just one building only. I sold the other building. Now I am doing this only. Here also there are 20–25 students.

Conclusion

In this chapter, we have developed a grounded theory analysis of the stories of seven case studies in order to gain a clearer picture of the conditions for women entrepreneurs in the tourism industry in Nepal. Through the constant comparison process of comparing data to data and voices to voices throughout the study, the research has demonstrated that the emancipation journey for Nepali women is shaped and motivated but also constrained by their social and cultural embeddedness.

Six key themes emerged from the data as a result of the grounded theory analysis process, and these themes were further integrated into two main categories that form the grounded theory of Nepali women's emancipation through tourism entrepreneurship. The grounded theory shows that the Nepali women are shaped, defined and also motivated by their personal environments, their lived experiences, and the social and cultural processes and practices; this provides the basis for their motivations to become entrepreneurs in the highly male-dominated culture and industry. It also represents a survival situation due to the gender inequality they experience in Nepal. Their pathways towards entrepreneurial activity are then created through and reflected in these lived experiences.

However, for the women in this study, their journeys of emancipation through tourism and entrepreneurship demonstrate the essence of emancipatory empowerment. As previously shown, empowerment as an agent of emancipation has several components that are ably demonstrated in the narratives of these Nepali women. They are individuals seeking to change their capacity and access to power. They struggle for freedom, self-identity and financial self-control. They struggle to control their own destiny; to rewrite the social and political laws that govern the positions of power in their immediate spheres of influence; and their physicality, psychology, economy and personality are affected and transformed through this process to achieve their 'self-dependence'.

References

Ateljevic, I. and Peeters, L.W.J. (2009) Women empowerment – entrepreneurship nexus in tourism: processes of social innovation. In: Ateljevic, J. and Page, S.J. (eds) *Tourism and Entrepreneurship: International Perspectives*. Butterworth-Heinemann Ltd, Oxford, UK.

Beeton, S. (2006) *Community Development Through Tourism*. Landlinks Press, Collingwood, Australia.

Bhushal, S. (2008) Educational and socio-cultural status of Nepali women. *Himalayan Journal of Sociology and Anthropology* 3, 139–147.

Biesta, G.J.J. (2012) Doing emancipation differently: transgression, equality and the politics of learning. *Civitas Educationis. Education, Politics and Culture* 1(1), 5–30.

Boyce, P. and Coyle, D. (2013) Development, discourse and law: transgender and same-sex sexualities in Nepal. IDS, Brighton, UK. Available at: www.ids.ac.uk/publication/development-discourse-and-law-transgender-and-and-same-sexualities-in-nepal (accessed 12 March 2018).

Charmaz, K. (2000) Grounded theory – objectivist and constructivist methods. In: Denzin, N. and Lincoln, Y. (eds) *Handbook of Qualitative Research*, 2nd edn,. SAGE, Thousand Oaks, California, pp. 509–535.

Charmaz, K. (2002) Qualitative interviewing and grounded theory analysis. In: Gubrium, J. and Holstein, J. (eds) *Handbook of Interview Research – Context and Method*. SAGE, Thousand Oaks, California, pp. 675–694.

Charmaz, K. (2006) *Constructing Grounded Theory – A Practical Guide Through Qualitative Analysis*. SAGE, London.

Connell, J. and Rugendyke, B. (2008) *Tourism at the Grassroots: Villagers and Visitors in the Asia-Pacific*. Routledge, London.

Das, D. (2000) Problems faced by women entrepreneurs. In: Sasikumar, K. (ed.) *Women Entrepreneurship*. Vikas Publishing House, New Delhi.

Dictionary.com Unabridged (2017) Independence. Available at: www.dictionary.com/browse/independence (accessed 1 March 2018).

Ferguson, L. (2010) Tourism development and the restructuring of social reproduction in Central America. *Review of International Political Economy* 17(5), 860–888. DOI: 10.1080/09692290903507219.

Ferguson, L. (2011) Promoting gender equality and empowering women? Tourism and the third Millennium Development Goal. *Current Issues in Tourism* 14(3), 235–249. DOI: 10.1080/13683500.2011.555522.

Garcia-Ramon, M., Canoves, G. and Valdovinos, N. (1995) Farm tourism, gender and the environment in Spain. *Annals of Tourism Research* 22(2), 267–282.

Getz, D., Carlsen, J. and Morrison, A. (2004) *The Family Business in Tourism and Hospitality*. CAB International, Wallingford, UK.

Giddens, A. (1991) *Modernity and Self-identity: Self and Society in the Late Modern Age*. Stanford University Press, Stanford, California.

Glaser, B. (1969) The constant comparative method of qualitative analysis. In: McCall, G. and Simmons, J. (eds) *Issues in Participant Observation*. Addison-Wesley, Boston, Massachusetts.

Glaser, B. and Strauss, A. (1967) *The Discovery of Grounded Theory: Strategies for Qualitative Research*. Aldine Publishing Company, Chicago, Illinois.

Guinee, N. (2014) Empowering women through education: experiences from Dalit women in Nepal. *International Journal of Educational Development* 39, 183–190. DOI: 10.1016/j.ijedudev.2014.07.007.

Hillman, W. and Radel, K. (eds) (2018) *Qualitative Methods in Tourism Research: Theory and Practice*. Channel View Publications, Bristol, UK.

Jones, N., Holmes, R. and Espey, J. (2008) Gender and the MDGs – a gender lens is vital for pro-poor results. ODI Briefing Paper No. 43. ODI, London. Available at: https://www.odi.org/publications/2386-gender-and-mdgs-gender-lens-vital-pro-poor-results (accessed 12 March 2018).

Kalma, P. (1994) Emancipatie in soorten. Sociaal-democratie en verzorgingsstaat. In: de Beer, P.T. and Bussemaker, M. (eds) *Verzorgingsstaat tussen individualisme en solidariteit*. Wiardi Beckman Stichting, Amsterdam.

Manyara, G. and Jones, E. (2007) Community-based tourism enterprises development in Kenya: an exploration of their potential as avenues of poverty reduction. *Journal of Sustainable Tourism* 15(6), 628–644.

Mezirow, J. (1977) Perspective transformation. *Studies in Adult Education* 9, 100–110.

Mezirow, J. (2000) Learning to think like an adult – core concepts of transformation theory. In: Mezirow, J. and associates (eds) *Learning as Transformation: Critical Perspectives on a Theory in Progress*. Jossey-Bass, San Francisco, California, pp. 3–31.

Moser, C. and Moser, A. (2005) Gender mainstreaming since Beijing: a review of success and limitations in international institutions. In: Porter, F. and Sweetman, C. (eds) *Mainstreaming Gender in Development: A Critical Review*. Oxfam, Oxford, UK.

Olesen, V.L. (2000) Feminisms and qualitative research at and into the millennium. In: Denzin, N.K. and Lincoln, Y.S. (eds) *Handbook of Qualitative Research*, 2nd edn. SAGE, Thousand Oaks, California, pp. 215–255.

Pascoe, V.A. and Radel, K. (2008) 'What are nice guys like them doing in a place like that?': education journeys from Australian indigenous students in custody. *International Journal of Learning* 15(1), 301–309.

Peshkin, A. (2001) Angles of vision: enhancing perception in qualitative research. *Qualitative Inquiry* 7(2), 238–253.

Radel, K. (2010) The Dreamtime Cultural Centre: A grounded theory of doing business in an Indigenous tourism enterprise. (Doctor of Philosophy), Central Queensland University, Rockhampton.

Radel, K., and Hillman, W. (2016) Disrupting poverty in rural Nepal: Transformations of women through tourism entrepreneurship. Paper presented at the 30th Australia and New Zealand Academy of Management (ANZAM) Conference, 'Under New Management – Innovating for sustainable and just futures', 6–9 December, 2016, QUT Brisbane.

Scheyvens, R. (1999) Ecotourism and the empowerment of local communities. *Tourism Management* 20(2), 245–249.

Scheyvens, R. (2000) Promoting women's empowerment through involvement in ecotourism: experiences from the Third World. *Journal of Sustainable Tourism* 8(3), 232–249.

Sofield, T. (2003) *Empowerment for Sustainable Tourism Development.* Pergamon, Oxford, UK.

Swain, M. (1995) Gender in tourism. *Annals of Tourism Research* 22(2), 247–266.

Thien, O. (2009) Women's empowerment through tourism – from social entrepreneurship perspective. Master of Science, Wageningen University, The Netherlands.

Thompson, J., Alvy, G. and Lees, A. (2000) Social entrepreneurship – a new look at the people and the potential. *Management Decision* 38(5), 328–338. DOI: 10.1108/00251740010340517.

United Nations (UN) Women (1995) Fourth World Conference on Women, Beijing, China – September 1995 Action for Equality, Development and Peace – Beijing Declaration. Available at: www.un.org/womenwatch/daw/beijing/beijingdeclaration.html (accessed 1 March 2018).

United Nations Department of Economic and Social Affairs (UNDESA) Population Division (2017) World population prospects: the 2017 revision. Available at: http://countrymeters.info/en/Nepal (accessed 1 March 2018).

United Nations Statistics Division (UNSD) (2017) Statistics and indicators on women and men. Available at: https://unstats.un.org/unsd/demographic/products/indwm/default.htm (accessed 1 March 2018).

van Teijlingen, E., Simkhada, B., Porter, M., Simkhada, P., Pitchforth, E., and Bhatta, P. (2011) Qualitative research and its place in health research in Nepal. *Kathmandu University Medical Journal* 9(36), 301–305.

Vermeulen, H. (1996) The concept of emancipation in ethnic studies. *Studia Rosenthaliana* 30(1), 21–32.

Weiermair, K., Siller, H. and Mossenlechner, C. (2006) Entrepreneurs and entrepreneurship in alpine tourism: past, present, and future. *Journal of Teaching in Travel and Tourism* 6(2 Special Issue: Travel and tourism education in a global marketplace: Key issues and challenges), 23–40.

Wilkinson, P. and Pratiwi, W. (1995) Gender and tourism in an Indonesian village. *Annals of Tourism Research* 22(2), 283–299.

Williams, G. (2007) Evaluating participatory development: tyranny, power and (re)politicisation. *Third World Quarterly* 25(3), 557–578. DOI: 10.1080/0143659042000191438.

Worldometers (2017) Nepal Population (LIVE). Available at: www.worldometers.info/world-population/nepal-population (accessed 1 March 2018).

Yang, L. and Wall, G. (2008) Ethnic tourism and entrepreneurship: Xishuangbanna, Yunnan, China. *Tourism Geographies* 10(4 Special Issue: Tourism in transition economies), 522–544.

Zeppel, H. (2006) *Indigenous Ecotourism: Sustainable Development and Management.* CAB International, Wallingford, UK.

Marta's Story: For My Son and My Island

Marta Muslin

My name is Marta Muslin, I am 36 years old and a single parent of one 10-year-old son. I am from Manggarai, West Flores, East Nusa Tenggara, Indonesia. I work as a community project manager and operations manager in a diving company in Labuan Bajo. Besides working in the company, I am also a chairman of Dive Operator Community Komodo, a legal committee of the Association of Indonesia Tour and Travel Agencies (ASITA) Manggarai Raya, an active member of the Association of Komodo Dive Guides, a coordinator of Flores Homestay Network, a coordinator of Indonesia Waste Platform and a mum.

People may ask how I manage my time, raising my child and supporting the whole family at the same time. Well, I have only been doing all these activities for 3 years now, but so far I am enjoying being busy, taking good care of my island, building the capacity of my people, and at the same time learning a lot of things from so many people I am working with.

The story of how I reached all those positions in my community and company is a long one. After my father passed away, I could not continue my studies and decided to work as a waitress in a restaurant in Bali. I had a dream of becoming a lawyer. So I talked to my boss about that dream, and asked for a loan, to continue my studies in the faculty of law at university. He laughed at me, but I convinced him. I remember I said, 'During 7 years of your company running in Indonesia, how many waitresses do you have that have dream to become a lawyer? You don't have to answer me now, but you can give your decision tomorrow morning, because if you say

Fig. S8. Marta and her son.

no, that's okay, but tomorrow is last day to register.' He started talking in Italian and I only remember he said, 'What a stubborn young girl'. Then, I met him and his wife the next morning, they gave me the money and told me, 'We will pay your registration fee, but we will deduct it from your salary monthly'. I was so happy, and then I started working in the afternoon and studying in the morning. But after some time, I couldn't pay the rent, so I ended up 'living' with my son in an office on the campus. Fortunately, my boss decided not to deduct from my salary, but gave me an additional job instead, and a promotion to become his personal assistant. Nine months before graduation, with all my loans paid, I applied to become assistant manager in a hotel in Bali, and got the job, and 3 months later, I was promoted to manager. I was the manager for only 6 months before graduating as a Bachelor of Law. I got a job in an international non-governmental organization (NGO) in Flores. That was the first time I finally came home after being away for 9 long and difficult years.

After 5 years with the NGO, I started to look for another challenge so I resigned and voluntarily worked as coordinator of Flores Homestay Network with Eco Flores. This programme suits my passion that tourism should benefit the community. While seeing the trend of increasing tourism in Flores and the number of divers coming to the island increase significantly, I applied for the job of community project manager at Wicked Diving, who have a programme to sponsor local people to become dive masters. After a year as community project manager, I was promoted to also become the operations manager.

As a single mother, I receive support from my son and my mother, and I can still do all those activities, but I still make time to take my son to school in the morning and pick him up after school. I always try to balance everything, but of course my son is my first priority.

In the beginning, it was not easy to prove that as a woman, and a single mother, I can be a decision-maker in all those positions I have now. Being a woman working in tourism is not as easy as it looks, especially if you are working on an island with a very patriarchal culture like mine. You need to work twice as hard to prove you are capable of making decisions. In the beginning, you are labelled as a prostitute and everyone is talking about you. It takes a big effort and commitment to make them realize that you are capable of doing that work.

However, in time, all my activities have been recognized locally, nationally and internationally (Australia Awards for Sustainable Regional Growth, 2016 and Indonesia Leadership Visitor Program for sustainable energy to USA 2017). Now people do not look at me as an ordinary Flores woman, who, in our patriarchal culture only acts as a supporter to all the decisions that men make for her. I have really proved that I can make the right decisions, not only for the company I manage, or the association that I lead, but also bigger decisions that relate to the sustainability of Flores, the new rising, but mismanaged, destination in the east of Indonesia.

9 Tourism and Women's Rights in Tunisia

Heather Jeffrey*

Middlesex University, Dubai, United Arab Emirates

Introduction

Tunisia is a small country on the north coast of Africa, which has become increasingly well known since the beginning of the Arab Spring in 2010, due in part to heightened media interest and coverage. The previous regimes of autocratic rulers Presidents Habib Bourguiba (1956–1987) and Zine el Abidine Ben Ali (1987–2011) had ensured a consistent narrative enveloped the country since gaining independence from France in 1956. This narrative simultaneously focused on women's rights and tourism in order to attack traditional society and garner support for the regime(s) both internally and externally, which had led to a weakened opposition and even support from the West. Even though the United Nations World Tourism Organization and UN Women (UNWTO and UN Women, 2011) stressed that tourism has the potential to empower women, as highlighted in Chapter 1 of this book there is no simple relationship between tourism and women's rights or empowerment.

The UNWTO has focused primarily on the industry's ability to economically empower women due to the majority of jobs requiring low skills or offering flexibility, but economic empowerment is arguably only possible when a woman is in control of her wage (Chant, 1997). This factor demands that studies on women in tourism or women and tourism are contextualized, as gender identities are context-dependent. Based on my PhD research, this chapter introduces perspectives of Tunisian women working in the tourism industry to highlight the importance of contextualized analyses. Drawing on interviews carried out with 15 women working in tourism, the chapter depicts an enduring ideology on what it means to be a woman in Tunisian society. At no point in the interviews did I explicitly introduce the topics of politicians, veiling practices or women's rights, but all of the participants discussed these areas with me. It is argued that discourses on veiled women hinder the ability of the tourism industry to empower all Tunisian women, and ultimately women's rights will never truly be women's rights, unless they include all women.

In 1881, emerging from a European power struggle and enabled by financial difficulty among the Ottoman Empire, France took Tunisia and began what would become more than a century of uninterrupted authoritarian rule (Gray and Coonan, 2013). The local elite considered the French colonialists a symbol of modernity and even today 'for

* E-mail: h.l.jeffrey@mdx.ac.ae

Tunisia, it is evident that modernity is composed of everything that came from the period of the French protectorate (...) an occidental epistemological system imposed by the coloniser' (Barnard, 2013, p. 74). The Carthage declaration of 1954 recognized Tunisian autonomy and in 1956 Tunisia was granted independence (Rossi, 1967). The newly independent Tunisia was led by President Habib Bourguiba; educated in France, Bourguiba not only figuratively, but literally, married himself to the French, only to divorce and remarry a Tunisian in 1962 (Hopwood, 1992).

In order to gain popularity and foment a nationalist movement, in the years prior to independence, Bourguiba drew on the most prominent cultural identity: Islam. The future president attempted to create a '*Tunisian personnalité*' distinctive to the French identity of the colonialists, and within this project, he vehemently advocated for Tunisian women to cover their hair by wearing a veil and traditional dress (Salem, 1984). Bourguiba's push to create a '*Tunisian personnalité*' centred on an Islamic identity was short-lived and, once elected president, Bourguiba shifted tack. Tunisia, under the rule of Bourguiba, began to weaken the constraints on women's productive freedom and public participation, in contrast to other North African territories (Marshall and Stokes, 1981). Yet, Bourguiba's policies, which have endured throughout the office of President Ben Ali, have shaped what it means to be a Tunisian woman.

Within the first decade of taking control of Tunisia, Bourguiba introduced a 'cultural liberation' programme in part delivered by the resurrected French education system, which was now aimed at delivering lessons in morality, and supported the implementation of the new legal system (Rossi, 1967). Bourguiba wanted to challenge cultural traditions he considered irrational, folkloric and pre-modern, he did this by focusing on both the family (at this time the family was based on clan-like kin groups) and religion. For the most part, this focus targeted Tunisian women, and for Bourguiba:

> The women of Tunisia were, as is known, for a long time victims not of the dynamic Islam that the religion was when it was

> founded, but of an Islam distorted by decadence, and also of an obscurantism which was the fruit of under-development. (Bourguiba in Rossi, 1967, p. 120)

Within the 'cultural liberation' programme lay tourism, which was far more than a mechanism to gain foreign exchange and development, it was a vehicle to instil new habits in the local population. Bourguiba was relying on tourists as his greatest ally to train the local population on what it meant to be a modern citizen (Rossi, 1967). However, it would eventually be Bourguiba's 'modernizing' ideology, which excluded many and incarcerated those who could not embody the '*Tunisian personnalité*' that would lead to his downfall, and in 1989 an Islamist uprising, his own senility and concerns over state intervention led to his replacement by President Ben Ali (Murphy, 1996; Hazbun, 2008). While the leadership changed, the ideology, temporarily masked, did not. During his first year in term the new president liberalized the media and released many political prisoners, but Ben Ali was ultimately to maintain Bourguiba's modernizing project, continuing to focus on tourism as a tool for development and attempting to secularize the nation (Louden, 2015). Both leaders used political Islam to justify their own policies, utilizing a fear of jihadism to legitimize authoritarian rule and secular policies (Dalmasso and Cavatorta, 2010; Louden, 2015). Whilst no exact figures are available for the number of political prisoners, they are estimated to be around 12,000 and, of those, the number of females could be anywhere between 300 and 1500 (Gray and Coonan, 2013). Ultimately, corruption, rising levels of youth unemployment and poverty, along with regional inequalities, culminated in the Jasmine Revolution, beginning in December 2010, and the downfall of President Ben Ali (Barnard, 2013).

Despite their autocratic regimes both Habib Bourguiba and Ben Ali achieved social and economic advances. One of the most notable areas of progress has been in gender equality, in which Tunisia has been hailed as leading the Middle East and North Africa (MENA) region by Western media (Murphy, 1996) and by the women in the MENA region

(Moghadam, 2011). Gender gaps in education are low, and the gender parity index for primary and secondary enrolment changed from 0.6 in 1971 (a disparity in favour of boys) to 1.01 (a disparity in favour of girls) in 2011 (World Economic Forum, 2016). Tourism and women's rights have been pivotal in all Tunisia's development plans (Bleasdale and Tapsell, 1999; Hazbun, 2008), and the relationship between women's rights and tourism is not one of cause and effect, but mutually constitutive. Bourguiba initiated a series of attacks on the family and religion, in the shape of both tourism development and the promotion of women's rights, in order to meet a wider goal of 'modernity' (Rossi, 1967). Moreover, the West has forgiven Tunisian leaders a multitude of sins, such as torturing their own citizens or a lack of political pluralism, democracy and freedom of expression, simply because the Islamist opposition is perceived as being far worse (Dalmasso and Cavatorta, 2010).

Women in the Tunisian Labour Market

Even though it might appear that many rights have been granted to women in Tunisia, they still lack one fundamental right: the right to an occupation of one's choosing (Moghadam, 2011). Women are legally entitled to an occupation and discrimination is outlawed, but in reality, there are many legal discriminatory mechanisms employers can utilize, and gender equality is yet to permeate the home. Restrictions may exist at the recruitment stage, such as targeting only those who have completed military service (at present only men are required to complete military service), or by creating an exam that only men can sit, as is the case with 'postmen' (Chékir and Arfaoui, 2011). Female labour force participation in Tunisia, although increasing from 25.4% in 1995 to 32.9% in 2009, remains low (Sinha, 2011). Married women only constitute 20% of the entire female labour force, which is primarily made up of single female heads of households (Chékir and Arfaoui, 2011).

There are several sectors that notably employ high numbers of women. One of these is the public sector, where women form 55% of the workforce as socially sanctioned teachers and nurses with maternity rights (Karkkainen, 2010). One of the most feminized sectors is the textile sector, where 80% of the workers are female and almost 60% of contracts are temporary (ILO, 2011). However, numerical representation on the textile workforce has not translated into managerial or union positions for women, and only one woman sits on the National Federation of Textiles Board (Chékir and Arfaoui, 2011). The textile industry is often supported by tourism as it creates demand for its products, and Bleasdale (2006) has previously warned of the possibility of female exploitation by the textile industry in Tunisia. Women who work in textiles receive no protection in cases of pregnancy, and in January 2004 the Mazallat workshop of blind women workers earned just 40 dinars (approximately US$32) per month (Chékir and Arfaoui, 2011).

In comparison to the textile industry, tourism employs relatively low numbers of women. In the hotel sector (most tourism jobs are hotel jobs in Tunisia) women comprise just 22.5% of workers, which was lower than the national average of female labour force participation (26%) in 2010 (Karkkainen, 2011). Women's low participation in the hotel sector is partly due to legislation preventing them from working nightshifts, but also because it is not socially acceptable for women to work with alcohol (Karkkainen, 2010). Yet, at the time of recruitment, this may also be a discriminatory ploy, as women are asked more than men if they are married or have children, and for the large part veiling is also considered an impediment to working in public areas (Karkkainen, 2011); under the previous regime, veiling was an illegal practice in public. There is also a lack of trained women as they comprise just 20% of the student body at the ten public vocational tourism schools in Tunisia (Karkkainen, 2010). These factors have led to horizontal and vertical segregation within the industry, and approximately 70.4% of the female workforce in hotels can be found in reception and housekeeping (Karkkainen, 2011). The male-dominated Tunisian tourism industry still has a long way to go if it is to support gender equality in Tunisia.

The Guardians of Tradition: Tunisian Women

Tunisia has been revered by Western media and some scholars as leading the way for gender equality in the MENA region (Megahed and Lack, 2011), which has arguably been wrongly linked to liberal values and has led to the overlooking of human rights violations (Dalmasso and Cavatorta, 2010). The penetration of European imperialism since the colonial period and the duplication of Western norms among the elite have reshaped the role of women and feminine identity in Tunisia (Marshall and Stokes, 1981). Sinha (2011) has argued that the improvement in women's status in Tunisia is a consequence of kin-based social reform. Yet, arguably kin-based social reform may also be a consequence of Bourguiba's push for women's rights (Charrad, 2001) as women were the guardians of tradition – by transforming women, Bourguiba could transform society.

The kin-based system has relied on women in order to achieve its goals and is arguably the source of the most visible elements associated with Islam in North Africa: the veil and the walled courtyard (Charrad, 2001). Both the veil and the courtyard can be linked to the demarcation of gendered space: the male space is outside, it is public, and men are free to wander in this space, but the female space is inside, it is domestic, and it is controlled (Barnard, 2013). Both the veil and the courtyard are mechanisms to ensure the honour of the kin group (Murphy, 1996; Sinha, 2011), which is dependent on the behaviour of the women who can shame the kin group (Charrad, 2001). The 'preoccupation with female purity and modesty is at the centre of social norms governing gender relations in the Middle East' (Charrad, 2001, p. 63). Bourguiba thought that by taking away the source of the honour he could also remove the tradition of kinship (and any opposition to the regime), so he attacked the veil[1] and promoted women's rights.

'Veil' is the English translation for Arabic hijab and women in Tunisia wear different styles, but the images in Figs 9.1 and 9.2 are used for illustrative purposes.

Fig. 9.1. Tunisian student wears hijab while holding an anti-violence sign in 2010. (From: FlickR User Magharebia (2010), https://www.flickr.com/photos/magharebia/6555267933.)

Fig. 9.2. Tunisian woman in the foreground wears traditional Sefsari in 2016. (From: Wikimedia Commons (2016), https://commons.wikimedia.org/wiki/File:Sefsari_tn.jpg.)

Bourguiba's reforms demanded women inhabit both the male and female space, that they drop the veil, but they were never meant to undermine their position in the home, which was reinforced by an education system restricted to training 'girls' in 'girls' trades' such as cooking, cleaning and sewing (Barnard, 2013). Existing and surviving gender inequality in Tunisia is a consequence of patriarchal societal values (Moghadem, 2005; Megahed and Lack, 2011; Sinha, 2011). Patriarchal values are a barrier to women's labour force participation and, if some women do work, for many their salary is controlled by the male head of the family (Sinha, 2011). Policies inciting dramatic changes to the role of the woman were seen in the Personal Status Code of 1956, initially outlawing polygamy, inspired by Turkey (Grami, 2008), and forced marriages, granting women citizenship and the right to vote. Other projects focused on the inclusion (not by law but persuasion) of women in the education system and a campaign against the veil (Perkins, 1986). Additional reforms introduced may not have directly targeted women, but promoted a further move away from the extended family (Perkins, 1986: Sinha, 2011) and directly attacked religion by, for example, abolishing religious courts (Grami, 2008).

In general, men's attitudes towards their women relatives working have become more positive. Yet, during times of political instability, economic uncertainty and especially high unemployment, some Tunisian men have desired 'a retreat into the culturally familiar realms of tradition' (Murphy, 1996: 139). The motivations of Bourguiba (and later Ben Ali) to attack tradition by promoting women's rights, rather than an actual desire to achieve gender equality, is highlighted by subsequent reservations towards CEDAW (the 1979 international Convention on the Elimination of all Forms of Discrimination Against Women promulgated by the United Nations) (Moghadam, 2011). Women's political rights in Tunisia have traditionally been nothing more than a 'democratic façade' (Grami, 2008). Bourguiba gained female support by promulgating legislation, but he did not listen to them and they were not able to express dissent due to restrictions on civil society groups[2] (Murphy, 1996). Most of the women's groups founded during the time of Bourguiba and Ben Ali were created by the leaders themselves, to serve their interests (Murphy, 1996).

In Tunisia more and more women are returning to the veil (Grami, 2008), and yet the explicit link between the veil and Islam is questionable, when women may choose to wear the veil for numerous reasons (Megahed and Lack, 2011). One of these reasons may be the popularization of the even 'trendy' veil via Arab cable television available since the 1990s and growing internet access since the turn of the new millennium (Grami, 2008). In Tunisia, some women may choose to wear a veil in order to show opposition to the previous autocratic government or to Western imperialism (Grami, 2008). Poirier (1995) has even suggested

that the return to the veil is directly related to a display of disapproval towards tourist behaviour. However, the separation of these supposed causes of a renaissance in veiling is complicated due to the political history of Tunisia, as is argued in this chapter. Horrific human rights violations occurred under both regimes, which targeted those considered visibly Muslim (Gray and Coonan, 2013), and a lack of freedom of expression has meant that any dissenting voice has been silenced (Murphy, 1996). So, perhaps more women are veiling in Tunisia simply because they can.

(Un)veiling Tunisian Women and Tourism

On 18 March 2015 there was a terrorist attack in the capital of Tunisia, Tunis. The attack at the Bardo Museum appeared to be aimed at tourists and, whilst it received messages of solidarity on social networks, it devastated the local population. I arrived in Sousse on the first of April, just 2 weeks later. As part of my PhD research I carried out 15 interviews with women who were involved in tourism in a myriad of ways, I interviewed henna tattooists, museum workers, hotel workers, handicraft makers and a representative from the Tunisian National Tourism Office (TNTO). Six women were in their 20s, six women in their 30s, and three were in their 40s. All of the women above 30 were married and one woman in her 20s was married, five women had never been married. This might be unrepresentative of the overall women's labour force participation, as previously stated married women form just 18% (Chékir and Arfaoui, 2011), or it might suggest that the tourism industry provides more opportunities than other industries for married women to work.

Interviews are one of the most popular methods of data collection within research on gender and tourism (Figueroa-Domecq et al., 2015), which is perhaps unsurprising, as the interview has long been associated with feminist research (Oakley, 1998). Semi-structured, in-depth interviews were carried out due to the ability to place importance on the participants' knowledge and understanding of situations (Hesse-Biber and Leavy, 2010). The interviews were shaped around the participants' experience of tourism.

Informal workers Mounira and Salwa, who work as henna tattooists, began their interview by highlighting their appreciation for Bourguiba and relating his opposition to traditional dress with freedom:

> Since the days of Bourguiba ... Bourguiba rid women of the 'Sefsari' [A 'Sefsari' is a large scarf that covers the entire body of the Tunisian woman]. He gave us (women) our freedom.

Mounira and Salwa continued by discussing how women from the south of Tunisia, whom they deemed more conservative as some still wear the Sefsari, could not do their job. When asked why, they suggested that they would be ashamed to work in public, talking freely to strangers the way that they do. The inverse relationship between traditional dress and freedom was discussed in all of the interviews, even by participants who chose to cover their hair with a head scarf or hijab. Of the women interviewed, three wore a hijab – a visitor attraction manager, a women's craft organization manager and a student. Safa, a visitor attraction manager, who wears a hijab, suggested that there were far more women wearing 'traditional Islamic dress' in her city than not. Safa was keen to dispel any myths associated with veiling practices, by highlighting that the women of Kairouen do leave the home and work, but she did not challenge the idea that the hijab was traditional or 'conservative', which shows that Bourguiba's politics permeated every part of society.

In recounting her fear that a woman wearing a niqab might 'blow herself up', Hela, an English teacher from a tourism institute, evidences just how clothing is still related to a fear of jihadism. To some extent this could be said to reflect Habib Bourguiba's use of a fear of jihadism to attack tradition and conservativism (Hazbun, 2008). Hela further explained her father's response to her sister's decision to veil and, in describing her father's reaction to

this event, she suggests that support for Bourguiba lives on long after his death.

> Even I do have my sister wearing a hijab and my father is a Bourguibist, the first time my sister came wearing a hijab, cos she's married and lives in Tunis she visited here and he told her 'Oh God that's not us', he said 'Come on what are you doing? It's not our customs we are not like,' that's what he said, and I said, 'Oh Dad, come on, it's her choice'. And he said 'I know but I didn't raise her like that'. So you see it's a generation gap.

Hela was adamant that the practice of veiling was from a bygone era, highlighting how the same Bourguiban discourses continue to circulate and (re)create what it means to be a Tunisian woman. Her father's reaction demonstrates that, for at least some women, the veil is not a paternal imposition. Hela went on to stress 'our parents are more modern than us now that's really strange it's the other way and it's disappointing'. On the other hand, Hela highlighted how her female students travelled from the south to study in the coastal school because they thought that tourism was 'cool'. She stressed that her students did not necessarily believe tourists were cool, but that women working in the tourism industry like her were. After having discussed her father, the Bourguibist, Hela described 'her group' as marginalized, suggesting 'We are a minority now, I think women without the veil', before (re)constructing herself as a daughter of Bourguiba, politicizing the wearing of the veil or perhaps the rejection of the veil as a symbol of support for a particular political regime:

> For me as a daughter of Bourguiba, because I am very proud to say it, to see this amount of people these women wearing this veil, it's a pity.

Bourguiba was not the only politician to be revered by the participants, and two hotel workers suggested that life was better with Ben Ali in power. The workers explicitly stated that life was more secure and there were more tourists and more money. A representative from TNTO described the changes in society since Ben Ali's downfall, but her reluctance to incorporate women who choose to wear a hijab perhaps suggests little has changed:

> Maybe 80% of girls don't wear the hijab, in my family you will find zero women wearing the hijab because we are not accustomed to that, but after the revolution these people they emerged from nowhere, they are there, they are part of the society, we cannot ignore them, but they have to accept us as we have to accept maybe them. I'm not talking about the terrorists of course.

The representative's positioning of women as 'these people' or even her reluctance to incorporate them in society: 'we have to accept *maybe* them' suggests that Bourguiban divisionary discourse lives on. Nour, a luxury hotel worker, described how being 'modern', which she related to clothing, helped her in her everyday life and her job. Nour stressed how she enjoyed speaking with new people every day and as she was a 'modern' woman she felt she could be more open-minded than other women. Nour went on to describe what she called a preference for 'modern' women:

> We can't hide it, there's not racism but there's preferences for women, modern women more than traditional or conservative women.

Finally, Hela finished her interview by reminiscing about her time in the UK. The number of women wearing a hijab or niqab struck Hela as unusual and she even stressed her feelings of fear when she passed them in the street, but she said that:

> When I came back home I said to myself 'Ahh its good they are better like that', but now it's changing here too, but it's okay I respect. I'm very tolerant but I cannot understand how a person, a woman can dress like that, how can she feel or see herself as a body I dunno, I cannot even for the hijab.

Again Hela's inability to accept women who wear the hijab evidences the continuation of the circulation of Bourguiban discourses on tradition and Islam. The discourses surrounding the practice of veiling as identified here permeate Tunisian society at all levels. Importantly, these discourses can have very material affects for women who choose to cover and attempt to gain employment in the tourism industry. The government representative, teacher in the tourism institute and managers in the hospitality industry all discussed the act of veiling derogatively.

Conclusion

Habib Bourguiba and Ben Ali both promoted and utilized a fear of jihadism in Tunisia to create support for the regime(s), and they both attacked tradition, which focused heavily on Tunisian women. The use of tourism within the 'cultural liberation' programme ensured Tunisians had 'modern' role models and Tunisia had Western support. It is thought that the political focus on women's rights might have tied the hands of these autocratic leaders, but many more women than those incarcerated were stalked and refused public services such as hospital treatment (Murphy, 1996). There have been some advances in gender equality in Tunisia, but visibly Muslim women are still discriminated against, as evidenced in the participants' accounts.

Even today, some Tunisians desire a return to a more stable past under the autocratic leader Ben Ali, and the participants' perspectives here evidence just how Bourguiban discourse lives on. The women working in the tourism industry show that there is a reluctance to accept women who do not fit the 'modern' ideal promoted by Bourguiba and Ben Ali. This strive for modernity includes showing hair and the 'cool' tourism industry; in general veiling is considered an impediment to working in public areas in hotels (Karkkainen, 2011). Their position towards the veil (as identified in this chapter) can have very material effects for women who veil and attempt to work in the tourism industry. Participants who hold prominent positions within the industry could not hide a negative stance towards practices of veiling during the interviews. This is not to say that they are to blame for this situation, but rather their stance highlights the circulation of anti-veiling discourses in Tunisian society.

The case of Tunisia highlights how an intersectional approach is necessary when studying the possibilities of tourism to empower women. The importance of contextualization, especially when considering economic empowerment, is supported by the chapter. In addition to these key points, the case of Tunisia supports the exploration of clothing as a site of politics for women involved in the tourism industry. Clothing here becomes part of the body politics as women fight for control over their bodies and what they wear, as such future research

on Tunisian tourism and women may choose to explore the subjectivities of women who choose to cover and work or are excluded from working in the tourism industry. In Tunisia the context has shaped what it means to be a woman, and therefore which women are included and excluded from tourism employment. Ultimately women's rights will never truly be women's rights, unless they include all women by bestowing a right to wear what they choose and work where they choose. The case of Tunisia highlights a necessity for a critical approach to gender and tourism, but also the context-dependent relationship between tourism, politics and women's rights.

Notes

1 https://youtu.be/Rx6N4CzE3_s
2 https://youtu.be/3x-dsibXl3o

References

Barnard, D. (2013) The necessity of having it both ways: tradition, modernity, and experience in the works of Hélé Béji. In: Sadiqi, F. (ed.) *Women and Knowledge in the Mediterranean*. Routledge, Abingdon, pp. 73–86.

Bleasdale, S. (2006) Connecting paradise, culture and tourism in Tunisia. *Journal of Intercultural Studies* 27(4), 447–460.

Bleasdale, S. and Tapsell, S. (1999) Social and cultural impacts of tourism policy in Tunisia. In: Robinson, M. and Boniface, P. (eds) *Tourism and Cultural Conflicts*. CAB International, Wallingford, pp. 181–203.

Chant, S. (1997) Gender and tourism employment in Mexico and the Philippines. In: Sinclair, M.T. (ed.) *Gender, Work and Tourism*. Routledge, London, pp. 119–178.

Charrad, M. (2001) *States and Women's Rights: The Making of Postcolonial Tunisia, Algeria, and Morocco*. University of California Press, Berkeley, California.

Charrad, M.M. and Zarrugh, A. (2014) Equal or complementary? Women in the new Tunisian Constitution after the Arab Spring. *Journal of North African Studies* 19(2), 230–243.

Chékir, H. and Arfaoui, K. (2011) Women's economic citizenship and trade union participation. In: Franzway, S., Fonow, M. and Moghadam, V.M. (eds) *Making Globalization Work for Women: The Role of Social Rights and Trade Union Leadership*. State of New York University Press, Albany, New York, pp. 71–92.

Dalmasso, E. and Cavatorta, F. (2010) Reforming the family code in Tunisia and Morocco – the struggle between religion, globalisation and democracy. *Totalitarian Movements and Political Religions* 11(2), 213–228.

Figueroa-Domecq, C., Pritchard, A., Segovia-Pérez, M., Morgan, N.J. and Villacé-Molinero, T. (2015) Tourism gender research: a critical accounting. *Annals of Tourism Research* 52, 87–103.

Grami, A. (2008) Gender equality in Tunisia. *British Journal of Middle Eastern Studies* 35(3), 349–361.

Gray, D.H. and Coonan, T. (2013) Notes from the field: silence kills! Women and the transitional justice process in post-revolutionary Tunisia. *International Journal of Transitional Justice* 7(2), 348–357.

Hazbun, W. (2008) *Beaches, Ruins, Resorts: The Politics of Tourism in the Arab World*. University of Minnesota Press, Minneapolis, Minnesota.

Hesse-Biber, S. and Leavy, P. (2010) In-depth interview. In: Hesse-Biber, S.N. and Leavy, P. *The Practice of Qualitative Research*, 2nd edn. Sage, Thousand Oaks, California, pp. 119–145.

Hopwood, D. (1992) *Bourgiba, Habib of Tunisia: The Tragedy of Longevity*. Macmillan, London.

International Labour Organization (ILO) (2011) *Studies on Growth with Equity, Tunisia a New Social Contract for Fair and Equitable Growth*. ILO, Turin, Italy.

Karkkainen, O. (2010) Women at work: access, limitations and potential in tourism and ICT. Egypt, Jordan and Tunisia. Publications Office of the European Union, Luxembourg.

Karkkainen, O. (2011) Women and work in Tunisia: tourism and ICT sectors: a case study. European Training Foundation, Turin, Italy.

Louden, S.R. (2015) Political Islamism in Tunisia: a history of repression and a complex forum for potential change. *Mathal* 4(1), 1–25.

Marshall, S.E. and Stokes, R.G. (1981) Tradition and the veil: female status in Tunisia and Algeria. *Journal of Modern African Studies* 19(04), 625–646.

Megahed, N. and Lack, S. (2011) Colonial legacy, women's rights and gender-educational inequality in the Arab World with particular reference to Egypt and Tunisia. *International Review of Education* 57(3–4), 397–418.

Moghadam, V. (2011) Toward economic citizenship: the Middle East and North Africa. In: Moghadam, V., Franzway, V.S. and Fonow, M. (eds) *Making Globalization Work for Women: The Role of Social Rights and Trade Union Leadership*. State of New York University Press, Albany, New York, pp. 25–46.

Murphy, E.C. (1996) Women in Tunisia: a survey of achievements and challenges. *Journal of North African Studies* 1(2), 138–156.

Oakley, A. (1998) Gender, methodology and people's ways of knowing: some problems with feminism and the paradigm debate in social science. *Sociology* 32(4), 707–731.

Perkins, K.J. (1986) *Tunisia: Crossroads of the Islamic and Mediterranean Worlds*. Westview Press, Boulder, Colorado.

Poirier, R.A. (1995) Tourism and development in Tunisia. *Annals of Tourism Research* 22(1), 157–171.

Rossi, P. (1967) *Bourguiba's Tunisia*. Matthews, R. (trans.). Kahia, Tunis.

Salem, N. (1984) *Habib Bourguiba, Islam, and the Creation of Tunisia*. Croom Helm, London.

Sinha, S. (2011) Women' s rights: Tunisian women in the workplace. *Journal of International Women's Studies* 12, 185–200.

United Nations World Tourism Organization (UNWTO) and UN Women (2011) *Global Report on Women in Tourism 2010*. UNWTO and UN Women, Madrid.

World Economic Forum (2016) The global gender gap report. The World Economic Forum, Geneva, Switzerland. Available at: www3.weforum.org/docs/GGGR16/WEF_Global_Gender_Gap_Report_2016.pdf (accessed 1 March 2018).

Leila's Story: A Moroccan Guide

Leila Lamara

Fig. S9. Leila Lamara.

My name is Leila Lamara and I'm 55 years old. I'm a mother of a 19-year-old daughter, whom I raised alone. I was born in the city of Fes, the oldest capital for the Moroccan nation. I'm the oldest of six brothers and sisters, born and raised in a very traditional conservative middle class family, in a multicultural, multireligious community. Jews and Christians were our neighbours; they were all Moroccan, the only difference was the kids were going to French mission school, and we were going to the Moroccan ones. My first contact with tourism started when I was studying in high school. The school was close to the famous gate of the old city of Fes. Every morning while I was getting off the bus, I saw tourists groups standing by the gate in a circle listening to the guides, and taking pictures. I was attracted by those people from different nationalities, and amazed by those tour guides in their beautiful elegant local dresses. Most of the time I couldn't go home for lunch, we only had 2 h break and home was 1 h drive. That was, in fact, my favourite break – I could follow the tours, sometimes I offered to show the sites to some tourists. Then, after my graduation, I decided what my future profession would be: a tour guide. I joined the Higher International Institute of Tourism in Tangier. My father did encourage me, but the rest of the family were all against it: this was not a job for a girl.

When I started I couldn't imagine that my situation would turn me into public enemy number 1 of the Moroccan society; my first 2 years were simply a daily fight against colleagues who were all men – there were no women working at all in tourism. I was not a decent woman. That pushed me to work hard to improve my skills to prove to myself and to the others that a Moroccan woman could do it. There were few people who supported me; they were not Moroccan, they were Spanish travel agents and tour leaders, and they became my best friends. I will be always thankful for their trust and their support.

The most common thing I faced is when I got to a hotel, the manager would tell me there was no room for me; the hotel was overbooked. I was booked with my guests, but later he would show me a key and tell me that the only room left was his room. Or the drivers would leave me behind while I was checking part of the group and go away with the other part! Other tour guides would take some of my group members and tell them that I was not qualified to be a guide because I'm a woman; the travel agents I used to work for at the time received phone calls from Moroccan tour guides asking them not to assign me tours. I paid them back by giving my guests the best travel experience in Morocco they could ever have. I kept learning about my country and discovering its beauty, and transmitting my knowledge and my passion to all my visitors. My job has allowed me to learn about life, to love people and share my culture with them.

10 Tourism Entrepreneurship and Gender in the Global South: The Mexican Experience

Isis Arlene Díaz-Carrión*

Facultad de Turismo y Mercadotecnia, Universidad Autónoma de Baja California, Tijuana, Mexico

Introduction

Tourism represents one of the main sources of employment for Mexican women (UNWTO, 2011). Employment in the sector, however, is mainly characterized by gender inequalities in access and segregation (Hernández *et al.*, 2005; Rodríguez and Acevedo, 2015; Martínez-Corona, 2003). As a feminist tourism scholar, I consider that feminist theorization can provide rich epistemological, conceptual and methodological tools for gender aware research in tourism. This chapter draws on Bourdieu's theory of social practice and the interpretations of one Mexican feminist to examine women's participation in ecotourism entrepreneurship. The study focuses on ventures, such as restaurants, lodging and ecotourist guiding in the Catemaco–Montepío corridor, located in Veracruz, Mexico, and examines women's strategies to transform unequal gender relations through entrepreneurship.

Becoming a female entrepreneur is not easy; women-owned businesses have historically been small, while suffering from a shortage of monetary goals, and tend to lack innovation (Clark-Muntean and Ozkazane-Pan, 2016). There is also the risk of business appropriation by men (Hernández *et al.*, 2005; Ratten and Dana, 2017). Following Bourdieu's theory on social capital-building (Lagarde, 2001; Bourdieu, 2013), Marcela Lagarde, a Mexican feminist and academic, has considered women as agents capable of either promoting gender roles or maintaining the status quo.

Among this study's empirical findings are the use of contradictory strategies: some women defy traditional gender roles, while others contribute to maintaining the status quo. Women entrepreneurs define success in terms of personal satisfaction, as opposed to the more traditional measure of business growth. Despite the perceived fragility of their businesses and the slow pace of social change, women overall value entrepreneurship as a positive experience.

Bourdieu and Mexican Feminists

Feminists in Latin America consider patriarchy, capitalism and neoliberalism as the main causes behind segregation, exclusion and inequality (Lagarde, 2001; Carosio, 2009). In their examination of inequalities, Mexican feminists have widely interpreted

---

* E-mail: diaz.isis@uabc.edu.mx

Bourdieu's theories. For example, drawing on Bourdieu's writings on social capital, Marcela Lagarde (2001) has conceptualized women as agents of change who can either promote transformational processes or defend the status quo. For this study status quo is the expression of traditional gender roles by dominant and controlling agents who, through their quotidian actions, reinforce the existing system of gender inequalities (Lagarde, 2001). In Lagarde's view, inequalities that limit women's social and political participation must be addressed in order to improve women's everyday lives and also in order to investigate how dominance occurs in the context of daily life.

There is a lack of agreement in defining social capital; for this study, social capital is considered as any social relations that generate benefits for women. Bourdieu's notion of social capital mainly considers macro processes and barely identifies individual processes. Nevertheless, any social process is the addition of several individual processes. For women, contestation begins at the individual level (Lagarde, 1996; 2001). Bourdieu (2013) and Bourdieu *et al.* (2008) consider micro processes that take place in everyday life not just as individual processes, but as a compendium of micro spaces where social conflict is always

part of the struggle for agency or power, and where context is also very significant.

The notions of reproduction and contestation have served as categories of analysis for tourism scholars in Latin America, mainly due to a common concern over the region's inequalities (Carosio, 2009). Tourism and gender research in Latin America also shows that women are contesting inequalities and becoming empowered through micro processes (Martínez-Corona, 2003; Ramos, 2004); this is also consistent with other findings in the global south (Tran and Walter, 2014; Kimbu and Ngoasong, 2016; Lenao and Basupi, 2016).

Female Entrepreneurship in Mexico's Tourism: An Interpretation from Tourism and Gender Research

Entrepreneurship is the 'pursuit of business opportunities for economic gain' (Ratten and Dana, 2017, p. 4), but other reasons – that is, social or environmental ones – are also important while deciding to become an entrepreneur (Martínez-Corona, 2003; Hernández *et al.*, 2005; Fernández-Aldecua and Martínez-Barón, 2010). As Fig. 10.1 suggests, empowerment, improved time management, ability

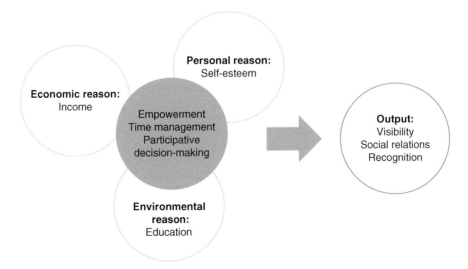

Fig. 10.1. Women have several motivations to become entrepreneurs. While engaging in empowerment they become visible and use this to improve their social relations, gaining recognition as a result. (Own elaboration from Martínez-Corona (2003), Fernández-Aldecua and Martínez-Barón (2010) and Kimbu and Ngoasong (2016).)

to participate in decision-making processes, becoming a 'visible' person, developing social bonds and getting public recognition are among the most important values for female entrepreneurs.

According to Anggadwita *et al.* (2017, p. 87), the entrepreneurial ability of women is highly dependent on the combination of several cultural factors, especially in societies where business has been considered as naturally suited to men (Hernández *et al.*, 2005). Critical authors maintain that entrepreneurship has been used to perpetuate gender stereotypes instead of promoting gender equality or poverty alleviation (Clark-Muntean and Ozkazanc-Pan, 2016), reproducing the message of a male-dominant sphere where women's results are peripheral (Ahl and Marlow, 2012, p. 557).

However, in several emerging destinations, like in Mexico, entrepreneurship has been considered as a key contributor to women's empowerment; women can use entrepreneurship as a tool for social transformation (Díaz-Carrión, 2014; Clark-Muntean and Ozkazanc-Pan, 2016). That is, by becoming entrepreneurs, women can gain social capital and use it to change gender roles in their communities by, for example, getting access to new resources and transforming gender roles not only as entrepreneurs but as rural women (Kimbu and Ngoasong, 2016; Apisalome and Dahles, 2017).

Tourism studies have not examined entrepreneurship through a Bourdieuian lens; however, to Bourdieu and Wacquant (2005) social agents develop strategies aimed at reproducing or changing society. As Fernández-Aldecua and Martínez-Barón (2010), Dreher and Ullrich (2011) and Lunardi *et al.* (2015) have considered, entrepreneurship can have a significant impact on social capital-building as well as improving gender roles. Some studies have looked at the effects of tourism entrepreneurship on women's empowerment, such as how empowerment changes traditional gender roles (Hernández *et al.*, 2005; Fernández-Aldecua and Martínez-Barón, 2010), with empowerment as a core element in social capital-building. As Martínez-Corona (2003, pp. 200–201) points out, women's empowerment processes in ecotourism initiatives generate the construction

of new power structures and gender relations. Fernández-Aldecua and Martínez-Barón (2010) also think tourism entrepreneurship has the potential to promote change in women's lives, improving their social capital.

However, social capital-building is not always a linear process. Female entrepreneurs can experience work overload when there is no sharing of domestic and care responsibilities with their partners at home (Costa *et al.*, 2016). As an entrepreneur, the lack of social recognition has a negative impact on women's social capital; the relevant literature reports work–family conflicts faced by female entrepreneurs (Ramos, 2004; Díaz-Carrión, 2014; Tran and Walter, 2014; Lunardi *et al.*, 2015; Kimbu and Ngoasong, 2016).

Female entrepreneurs are not always aware of changes generated while building social capital. For example, they can recognize the way participation in tourism has changed their lives, but often, they are unaware of the underlying implications regarding how gender roles are changing (Fernández-Aldecua and Martínez-Barón, 2010). This results in contradictory opinions between traditional and new gender roles and places extra burden on women that challenge the status quo. These conflicts stand at the core of the debates on whether women's entrepreneurship helps maintain the status quo of patriarchal norms and values. The cycle starts with women having to ask for their partner's permission before engaging in any entrepreneurial activity. Usually, women's type of participation is moulded around their care responsibilities, perpetuating women's role as caregivers, and doubling or tripling their workload (Díaz-Carrión, 2014; Rodríguez and Acevedo, 2015) while promoting undervaluation of care work (Carrasco *et al.*, 2011).

At first glance, tourism may contribute to maintaining the status quo and generate limited gains for women (Smrittee and Brijesh, 2017). Women in tourism face additional challenges since any activity that attempts to change the status quo tends to face resistance, so women's advancement through tourism is a slow process (Bourdieu, 2000; 2004; Lagarde, 2001). Through a more critical lens, despite the high number of care activities, women's involvement in tourism can open a path for social capital-building, aiding in the transformation of traditional gender roles (Lenao and Basupi, 2016). The potential for tourism to bring about meaningful change particularly increases when women participate as business operators in community-based organizations (Apisalome and Dahles, 2017) and as entrepreneurs in hospitality and lodging (Tshabalala and Ezeuduji, 2016; Smrittee and Brijesh, 2017).

Women involved in ecotourism as entrepreneurs have reported both benefits and constraints. Economic opportunities in rural areas characterized by a shortage of employment are the main benefit. Another benefit is women's enhanced self-confidence due to direct interaction with tourists or indirect access to business networks, as well as their recognition as successful entrepreneurs (Martínez-Corona, 2003; Hernández *et al.*, 2005; Tshabalala and Ezeuduji, 2016; Smrittee and Brijesh, 2017). On the other hand, small improvements do not guarantee the transformation of power relations. Women's participation in ecotourism ventures could increase their work burden (Díaz-Carrión, 2014; Rodríguez and Acevedo, 2015). There is also the risk of male appropriation of women-run businesses once these become economically profitable (Hernández *et al.*, 2005).

Following Bourdieu (2000; 2013), small changes are fundamental in the construction of social capital, and could trigger broader changes. For instance, the economic or social gains brought by ecotourism entrepreneurship can contribute towards women's financial security or public recognition, which is a prerequisite for social capital-building in daily life (Lagarde and Aliaga, 1997; Lagarde, 2001). By becoming entrepreneurs, women might also increase their social capital through networking opportunities, increased self-confidence and sense of fulfilment (Fernández-Aldecua and Martínez-Barón, 2010; Kimbu and Ngoasong, 2016). Figure 10.2 shows that female entrepreneurs can use diverse contestation strategies in order to consolidate their social capital and change gender roles; on the contrary, reproduction strategies maintain status quo and legitimize women's subordination (Ahl and Marlow, 2012).

The next sections will focus on female entrepreneurs' experiences in various rural destinations in the Catemaco–Montepío corridor, Mexico, in order to explore the effects on female entrepreneurs' social capital as a consequence of their entrepreneurial involvement.

Ecotourism in Catemaco–Montepío Corridor in Los Tuxtlas, Veracruz

Los Tuxtlas, south of Veracruz, Mexico, is a volcanic island with two outstanding volcanoes, San Martín and Santa Marta, separated by low-lying land, which contains two important water bodies, the Catemaco Lake and the Sontecomapan Lagoon (Siemens, 2004).

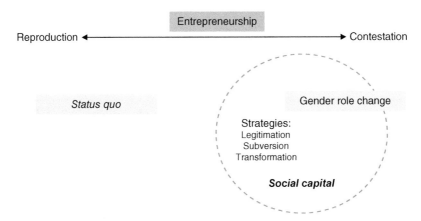

Fig. 10.2. Entrepreneurship and social capital. (Own elaboration from Bourdieu (2000; 2013) and Lagarde (2001).)

The region is also a conglomerate of rural destinations usually used by locals for leisure purposes, and has been protected for the past 80 years, and even more so during the past 30 years (Díaz-Carrión and Neger, 2014, p. 192).

In Los Tuxtlas, ecotourism has existed in some of the small rural communities since the 1980s. Ecotourism businesses are mainly located around Lake Catemaco and in the northern coastal area of Los Tuxtlas (Díaz-Carrión and Neger, 2014, pp. 195–196). The study area for the present research is the so-called Catemaco–Montepío corridor, a well-known tourist destination that connects the main urban areas of the region, San Andrés Tuxtla and Catemaco, with the northern coastal area. In the Catemaco–Montepío corridor, the declaration of the Biosphere Reserve led to the promotion of community-based enterprises, with the purpose of promoting environmental conservation and poverty alleviation. Some public funds have also introduced a 'gender clause', to promote women's participation, however with limited success.

This qualitative study examines the entrepreneurship experiences of 25 women in different ecotourism-related businesses: 19 own or are partners in restaurants, lodging or tour guiding ventures in rural destinations located in the Catemaco–Montepío corridor; while the other six run their business in the broader Los Tuxtlas region. I used snowball sampling to identify participants after initial contact was made through the region's tourism office. Officers referred me to the ecotourism enterprises (either community-based organizations or private enterprises) and other relevant informants in the area. Oral consent was obtained from all women interviewed. In-depth interviews and indirect observation were used to explore everyday experiences from a gender perspective (Ayres, 2008, pp. 810–811). The interviews were recorded and content analysis was performed on the resulting transcriptions (Ruiz, 2012, p. 194).

How to Be a Woman Entrepreneur and Not Die Trying

The main findings and discussion are structured in three subsections.

To be or not to be?

In general, women value their involvement in ecotourism as a positive experience, as one entrepreneur stated: 'to me, it was through my participation [in ecotourism] that I could get access to many things and it is enriching at the end' (*Interviewee 1*). The decision to get involved in ecotourism entrepreneurship is influenced by various factors. However, the economic factor is regarded as an important motivation. In the words of a participant: 'when you depend on your husband to have money, you have to do many things to please him, sometimes you endure situations that make you feel unhappy and you are not okay' (*Interviewee 4*). Economic benefits from engaging in tourism entrepreneurship may generate changes at the personal level: 'when I opened this restaurant again I could earn my own money again so I didn't have to ask my husband for money, I appreciate having my own money' (*Interviewee 4*).

Ecotourism is affected by macro and micro processes, which are defined by the neoliberalist prioritizing of economic or financial gain over non-monetary economic or social values. For the women interviewed, there were several reasons besides economic gain that motivated them to become involved in ecotourism. For example, overcoming isolation was an important motivation, since women regarded it as a negative aspect of their lives. They recall that before becoming entrepreneurs: 'we were neighbours, but we never lived together as true neighbours' (*Interviewee 7*).

Women appreciated establishing links with other members of their communities through participation in ecotourism ventures. This gain was particularly noted by older women, who saw their involvement in ecotourism as a vital step towards obtaining recognition in the public sphere: 'I am 52 years old and have always been at home, to participate in this venture ... I am not just "the wife" or "the mother" ... when tourists arrive to the community they are sent to me, they are told go to that place and ask for me' (*Interviewee 11*). The creation of spaces in which women can socialize is necessary, in order to expand the impact of individual changes and to consolidate women's social capital in rural communities. In rural communities public life tends to be restricted to men, particularly among the older women (Lagarde and Aliaga, 1997; Lagarde, 2001), who have a more restricted social role and everyday life is centred around private spaces for them.

Environmental motivations were also present in the decision to become entrepreneurs, as exemplified in a woman's remarks: 'I wanted to do something for my community, when I was a child there were many trees everywhere but now it is very dirty and without trees' (*Interviewee 1*). Not all entrepreneurs were environmentally conscious from the beginning, but eventually got involved in conservation activities: 'I was not interested until I met a friend, she ... she told me about the importance [of the environment] and ... invited me to attend the meetings where people from different communities were already participating' (*Interviewee 4*). Women's level of participation in conservation activities varies across ventures; however, the location of their communities in a Protected Area (Biosphere Reserve) along with the institutional incentives provided to local entrepreneurs (e.g. workshops and public funding), have contributed to reinforcing women's environmental consciousness. They have also increased their social capital by generating spaces where female entrepreneurs can exchange experiences and promote sororities (*Interviewee 2, Interviewee 10*).

Only three women among the participants recognized personal reasons as the main motivator to become an entrepreneur. The first woman expressed that since her mother was a restaurant owner, this provided her with the motivation to start her own business. Nonconformity with traditional gender roles was also crucial in her decision: 'I used to work in my mother's restaurant in the kitchen ... but when she decided to name my brother as the administrator ... because he was male ... I felt disappointed and ... when I got an opportunity to start my own restaurant, a very tiny one, and after pondering it a lot ... I made up my mind' (*Interviewee 4*). For the second woman, participation in ecotourism entrepreneurship was a consequence of her family's involvement: 'My father started the

business and when he became old, my sister and I inherited it and have kept it going on [...] I don't have a brother, it's just my sister and I' (*Interviewee 16*). Finally, the third case was a young woman who struggled to become a tourist guide in a community enterprise. She was denied involvement because she was young (under 18 years old) and female (*Interviewee 5*), but she negotiated with old, male partners and eventually became accepted.

As the previous three examples show, local entrepreneurs in these rural communities defined active participation and decision-making as predominantly male attributes. Women faced restrictions to their participation in community enterprises, due to the widespread belief that business was not a suitable activity for women. This belief corresponds with the expectations associated with traditional gender roles, that women lack initiative, independence or interest in becoming entrepreneurs and are only interested in getting money from their husbands (*Interviewee 7, Interviewee 2*).

In Los Tuxtlas, land tenure has historically been a male right. Women have only accessed this asset as widows (with a son frequently named as administrator), or when inheriting less productive or smaller pieces of land (Almeida, 2012, p. 73). Land entitlement is an important prerequisite to obtain government funding to start or consolidate a business: 'If you don't have the rights [of land] you can't have access to any aid or financial programme' (*Interviewee 16*). Land requirements help perpetuate the notion of business as a male activity: 'When there is any funding, officials come to the Ejido Assembly (the main ruling body), where most members are men, so it is ... like the projects are for men ... it was in this way that communal land holders (ejidatarios) decided ecotourism was for men, and women were not allowed to participate until they needed somebody to cook, or participation was mandatory for us as partners' (*Interviewee 5*).

In recent years, government programmes have introduced a 'gender clause' to increase the presence of women in ecotourism projects. Women saw this as a positive measure, but recognize that this action alone will not solve the lack of gender equity (*Interviewee*

16). Gender awareness programmes will also be necessary for women and men to change '*machete*' attitudes and behaviours (*Interviewee 10*).

Women's enterprises: the role of family

Ecotourism businesses in the Catemaco–Montepío corridor can be classified into two categories: (i) community-based enterprises (e.g. cooperatives), where women are partners; and (ii) individual businesses (financed with personal or borrowed capital), where women can be sole proprietors or partners (see Fig. 10.3).

The majority of rural women participate in community-based enterprises, whereas neo-rural women more likely engage in individual businesses. Some women entrepreneurs live in the municipality, but all the women interviewed moved from urban cities to communities in this rural destination and are categorized as neo-rural. The educational level is higher for neo-rural entrepreneurs than for rural entrepreneurs, and younger rural women show higher educational attainment compared to their middle-aged counterparts.

Family has been an important support for women starting their business. All women have at least one relative as partner or employee. This is more frequently true in community-based enterprises that received public or international funds. Such aid was targeted towards community-based initiatives as opposed to private ventures, and facilitated the incorporation of kin (*Interviewee 15*, Los Tuxtlas Biosphere Directorate). Women-led private enterprises also count on family members' work (e.g. husband/partner,

parents or siblings). As a result, women define their business as a family enterprise rather than an individual venture (*Interviewees 4* and *6*). One woman openly used this strategy to circumvent her husband's prohibition to run a business: 'He didn't like that I worked in my mother's restaurant very much ... I was afraid he wouldn't want me to have my own place either ... so I used to say that it was for the family' (*Interviewee 4*).

For another entrepreneur, running the business along with her sister has provided a strategy to manage critical stages in their life cycles: 'I have been running the Rancho since my sister had a baby ... so she could enjoy the baby ... and now she will start running it so I can keep studying' (*Interviewee 16*). Overcoming family supervision has been a challenge for women entrepreneurs. Feminist perspectives on the family view it as a patriarchal institution or a tool for oppression (Lagarde 1996; Lagarde and Aliaga, 1997; Bourdieu, 2013). Nevertheless, in some instances, families can promote egalitarian relations. One woman explained how after she got divorced, she made sure she educated her children (one son and two daughters) in a less oppressive environment (*Interviewee 10*). Supportive family arrangements may mean more women choose motherhood as they can get help with childcare. These types of domestic arrangements fill in for the lack of public childcare assistance, especially in remote rural locations: 'We work on our own ... so we can't get access to government assistance ... the only available childcare is the one you pay for, and my sister wanted to stay with her baby for a while ... and we are isolated' (*Interviewee 16*).

Social norms define what activities are more suitable for women, but age and educational level were contributory factors in the

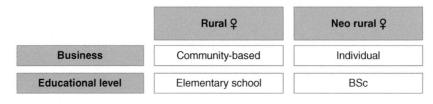

Fig. 10.3. Women's profile for entrepreneurship in ecotourism in Catemaco–Montepío.

types of business activities. Women over 30 years old run or are partners in restaurants, lodgings or combined ventures. whereas younger women are more likely to join initiatives as tourist guides (*Interviewees 3, 6, 15* and *16*). The younger generations (women with higher levels of education) participated in activities traditionally deemed as masculine (e.g. tour guiding) and in traditionally male spaces (e.g. the lagoon, the lake or hiking trails). 'Some of us went to school and also took courses to be ecotourist guides so it is easier to interact with the tourists ... The others [older males] do not feel very comfortable interacting with them because they did not go to school' (*Interviewee 3*).

Changing gender roles?

As stated by Bourdieu (2000), women tend not to be aware of the gender system transformations they promote until recognition comes, usually from the outside. Initially, female entrepreneurs in the Catemaco–Montepío corridor were not motivated by potential changes in gender roles to participate in ecotourism. However, some female entrepreneurs became conscious of gender inequities at several stages of the process. Through this 'awakening', women started questioning traditional gender roles and eventually developed strategies to challenge gender norms. For some women, these changes have reached the domestic sphere: 'To me it was very important to be conscious of gender inequalities and very sad too because I realized that my husband was *machista* and at the end I decided to get a divorce, I was the first divorced women in my town' (*Interviewee 10*). However, both older and younger women have occasionally deployed strategies to maintain the status quo.

For female entrepreneurs in the Catemaco–Montepío corridor, the use of transformative or compliance strategies was related to age rather than to social hierarchy. As one woman suggested, 'new arrangements are for young woman, for older women ... like me, it is too late' (*Interviewee 12*). Interest in promoting gender changes was indeed more frequent among young female entrepreneurs.

These women seek access to education; participation in decision-making processes; a more egalitarian relationship; or a professional career (*Interviewees 3, 9* and *16*). The question is whether these younger women will have enough social capital to achieve and promote gender changes, not only at the personal or domestic levels, but also within the community.

A significant number of study participants recognized that women must pursue a more active role to gain visibility as entrepreneurs. In the words of one of the participants: 'I think women entrepreneurs do many successful things, but you know, if a man does something successful they tell everybody to get recognition and we don't, so we also have to announce [our successes] as a means to get recognition' (*Interviewee 9*). Through building social capital, social recognition can support women's transformation strategies (Kay and Laberge, 2004; Tran and Walter, 2014).

Some groups received gender aware training and in others, the 'gender clause' was institutionalized. Both official measures have been effective in promoting some gender changes, mainly in the domestic sphere (*Interviewees 1, 3* and *10*). As *Interviewee 1* stated: 'Some women realized they do not need their husband's permission, that it is not okay ... and they are adults ... and started to negotiate within their family to make some changes'. However, these measures do not guarantee gender transformation per se. Changes prove difficult to attain for the following reasons:

- Some women do not value gender change because they perceive benefits in traditional gender arrangements, in some cases they prefer to stay at home and embrace domesticity without being interested in negotiating gender role changes.
- Lack of intergenerational sisterhood. This reinforces the differences between older and younger generations.
- Lack of gender awareness training. Since tourism plans and enterprises are still gender-blind, contexts are ignored and inequalities are reinforced.

Conclusion

The purpose of this chapter was to explore Bourdieu's concept of social capital from a Mexican feminist perspective, and to apply this theoretical construct to the analysis of tourism entrepreneurship in rural areas. The experiences of 16 women entrepreneurs were examined in this chapter.

As a *mestizo*, feminist, urban and heterosexual academic, I see women ecotourism entrepreneurs in Catemaco–Montepío presenting strategies of legitimization, subversion and transformation. They follow diverse strategies concerning gender relations. Some women use their social capital to defy traditional gender roles to get access to resources or activities not considered suitable for women, while others contribute to maintaining the status quo. Despite the negative outcomes identified by scholars, female entrepreneurship can become a strategy to generate changes in traditional gender systems, and to increase women's social capital (Kay and Laberge, 2004; Ahl and Marlow, 2012). Sometimes women alternate strategies, first promoting the maintenance of the status quo to later realize the inequalities in this approach, and shift to subversive or transformative strategies, as in the case of *Interviewees 4* or *10*, who pursue more egalitarian gender relations within their families and promote entrepreneurial roles in their communities.

As shown in the present research, some female entrepreneurs have notably taken advantage of the aforementioned limitations, that is, the fact that entrepreneurship is still defined as a male activity in their society, plus the extra burden, and have transformed them into positive improvement strategies. For these women, becoming a tourism entrepreneur has been a strategic platform to increase their social capital and to gain community and domestic recognition, all necessary steps towards social capital-building (Lagarde, 2001). The changes produced by social capital are concentrated at the micro level; that is, in the everyday life spaces where women work and interact. The accumulation of everyday changes may eventually generate broader social transformations, in what I see as a slow revolution.

In the Catemaco–Montepío corridor, female entrepreneurs define success in terms of personal satisfaction, as opposed to the more traditional measure of business growth. Participation in ecotourism is not the only space for these women to generate social change, but ecotourism represents one of several complementary strategies to obtain income in their area. The transformational potential of ecotourism entrepreneurship appears more closely related to women's increase in *social status*. The strategies adopted by female entrepreneurs seldom contest gender inequalities directly; however, in the process of empowering themselves, women generate a set of mechanisms necessary to improve gender relations in their personal and community spheres.

References

Ahl, H. and Marlow, S. (2012) Exploring the dynamics of gender, feminism and entrepreneurship: advancing debate to escape a dead end?' *Organization* 19(5), 543–562. DOI: 10.1177/1350508412448695.

Almeida, E. (2012) Herencia y donación. Prácticas intrafamiliares de transmisión de la tierra. Caso de un ejido veracruzano. *Revista Cuicuilco* 54, 55–79.

Anggadwita, G., Luturlean, B., Ramadani, V. and Ratten, V. (2017) Sociocultural environments and emerging economy entrepreneurship: women entrepreneurs in Indonesia. *Journal of Entrepreneurship in Emerging Economies*, 9(1), 85–96.

Apisalome, M. and Dahles, H. (2017) Female empowerment and tourism: a focus on businesses in a Fijian village. *Asia Pacific Journal of Tourism Research*, 1–12.

Ayres, L. (2008) Semi-structured interviews. In: *The Sage Encyclopedia of Qualitative Research Methods*. SAGE, Thousand Oaks, California, pp. 810–811.

Bourdieu, P. (2000) *Intelectuales, política y poder*. Editorial EUDEBA, Buenos Aires.

Bourdieu, P. (2004) *Cosas dichas*. Editorial Gedisa, Barcelona, Spain.

Bourdieu, P. (2013) *La dominación masculina*. Anagrama, Barcelona, Spain.

Bourdieu, P. and Wacquant, L. (2005) *Una invitación a la sociología reflexiva*. Siglo XXI, Buenos Aires.

Bourdieu, P., Chamboredon, J.C. and Passeron, J.C. (2008) *El oficio del sociólogo: presupuestos epistemológicos*. Siglo XXI, Buenos Aires.

Carosio, A. (2009) Feminismo Latinoamericano: imperativo ético para la emancipación. In: Girón, A. (ed.) *Género y globalización*, 1st edn. CLACSO, Buenos Aires, pp. 229–252.

Carrasco, C., Borderías, C. and Torns, T. (2011) *El trabajo de cuidados. Historia, teoría y políticas*. Catarata, Madrid.

Clark-Muntean, S. and Ozkazanc-Pan, B. (2016) Feminist perspectives on social entrepreneurship: critique and new directions. *International Journal of Gender and Entrepreneurship* 8(3), 221–241. DOI: 10.1108/IJGE-10-2014-0034.

Costa, C., Breda, Z., Bakas, F., Durão, M. and Pinho, I. (2016) Through the gender looking-glass: Brazilian tourism entrepreneurs. *International Journal of Gender and Entrepreneurship* 8(3). DOI: 10.1108/IJGE-07-2015-0023.

Díaz-Carrión, I. (2014) Ecoturismo y vida cotidiana de las mujeres en Sontecomapan (Veracruz, México). *Cuadernos de turismo* 34, 69–88.

Díaz-Carrión, I. and Neger, C. (2014) Ecotourism in the Reserva de la Biosfera de Los Tuxtlas (Veracruz, Mexico). *Athens Journal of Tourism* September, 191–202.

Dreher, T. and Ullrich, D. (2011) Gestión de las empresas turísticas: la representación de las mujeres en Blumenau – SC, Brasil. *Estudios y Perspectivas en Turismo* 20(2), 425–440.

Fernández-Aldecua, M. and Martínez-Barón, L. (2010) Participación de las mujeres en las empresas turísticas privadas y comunitarias de Bahías de Huatulco, México ¿Hacia un cambio en el rol de género? *Cuadernos de Turismo* 26, 129–151.

Hernández, R., Bello, E., Montoya, G. and Estrada, E. (2005) Social adaptation ecotourism in the Lacandon forest. *Annals of Tourism Research* 32(3), 610–627.

Kay, J. and Laberge, S. (2004) 'Mandatory equipment': women in adventure racing. In: Wheaton, B. (ed). *Understanding Lifestyle Sports: Consumption, Identity and Difference*. Routledge, New York, pp. 154–174.

Kimbu, A. and Ngoasong, M. (2016) Women as vectors of social entrepreneurship. *Annals of Tourism Research* 60, 63–79.

Lagarde, M. (1996) *Género y feminismo. Desarrollo humano y democracia*. Horas y Horas, Madrid.

Lagarde, M. (2001) *Claves feministas para la autoestima de las mujeres*. Horas y Horas, Madrid.

Lagarde, M. and Aliaga, S. (1997) *Entre decir y vivir*. Centro de Información y Desarrollo de la Mujer (CIDEM), La Paz, Bolivia.

Lenao, M. and Basupi, B. (2016) Ecotourism development and female empowerment in Botswana: a review. *Tourism Management Perspectives* 18, 51–58.

Lunardi, R., de Souza, M. and Perurena, F. (2015) O trabalho de homens e mulheres no turismo rural em São José dos Ausentes: o 'leve' e o 'pesado' – *Visão e Ação* 17(1), 179–209.

Martínez-Corona, B. (2003) Género, sustentabilidad y empoderamiento en proyectos ecoturísticos de mujeres indígenas. *La Ventana* 17(July), 188–217.

Ramos, T. (2004) Artesanas y artesanías: indígenas y mestizas de Chiapas construyendo Espacios de cambio. *LiminaR. Estudios Sociales y Humanísticos* II(1), 50–71.

Ratten, V. and Dana, L.-P. (2017) Gendered perspective of indigenous entrepreneurship. *Small Enterprise Research* 4–11. DOI: 10.1080/13215906.2017.1289858.

Rodríguez, G. and Acevedo, A. (2015) Cambios en la vida cotidiana de las mujeres a través de la incorporación al trabajo turístico en la Reserva de la Biosfera de la Mariposa Monarca. *El Periplo Sustentable* 29, 5–33.

Ruiz, J. (2012) *Metodología de la Investigación Cualitativa*. Deusto, Bilbao.

Siemens, A. (2004) The landscapes. In: *Los Tuxtlas: The Landscape of the Mountain Range*. INECOL, Xalapa, pp. 41–58.

Smrittee, K. and Brijesh, T. (2017) Entrepreneurship and women's empowerment in gateway communities of Bardia National Park, Nepal. *Journal of Ecotourism* 17(1), 20–42. DOI: 10.1080/14724049.2017.1299743.

Tran, L. and Walter, P. (2014) Ecotourism, gender and development in northern Vietnam. *Annals of Tourism Research* 44, 116–130.

Tshabalala, S. and Ezeuduji, I. (2016) Women tourism entrepreneurs in KwaZulu Natal, South Africa: any way forward? *AUDOE* 12(5), 19–32.

United Nations World Tourism Organization (UNWTO) (2011) *Global Report on Women in Tourism 2010*. UNWTO, Madrid.

Sari's Story: Labuan Bajo's First Female Dive Guide

Sari Sehang

The youngest of four children from a remote village on the island of Rinca, Indonesia, I always thought I would be a police officer. During middle school, I saw how tourism was growing in the nearest town and around my island and decided to study tourism and travel at vocational high school. During my 3-month work experience at Wicked Dive, I went out on the dive boats to practise my English. When I saw how excited the guests were when they saw manta rays and turtles I wanted to try diving. A British female dive guide encouraged me to try it out, and I loved it! There was a lot to learn and many challenges to overcome. My father did not agree at all; he was scared about aggressive sharks, he thought it was a heavy job, not suited to women. When I told him there were plenty of foreign female dive guides, he said they were different, different culture, stronger, braver, but I remained determined. My father accepted my chosen profession and I think he might even be proud of me but he doesn't say so. In 2015 I qualified as a dive master. I felt respected by my peers on the boats, despite being the only female dive guide, but I worried if I'd ever find a husband who would accept me and let me carry on working. Good news, within a year I did, and married another dive guide who shares and understands my passion!

Sari had hoped to be able to combine her career with having children too and wanted to open the minds of other local women to try diving and break into the male-dominated profession. However, on marriage she immediately became pregnant and, despite Wicked Dive giving her the role of outreach to talk to young women,

Fig. S10. Scuba dive master.

she quickly resigned. Local tradition dictates that women should give up work when they are married, and many local companies use this as an excuse not to employ and train women. Wicked Dive invested a lot in their first female dive guide but have not given up trying to persuade others to enter the profession.

11 Tourism, Dolls and Dreams: The Last Generation?

Hazel Tucker*

University of Otago, Dunedin, New Zealand

Introduction

All over the world, from Latin America and Africa to Eastern Europe and Asia, women in developing economies endeavour to improve the lives of their families by creating and selling exquisite indigenous crafts. The weavers of Guatemala, the Ndebele beaders of South Africa, the flower painters of Poland, the batik artists of Indonesia, the doll-makers of Turkey, the mirror embroiderers of India – all these women artisans draw from past traditions as well as make eloquent contributions to the future of their children and their cultures.

These words are from the cover of a book entitled *In Her Hands: Craftswomen Changing the World* (Gianturco and Tuttle, 2000), a coffee table-style book that is a photographic documentary of 'ninety women living in twelve countries on four continents'. The book is described as a portrait of the women's 'diverse lives and surprisingly universal aspirations', those aspirations being to 'create beautiful crafts that contribute to a better life for themselves and for future generations'. Among the women documented in the book is Hanife, from Soğanli in central Turkey, who, in the 1960s, had made the first Soğanli doll that was sold to passing tourists. The story talks of Hanife's aspirations for her children to become better educated than herself so that they would be able to leave the village and have a better life than the one she had had. Her life she described as one of always relying on selling dolls to tourists in order for her and her family to get by.

During fieldwork visits I made to Soğanli, most recently in 2015, however, among the doll-maker women I visited and chatted with while they sat with their dolls waiting for tourists to come by were the great-granddaughters of Hanife. They, and their mothers and grandmothers, had not, it seems, managed to leave the village to secure a 'better life'. In their expressing the desire for each generation to be the last generation of doll-maker women, therefore, the Soğanli women's stories serve to form a critique of the romanticization of women craft-makers and craft-making that is often apparent in tourism and development contexts (see Jimenez-Esquinas, 2017). This chapter tells those stories and, based on conversations with Soğanli doll-maker women, including those written about in the *In Her Hands: Craftswomen Changing the World* (Gianturco and Tuttle, 2000) book and those had

---

* E-mail: hazel.tucker@otago.ac.nz

during ethnographic fieldwork conducted in Soğanli Valley, the chapter is intended to bring into view a longitudinal, generational focus on women and tourism contexts.

Women's making and selling of handicrafts to tourists is widely considered to be typical home-based self-employment that women are able to engage in within tourism contexts in order to achieve some level of economic empowerment. Such 'empowerment' is argued by Kabeer (2005, p. 13) to be the process 'by which those who have been denied the ability to make choices acquire such ability'. However, the notion of 'empowerment' is far from straightforward, since it is not only a process demanding significant change, but also is one inevitably associated with contradiction and ambivalence (Tucker and Boonabaana, 2012). As Chant notes, for example, a problem exists in the tendency for gender and development projects to lead to 'women working for development' rather than a situation of development 'working for women' (2006, p. 102). Moreover, even where women's involvements in tourism do appear to empower women, the longitudinal, or ongoing, implications of such involvements for women, men and the broader community need to be considered.

In the gender and tourism literature, certainly, the relative benefits of tourism development to women and men are widely understood to reflect local socio-cultural norms regarding gender relations and the division of labour based on sex (see, for example, Kinnaird *et al.*, 1994; Harvey *et al.*, 1995; Wilkinson and Pratiwi, 1995; Long and Kindon, 1997; Scott, 1997; Apostolopoulos and Sönmez, 2001; Gibson, 2001; Ferguson, 2009). Within this context, however, Scheyvens (2000) has noted, based on her survey of a wide range of developing contexts, that it is small-scale tourism initiatives that tend to offer the highest potential for enhancing the lives of economically marginalized groups, including rural women. Gentry (2007) similarly argues that alternative forms of tourism, which emphasize small-scale businesses, are likely overall to be more beneficial to local women than mass tourism developments. This issue of scale is

why it is that many 'pro-poor' tourism initiatives, such as the World Bank's gender and poverty-reduction tourism projects in Central America, are often based predominantly on small-scale and 'alternative' forms of tourism development (Ferguson, 2010).

Indeed, among the 90 women from throughout the world featured in Gianturco and Tuttle's (2000) book, many of those who are engaged in tourism-related handicraft production and sales are likely to be involved in small-scale or 'alternative' forms of tourism development as some sort of poverty-reduction strategy. As the book's authors explain: 'Often driven by the harsh realities of poverty, little education, and lack of even basic health care, these female artisans are motivated by the desire to provide for their children: to dress them properly, to feed them well, and most of all, to educate them'. The Soğanli doll-maker women are depicted among the 'highlights' of the book:

> The doll-makers of Soğanli, Turkey are the only wage earners of the village. Men work in the fields and gather firewood for their families, but there are no cash crops or 'men's jobs' in manufacturing or construction to provide income. Fifty women (the town has fifty families) create dolls dressed in bright silky costumes accented with sequins – much like the clothes they wear themselves.

During fieldwork I was undertaking in the Cappadocia region of central Turkey in 2015, I got to know some of the current generation of Soğanli women who make dolls to sell to tourists. My research in Cappadocia began in 1995 and is a longitudinal ethnographic study into the socio-cultural change brought about by tourism development in the region. A key focus of the research has been the ongoing dynamics of the relationship between tourism development and gender relations in this socially conservative society (see, in particular, Tucker, 2003; 2007; 2011). Whilst my fieldwork has predominantly focused on the township of Göreme, which, along with the towns of Ürgüp and Avanos, is considered to be in the heart of the tourism developments in Cappadocia, I have periodically extended my fieldwork area to other parts of the Cappadocia region, including the Soğanli Valley. I therefore have visited Soğanli many times over a period of more than two decades, and have been able to observe many aspects of the tourism, and other 'developments' there. In 2015, during a 4-month stay in Cappadocia throughout the summer tourism season, I made multiple fieldwork visits to Soğanli and conducted participant observation there, including numerous conversational interviews with doll-maker women and other Soğanli villagers. Before going on to discuss the Soğanli doll-maker women's stories, the next section will provide an outline of the tourism context in the region.

Cappadocia and Soğanli Tourism Context

Known for its 'moonlike' landscape of giant rock cones, historic Byzantine churches and cave dwellings, the Cappadocia region has, in recent decades, become a major focus of Turkey's 'cultural tourism' development. 'Tourism Encouragement Act' legislation enacted throughout Turkey in the early 1980s, together with the listing of the Cappadocia region as a United Nations Educational, Scientific and Cultural Organization (UNESCO) World Heritage Site area in 1985, prompted a surge in tourism development throughout the 1980s, 1990s and 2000s. The main tourism development is centred around the Göreme, Ürgüp and Avanos area, where the Göreme National Park and Göreme Open-Air Museum have attracted considerable tourism investments, both from external hotel chains and tour operators developing large-scale tourism facilities and from local entrepreneurs developing smaller-scale tourism facilities. Most tourists visiting Cappadocia and staying in this central part of Cappadocia undertake at least one regional tour, which would usually include a visit to an 'underground city', also part of the World Heritage Site listing, plus one or two further afield areas where there are notable concentrations of Byzantine churches or landscapes of interest.

Soğanli Valley is one of these areas and it is generally considered rather remote,

situated as it is in the southeast corner of the Cappadocia region approximately 60 km from Göreme and Ürgüp townships. Soğanli has been particularly popular over the years with German, French and Italian tour groups, and throughout the late 1980s and 1990s Soğanli was one of the main stops on a popular day-long tour package sold to the independent traveller market by the many small tour agencies in Göreme and Ürgüp. Soğanli became an attraction for these tourist markets not only because of its Byzantine churches and their well-preserved frescoes, but also, being relatively 'remote' and situated at the far end of a long ravine with high cliffs soaring high above the valley floor, Soğanli village was considered by tourists to be particularly scenic and to have an 'authentic' character (see Tucker, 2003). Arriving by tour coach, or minibus in the case of the independent traveller tours, besides visiting the churches and viewing the spectacular landscapes, tourists would spend time roaming around the village with its stone houses, donkeys and 'peasant' inhabitants (see Tucker, 2010, for discussion of the use of the term 'peasant' in the Cappadocia context). The tour buses would stop in the bus park area in the centre of the village beside the main tea house. As well as going for a wander around the village, tourists bought tea and snacks in the tea house, had lunch at the open-air restaurant set up to cater especially to the tour groups and shopped at the many souvenir stalls set up near the bus park area. The Soğanli doll-maker women were the main holders of these stalls.

The period from the late 1980s through to the end of the 1990s was considered the heyday of Soğanli's tourism, with its popularity fluctuating over the years, depending not only on the state of tourism in Cappadocia and Turkey more generally, but also on the whims of the tour companies and tour guides operating in the region. For example, throughout the 2000s the hot air ballooning tourism industry rapidly developed there, again centred around the Göreme and Ürgüp area of Cappadocia. Since the tour companies were able to receive hefty commissions from encouraging their customers to go hot air ballooning, they were keen to keep them in the Göreme and Ürgüp area rather than taking them on tours to other parts of Cappadocia. Also, at the end of the 1990s tourism developments in another valley in the western part of Cappadocia meant that the local tour agencies selling tours to the independent traveller market changed their itineraries to include that other valley. Soğanli therefore fell out of favour to some degree. Those developments in the competing valley included the creation of scenic walking tracks along the valley floor, and some restaurants in that valley offering lunch packages to minibus groups for less than the prices at the Soğanli village restaurant. With many of the tour agencies in Göreme and Ürgüp, as well as the larger tour companies and their guides, chasing better profit margins and higher commissions, the number of tour buses, both large and small, visiting Soğanli dropped considerably from the early 2000s onwards.

Another major occurrence in Soğanli around that time was the relocation of the village to another site nearby due to rock fall in the ravine deemed to be a danger to inhabitants. In the year 2000 a section of the cliff high above the village collapsed and some large boulders fell down onto the upper parts of the village. The government immediately enforced the removal of the villagers from their stone houses in the old village and housed them in rows of newly built prefabricated houses at a 'new village' site nearby. Only two or three houses in the old village remained 'habitable', including a tourist guest house that is the only tourist accommodation available in Soğanli Valley. Otherwise, the old village has become something of a ghost village, including the lower central area where the tea house, restaurant and shops used to be, and is no longer the lively and 'authentic' Cappadocian village tourists used to enjoy wandering around. Moreover, to reach the section of the valley where the churches are located, tourists must travel past the new village site, which, with its rows of small prefabricated houses, is considered to spoil the 'authentic' appearance of the entire valley.

All of these factors have further reduced tourist visitation to Soğanli during the past decade and a half. Despite this, however, the doll-maker women continue to make dolls, as well as knitting coarse wool socks and gloves in distinctive Soğanli styles. Every morning they walk the 2 km from the new village site to set up their stalls either in the old village at the original site, beside the now derelict tea house, or outside one of the churches further along the valley. The small number of minibuses that still go to Soğanli, plus a growing number of independent tourists driving around the region in rental cars, now tend to bypass the old village site and go directly to visit the three or four churches further along the valley. Those that do still stop in the original bus park area now park beside what has become a derelict row of shops, and the tourists may get out of the bus to wander around a 'ghost village'. Wherever they visit in Soğanli, tourists tend still to be greeted by Soğanli doll-maker women, whose wares are laid out on a cloth sheet or a wooden stall, forever in hope of making a sale.

Conversations with Soğanli Women: Dolls and Dreams

Prior to tourism opportunities arising in the Cappadocia region, the local economy was primarily one of subsistence farming, although, driven by economic hardship, many families had moved to cities to find work and some had taken advantage of migration programmes to northern Europe. Despite significant social and economic change in Turkey over some decades, the Cappadocia region remains a pocket of rural conservatism. The population is predominantly Muslim and there are strict societal codes with a well-defined distribution of economic and social activity according to gender upheld by principles of shame and honour (Tucker, 2003; 2007). Consequently, since tourism has developed in the region, it is mainly the men who have become the tourism entrepreneurs, opening guesthouses, tour agencies and restaurants, while women remained occupied with domestic-related work (see Tucker, 2003; 2007; 2009).

In Soğanli too, it has been the men of the village who have opened restaurants for tourists. As mentioned, during the heyday of Soğanli's tourism the main tourist restaurant was in the village centre next to the old village tea house. Over the years of tourism development in Soğanli there have been four restaurants set up in total, with two opening in recent years on the owners' garden or orchard land and near to where the churches are situated along the valley. Other than these, it is interesting to note that, unlike the other parts of Cappadocia where it was predominantly the men who became the tourism entrepreneurs, in Soğanli it is the women who have led most of the tourism-related entrepreneurial activities. This has been mainly through doll-making and selling, but it also includes the guest house, which is managed and run by the daughters of the elderly man who, in 1995, used his retirement fund to buy a dilapidated stone house in the heart of the old village to restore and convert for tourist accommodation. Besides most families receiving a modest income from tourism, they have retained their garden and orchard land in order to continue their subsistence farming practice (retaining land as a fallback is a way of 'safeguarding peasant survival in the face of adversity'; Bryceson 2000, p. 312; see also Tucker, 2010). Some families now grow enough wheat for it to be considered a modest 'cash crop'. In Soğanli it is predominantly the men who go out to work in the fields, while the women make dolls and knit socks and gloves and set up stalls to sell their craftwork to tourists.

The first Soğanli doll-maker women I met were set up with their dolls and knitted items laid out on a sheet in front of the church, which tends to be the first one tourists visit along the valley. They were three women, sitting in the shade of the rock wall of the church, plus the husband of the youngest of the women, who was there as a chaperone, snoozing in the shade a few metres away. As well as the dolls for sale on the sheet, there were many part-made dolls beside where the women sat. They were busy sewing skirts for them, adding sequins and drawing faces onto the dolls with felt-tip

pens. They told me they sit by this particular church from morning until dusk 3 or 4 days per week, and on the other days they set up their stall at the bus park area by the derelict tea house in the old village. They told me that some years ago, during tourism's 'heyday', the doll-maker women had organized a 'cooperative' that all the Soğanli doll-maker women belonged to. They continued to say that the formal structure of the cooperative had since disintegrated and that now there is merely an unwritten arrangement among the 11 women who sell dolls whereby they alternate and therefore 'share' the different locations. They said that sales were better when they sat by the church since tourists tended to stop there first rather than in the village. They also added that, these days, many tourists did not go to the old village at all and they felt sad when they sat there because it used to be quite vibrant there but now it is empty and lifeless. While I sat and chatted with the women, a number of tourist cars and minibuses stopped to visit the church. Many of the international tourists walked straight past the women and their wares, avoiding eye contact seemingly to avoid being drawn into making a purchase. Most Turkish tourists who came by stopped and chatted with the three doll-maker women for a short while, but again, few of them made a purchase.

On a later visit to Soğanli, when, together with my family, I planned to stay overnight in the guest house, our three doll-maker friends, Ayşegül, Hacer and Havva (pseudonyms), whom again we met by the church, invited us to visit them in the 'new village' after their return home in the evening. We accepted the invitation and, when we arrived in the new village that evening, we were greeted by our three friends and taken to the cow shed at Ayşegül's house to watch her milking her family's three cows. Afterwards we went to Havva's house, the youngest of the three women. We were given a 'tour' around the house and shown its small living room leading to two small bedrooms, and its tiny kitchen and bathroom. The women explained that the prefabricated houses were terrible to live in because of having walls only 1–2 cm thick and no insulation and so, unlike their old houses, which had thick stone/rock walls, they were freezing in winter and too hot during the summer months. Their biggest complaint was the size of the new houses and that they felt too small and crowded compared to their houses in the old village. One hundred prefabricated houses had been built to replace 50 much larger houses in the old village, in which whole extended families had lived together. Now families were split into living in 'nuclear family' groups and so the village move had changed their way of living substantially, they said. The village move had also created the impetus for many of the younger families to move away to towns and cities in other parts of Turkey, and so the remaining village population was much smaller than it was when occupying the old village site. The fall in the younger population had led to the closure of the village school and so children now had to go by bus to town to attend the primary school there.

After our tour of the house, we were shown to a large covered area and invited to sit down to have tea. The covered area was outside at the front of the house and, due to a lack of space around the rows of compact houses, it was directly adjacent to the road. Various male relatives of our three women friends arrived to drink tea with us and they explained that they had just come home from the wheat fields where they had been working all day. Piled up at one end of the covered area where we sat were sacks of wheat waiting to be taken to market to sell. Apart from wheat, and some surplus apricots, which are dried to be sold, the men told us that the farming activities of Soğanli villagers are for home consumption. I asked the men if they had any other work apart from farming and they said they also sometimes helped out the women in the making of the dolls. While we sat waiting for the tea to brew, Aysegül and Hacer, the two older doll-maker women, took out some fabric and sequins and began sewing skirts onto part-made dolls. They apologized for continuing to work during our visit, and explained that they had a big wholesale order that had to be ready to send away in 2 days' time. I was interested in where the wholesale dolls were

going but they were not able to tell me because the male relative who had organized the sale was not present to answer my question. Interestingly, because it was always the men who did the larger 'wholesale' business transactions, the women did not know exactly who or where the orders came from, but they assumed that the dolls were being purchased by a large tourist shop in another part of Turkey. After drinking our tea, my family and I returned to the old village to have our evening meal in the guest house. An Italian couple were also staying in the guest house that night. We chatted over dinner and they said that they were glad we were staying there too, otherwise it would have been rather unnerving given that the guest house was the only inhabited building in what was now a 'ghost village'.

The following morning when we went out of the guest house, our three doll-maker friends had already arrived in the old village and had taken up their 'stall' position. As there were no tourists around yet, they sat continuing to produce more dolls for the wholesale order. They said that because of the rush on the order, their husbands were also helping out, although back at their houses and so 'behind the scenes'. They said the men were 'painting' the flowers on the skirts of the dolls, and then quickly added that they had already drawn the pen outlines of the flowers and so the men only had to 'colour them in'. The women explained that when there was a big order to make, the men often helped out, particularly with the machine sewing of the dolls' clothes. This conversation prompted me to look more closely at the dolls' clothes and I noticed that some of the dolls wore long, often sequin-covered, skirts, while some wore 'şalvar', or the baggy trousers worn by village women in Cappadocia when working in the fields. I asked the women why there was this variety in clothing on the dolls. They held up dolls wearing şalvar and said 'They are peasants, like us'. Then they held up dolls wearing skirts and said 'These are town women – "high society" women, so not like us". A little later, a minibus full of tourists arrived in the bus park. The women from the other stalls rushed forward and held out dolls and knitted socks, shouting 'hello' in different languages to try to get the attention of at least some of the mixed nationality tourist group. My doll-maker friends continued sitting and working on their dolls. They raised their eyebrows in the direction of the other women, to communicate to me a disapproval of the others' more aggressive selling style.

Leaving my friends alone for a while so that they could approach the tourists if they wished, I wandered behind the stalls to where the derelict shops were. On the inside of one of the empty shop's window, taped onto the glass were the pages from a book. It was the chapter on the Soğanli doll-maker women in Gianturco and Tuttle's *In Her Hands: Craftswomen Changing the World* (2000). The pages displayed photographs and text with stories of a few of the doll-maker women living and working in the village during the 1990s, hence before the Soğanli villagers were relocated to the new village site. In the book, the authors talk about being invited by a doll-maker woman named Ayse to visit her family's old stone house in an upper neighbourhood. They describe walking up through the winding streets, past a communal oven and entering the house where they met Hanife, Ayse's elderly grandmother. Hanife told the authors of how, in the 1960s, she had made a doll out of twigs and scraps of fabric for her daughter, Dondu, to take for 'show and tell' at school. Dondu had sold the doll to a tourist she met on her way home from school and then urged her mother to make more dolls to sell so that they could earn a bit of money. Hanife had acted on the idea and it was not long before other women saw her success and started doing the same, copying her doll design. Hanife said that those other women were more successful because they were more 'aggressive' in their selling tactics than she was. Ayse's sister and sister-in-law came to Hanife's house too while the *In Her Hands* authors were there and joined in the conversation. They all talked together about how there were no jobs for the men in Soğanli and so the women had had to 'seize the economic opportunity' that tourism presents. They wondered about what would

happen if tourists for some reason stopped coming to Soğanli; how would they live then?

The *In Her Hands* authors describe how: 'Every Soğanli mother we talk to hopes her children will leave this village to continue studying after completing the local primary school' (Gianturco and Tuttle, 2000, p. 154). The doll-maker women told the *In Her Hands* authors of how they invest in gold bracelets, which are easy to convert to money for tuition fees and books later on. As well as chatting with Hanife and her daughters, the authors had talked with a doll-maker called Hatice, together with her 15-year-old daughter Gülsen, who had been making and selling dolls for 3 years already. Hatice said that her son, Gülsen's brother, had been sent away to stay with relatives elsewhere in order to attend secondary school. She hoped that one day they would be able to afford to also send Gülsen to secondary school because, Hatice said, 'only with education is self-sufficiency possible' (p. 154). She said that she wanted her children to be educated so that they could leave the village and do better things with their life than make dolls to sell to tourists. The book's authors asked Hatice what dreams she had for her own life. She answered: 'My future will be good if the children are well, happy, and self-sufficient' (p. 154). Indeed, according to the blurb on the cover of the *In Her Hands* book, the women artisans from all around the world who are portrayed in the book are 'motivated by the desire to provide for their children: to dress them properly, to feed them well, and most of all, to educate them'.

After I had read the pages of the book on the shop window, I returned to chat with Aysegül, Hacer and Havva at their stall. I told them I found the book interesting in that the women interviewed had expressed a desire for their children to be well-enough educated that they would be able to leave the village and have jobs other than having to sell dolls to tourists. Aysegül, Hacer and Havva told me that Ayse in the book was their aunt and that Hanife was their great grandmother. They said that, whilst some others of their generation had managed to leave and get 'city jobs', such as becoming teachers or doctors, they themselves had not attended school beyond primary level: 'This is our life, we are stuck', they said. Nonetheless, they expressed hope that they would be the 'last generation' of Soğanli doll-makers, telling me that they certainly have higher aspirations for *their own* children. Aysegül said that her daughter was in high school, getting 'a good education'. Hacer said that her son had finished high school and worked in the ticket office of a historic site elsewhere in Cappadocia. We talked further about how, if they were to be the last generation of Soğanli doll-maker women, after they stop there will be no more Soğanli dolls produced. In response to that thought, Havva exclaimed: 'Thanks to God, our children won't have to do this work!'

During a fieldwork visit to Soğanli later in 2015 when the women were able to sit comfortably by the church in the not-so-hot autumn sun, some Turkish tourists stopped by to visit the church. The touring couple got chatting and took photos with Aysegül, Hacer and Havva. The doll-maker women asked where the couple were from and they said that they came from Kayseri, the largest city close to Cappadocia. While the woman was browsing the wares on the stall, the Soğanli women continued their conversation with the man and asked him what his work was in Kayseri. He said he worked for an accountancy firm, to which the Soğanli women responded with apparent approval and said that the couple's life in the city must be 'good' and 'comfortable'. The man agreed but then added that, from what he could see, the Soğanli women had a pretty good life too, sitting out here in the peaceful valley all day, looking at the beautiful view, and chatting with different tourists who came by. The Soğanli women disagreed, arguing that what they did was hard work and earned little, that it made their backs ache and their fingers sore from the needles. They added that they had to live in those terrible prefabricated houses whilst he lived in a comfortable apartment in Kayseri. The Kayseri man then retorted that, unlike him, the Soğanli women worked for themselves, so they had no boss and could relax all day if they so wished. The conversation continued as an increasingly jokey competitive banter until each party laughed and agreed to accept that they clearly both had a 'the grass is always greener elsewhere' view on things.

The conversation the women had with the Kayseri man serves as a reminder of the ease with which the lives of the Soğanli doll-maker women, and other women like them particularly in tourism contexts, might tend to be romanticized by people visiting from elsewhere (see Jimenez-Esquinas, 2017, for interesting discussion on the 'heritagization' and 'touristification' of craftswomen particularly in rural tourism contexts). Indeed, a romanticizing tone is apparent in Gianturco and Tuttle's *In Her Hands* book, where the 'female artisans' from around the world are portrayed as 'creating and selling exquisite indigenous crafts'. So, although the book describes the women as often living with the 'harsh realities of poverty, little education, and lack of even basic health care', it is explained that '*In Her Hands* celebrates a different kind of women's movement – a movement in which mothers, grandmothers, sisters and friends join together to create beautiful crafts that contribute to a better life for themselves and for future generations'. Linked to this idea of a 'women's movement', also, many of the book's chapters, including the Soğanli doll-makers chapter, talk about cooperatives organized among the craftswomen. This is perhaps another aspect of the romanticized portrayal of such women, and what is not often mentioned is that many such cooperatives may be short-lived and fall apart, as had the Soğanli doll-maker cooperative at the time of my research. In addition, portrayals of such tourism-related handicraft producers seldom discuss how working towards 'a better life for themselves and for future generations' may include, in the women's dreams at least, their *leaving* their handicraft production and, maybe, even leaving their place and way of life altogether. It is interesting, then, that this was the very dream expressed by all of the Soğanli women with whom the *In Her Hands* authors and I had conversations during our research.

Conclusion

In the concluding chapter of *In Her Hands*, it is written:

> Perhaps the most important social legacy craftswomen will leave is a better educated next generation. As more girls attend school, the chances increase of subsequent generations attending school. A mother's education determines her children's – education begets education.
>
> (Gianturco and Tuttle, 2000, p. 219)

Generations of Soğanli women have now been involved in tourism and doll-making in the hope that the income from selling the dolls will enable them to provide opportunities for their children and grandchildren to gain a good education and hence have opportunities for a 'better life' than that of making dolls to sell to tourists. However, women there are *still* making dolls and they *still* wait all day with their wares in the hope that tourists might buy something. Nonetheless, the women continue to express hope that their doll-making and selling endeavours will allow their children not to be stuck in the same situation. Indeed, the copy of the chapter entitled 'Hanife and the Doll-makers' in Gianturco and Tuttle's book acts as a reminder that, generation after generation, the Soğanli women hope that they will be the last generation of doll-makers. So, whilst Gianturco and Tuttle suggest, with a somewhat romanticizing tone, that the women portrayed in their book have the 'surprisingly universal aspirations' to 'create beautiful crafts that contribute to a better life for themselves and for future generations', what the Soğanli women aspire to is no longer having to 'create crafts' to make their living. There is no romanticizing among the Soğanli women of their craft or their lives; rather, they dream of creating a future in which their children will not have to make dolls for a living.

Fig. 11.1 Soğanli valley from above derelict village.

Referring back to a definition of 'empowerment' quoted earlier in this chapter, which was the notion of empowerment being the process whereby 'those who have been denied the ability to make choices acquire such ability' (Kabeer, 2005, p.13), for the Soğanli women empowerment would be acquiring the ability to choose whether or not to make and sell dolls for a living, and also to choose whether to leave or stay in Soğanli village. Indeed, although the past five decades have shown tourism in Soğanli to ebb and wane, which is especially problematic for such economically marginalized groups as rural women from Soğanli, the doll-maker women's tourism endeavours do nonetheless appear to be paying off at last. Today, increasing numbers of young people, both boys and girls, are leaving the village and attending school to higher levels; for example, as

mentioned already, both Hacer's son and Aysegül's daughter have attended secondary school. Moreover, scholarships are becoming more readily available across Turkey, meaning that the ability of young people from rural areas such as Soğanli to complete secondary, and even tertiary, education is less dependent on their families' ability to raise the money themselves to meet the education costs. Indeed, a young woman helping her aunty run the Soğanli guest house during the summer of my fieldwork was home for the holidays from university where she studies international trade. Perhaps, then, with their children acquiring the ability to make choices they never had, Hacer, Aysegül and Havva's generation really will be the last of the Soğanli doll-maker women. To quote Havva's words once more, 'Thanks to God, our children won't have to do this work!'

References

Apostolopoulos, Y. and Sönmez, S. (2001) Working producers, leisured consumers: Women's experiences in developing regions. In: Apostolopoulos, Y., Sönmez, S. and Timothy, D. (eds) *Women as Producers and Consumers of Tourism in Developing Regions*. Praeger Publishers, Westport, Connecticut, pp. 3–18.

Bryceson, D. (2000) Disappearing peasantries? Rural labour redundancy in the neo-liberal era and beyond. In: Bryceson, D., Kay, C. and Moooij, J. (eds) *Disappearing Peasantries?: Rural Labour in Africa, Asia and Latin America*. ITDG Publishing, London, pp. 299–326.

Chant, S. (2006) Contribution of a gender perspective to the analysis of poverty. In: Jaquette, J.S. and Summerfield, G. (eds) *Women and Gender Equity in Development Theory and Practice: Institutions, Resources and Mobilisation*. Duke University Press, Durham, North Carolina, and London, pp. 87–106.

Ferguson, L. (2009) Analysing the gender dimensions of tourism as a development strategy (No. pp03/09). ICEI Working Paper, Universidad Complutense de Madrid, Madrid.

Ferguson, L. (2010) Interrogating gender in development policy and practice: the World Bank, tourism and microentreprise in Honduras. *International Feminist Journal of Politics* 12(1), 3–24.

Gentry, K.M. (2007) Belizean women and tourism work: opportunity or impediment? *Annals of Tourism Research* 34(2), 477–496.

Gianturco, P. and Tuttle, T. (2000) *In Her Hands: Craftswomen Changing the World*. Powerhouse Books, New York.

Gibson, H. (2001) Gender in tourism: theoretical perspectives. In: Apostolopoulos, Y., Sönmez, S. and Timothy, D. (eds) *Women as Producers and Consumers of Tourism in Developing Regions*. Praeger Publishers, Westport, Connecticut, pp. 19–43.

Harvey, J.M., Hunt, J. and Harris Jr, C.C. (1995) Gender and community tourism dependence level. *Annals of Tourism Research* 22(2), 349–366.

Jimenez-Esquinas, G. (2017) This is not only about culture: on tourism, gender stereotypes and other affective fluxes. *Journal of Sustainable Tourism* 25(3), 311–326.

Kabeer, N. (2005) Gender equality and women's empowerment: a critical analysis of the third Millennium Development Goal. *Gender and Development* 13(1), 13–24.

Kinnaird, V., Kothari, U. and Hall, D. (1994) Tourism: gender perspectives. In: Kinnaird, V. and Hall, D. (eds) *Tourism: A Gender Analysis*. John Wiley & Sons Ltd, Chichester, UK, pp. 1–28.

Long, V. and Kindon, S. (1997) Gender and tourism development in a Balinese village. In: Sinclair, M.T. (ed.) *Gender, Work and Tourism*. Routledge, London.

Scheyvens, R. (2000) Promoting women's empowerment through involvement in ecotourism : experiences from the third world. *Journal of Sustainable Tourism* 8(3), 232–249.

Scott, J. (1997) Chances and choices: women and tourism in Northern Cyprus. In: Sinclair, T. (ed.) *Gender, Work and Tourism*. Routledge, London, pp. 60–90.

Tucker, H. (2003) *Living With Tourism: Negotiating Identities in a Turkish Village*. Routledge, London.

Tucker, H. (2007) Undoing shame: tourism and women's work in Turkey. *Journal of Tourism and Cultural Change* 5(2), 87–105.

Tucker, H. (2009) The cave homes of Göreme: performing tourism hospitality in gendered space. In: Lynch, P., McIntosh, A. and Tucker, H. (eds) *Commercial Homes in Tourism: An International Perspective*. Routledge, London.

Tucker, H. (2010) Peasant-entrepreneurs: a longitudinal ethnography. *Annals of Tourism Research* 37(4), 927–946.

Tucker, H. (2011) Success and access to knowledge in the tourist-local encounter: confrontations with the unexpected in a Turkish community. In: Theodossopoulos, D. and Skinner, J. (eds) *Great Expectations: Imagination, Anticipation, and Enchantment in Tourism*. Berghahn Books, Oxford, pp. 27–39.

Tucker, H. and Boonabaana, B. (2012) A critical analysis of tourism, gender and poverty reduction. *Journal of Sustainable Tourism* 20, 437–456.

Wilkinson, P. and Pratiwi, W. (1995) Gender and tourism in an Indonesian village. *Annals of Tourism Research* 22(2), 283–299.

Arzu's Story: Rural Tourism – a Necessity for Women's Empowerment in Turkey

Arzu Kutucu Ozenen

Fig. S11. Arzu and Misi women.

I, Arzu Kutucu Ozenen, am the founder and chairperson of Yesil Valiz Association for Responsible Tourism, an association promoting responsible tourism in Turkey. A graduate of Ankara University, I received a BA in law. Having been interested in community development since my university years, I have participated in several civil society activities. With the dream of a better future for all, I focused on educational opportunities for disadvantaged groups. Rural young women, who were far more disadvantaged than any other group in Turkey, became the top priority in my work. Seeing the growing interest in rural tourism as a window of opportunity for women, I worked with several municipalities and village women's associations in areas of skills development, entrepreneurship, local value chains and informed political participation, which will enable women to ask for more.

Since I started to work for women's empowerment, I have always seen rural tourism as a wonderful opportunity to increase registered women employment in the villages. That is, until a new law entered the system as a game changer and rural tourism became a necessity rather than an opportunity.

In 2013, Law No. 6360 On Metropolitan Municipality System in Turkey was accepted by parliament. The law resulted in changes in the administrative boundaries and system of governance, changing central and local government relations. The government emphasized the need for strong local administrations through creating metropolitan cities. Code 6360 brought significant administrative changes to locals like abolishing the legal entity of county municipalities and villages in the provinces. In addition 14 municipalities that have more than 750,000 residents will be transformed into metropolitan municipalities. The changes mean 56 million out of Turkey's population of 75.8 million will live within the boundaries of metropolitan municipalities. Villages have lost their legal entities, along with their sense of community. The Code will fully come into force in 2018, and then, the regulations will touch rural people's everyday lives. Villages will not be able to decide on their infrastructure, will have no say in mining contracts in their region and will have to pay for their water even if they built the infrastructure themselves, which would certainly mean the end of family farming.

This transformation has triggered depopulation of the villages and created many more rural migrant women, who have no skills, to seek work in the city. The majority of these women became house workers without any security. The traditions have been lost in the wilderness of the metropolis, the family farms were left without care. In addition to a certain sociological decay, the food supply safety is under threat.

This has made rural tourism, once a wonderful empowerment opportunity for rural women, a must, not only for women's economic empowerment, but also to give them the motivation to be a part of decision-making process. So we did something different and did not start with 'tourism entrepreneurship training' as usual. Instead we started a project called 'Vocal Women, Local Solutions'. The first aim of the project was to increase rural women's informed and active participation in the decision-making processes for socio-economic development plans of their region, Erdek. The objectives were to encourage rural women to learn about their territories' social, economic and historical facts; enabling them to analyse their territorial problems, express their opinions, ask the right questions and suggest ideas, thus becoming a real participant in formal meetings. This project was to support and develop processes that enable rural women to engage with the elected political representatives, have a say in the budgets and development plans for their territories. We also wanted them to decide on the path they want to take, rather than imposing rural tourism as the only solution.

There were natural leaders in every group we worked with. In most of the cases it was the wife of the village local authority. One might say that these women are using the authority of their husbands. But usually it was vice-versa: the husbands were using the organizational skills of their wives in order to be selected in the villages. So we wanted them to use their skills for themselves. In one of the villages, Nagihan, wife of the chair of the local authority was proposed as a candidate in the next election.

So far we have finished training in seven villages and four of the villages have decided to continue with the tourism entrepreneurship training. The other villages have decided to benefit from the supply chain that will be created by the rural tourism activities in the neighbouring villages, and thus will continue with sustainable farming training. Before anything else, we have engaged the villages in a festival. We organized trekking routes around the villages and created camping spots near the villages. The catering was done by the village women. These activities introduced women to tourism.

Furthermore, they have a voice loud enough to be heard from the metropolitan city Balıkesir, especially now, when it is only a year away from the local elections. We dare say that democracy is blooming in the fields of Erdek this year.

12 Conclusions: Beyond Empowerment

Stroma Cole*

University of the West of England, Bristol, UK

This book has taken a critical gendered perspective of women's involvement in tourism development and women's empowerment. The volume has provided a global perspective with contributions and stories from around the globe. Women's stories ranged from the unsatisfied, unfulfilled doll-makers in Turkey who seize the economic opportunities that tourism can bring; those that are desperate to support their families however they can; through to those who have used the transformative powers of tourism to change their own lives and are now going about transforming the lives of others.

This conclusion will highlight the commonalities in the women's stories before looking at the possibilities of shifting a gear towards further speedier, deeper change. It finishes with some suggestions for extending this work. The stories speak to:

- a need for a new interpretation of empowerment;
- that women help women;
- the barriers women face in pursuing careers in tourism;
- the hopes but also the fears that tourism work can bring;
- how indecent work tourism can be, and that the situation is far worse for some women than others.

The women in this book are involved in a slow revolution of change, and a number of factors were identified that could aid a transformation of gender relations in tourism, including better definitions and the enforcement of gender equality as a human right; the need to take account of reproductive labour; ensuring women's voices are heard and using gendered action plans; using gender auditing and impact analysis; gender awareness training; and improved disclosure of best practice.

Empowerment: Beyond Economics

According to the United Nations World Tourism Organization (UNWTO):

> tourism can empower women in multiple ways, particularly through the provision of jobs and through income-generating opportunities in small and larger-scale tourism and hospitality related enterprises. As one of the sectors with the highest share both of women employed and of entrepreneurs, tourism can be a tool for women to unlock their potential. It can help them to become fully engaged and lead in every aspect of society and thus contribute to SDG 5 'Achieve gender equality and empower for all women and girls'.
>
> (UNWTO, 2015)

---

* E-mail: stroma.cole@uwe.ac.uk

However, as the authors of this book have demonstrated, there is no direct or automatic relationship between women's employment and empowerment, and, in any event, policy does not support it. Employing women or supporting them to become entrepreneurs does not necessarily change the gendered dynamics in which they are embedded: their relationships with men; inequitable relations in society; and in some cases their work can lead to greater exploitation and reinforced stereotypes. Women working as cheap labour for an exploitative industry is far more likely to lead to double burden and increased gender inequality. Empowerment, understood in economic terms, also makes a division between productive and reproductive labour. This is not a new point but is critical and needs to be restated.

While women's empowerment as conceived by neoliberal capitalism and promoted in the tourism context by the UNWTO and others, is a hollowed out notion that will do little to improve gender equality, the stories in this book have illustrated that tourism can improve gender equality, especially if we look to the other forms of empowerment discussed in the introduction. As Meghan Muldoon discusses in Chapter 7, empowerment comes from pride and the opportunity to show tourists a counternarrative: that African women are strong and resilient. For others like Thinlas and her trekking guides in Ladakh and Neussa in Cape Verde, empowerment comes from the satisfaction of breaking gender stereotypes. There were various ways that psychological empowerment was expressed: dignity, self-worth, self-confidence (Chapter 10), gaining respect (María, p. 55) soulful rewards (Giota, p. 12) and recognition in the public sphere (Chapter 5). These aspects of personal satisfaction were more important than business growth for some of the women (Chapter 10).

For many of the women, tourism brought them the opportunity to learn new skills: photography (Chapter 7), diving (Sari, p. 118), kayaking (one of the Nepali participants in Chapter 8), as well as learning languages, particularly English (see Chapter 6). These skills were not learnt formally but from individual (female) tourists. However, as Priscilla (p. 80) so readily explains, informal learning and skills possessed by women do not count as much as formal qualifications in many tourism contexts.

The women also recounted how tourism helped them overcome isolation (Chapters 5 and 10). Meeting people increased women's links to the wider world and the internet (Nukul, p. 23). As Isis Díaz-Carrión explores in Chapter 10, this increased social capital is a step on the path to transforming gender roles. Changes in the consciousness and agency of individual women, while not removing systemic inequality, are important starting points, stepping stones on a long journey. They help to create the critical consciousness of inequality and injustice to generate the impetus for societal change.

Women Help Women

One of the commonalities from the stories and analysis in this book is that women help women. Nukul (p. 23), a young single mother from Thailand, suggests that power is realized through providing opportunities to learn, to work and to be in community with other women who lift one another up. Meanwhile in Ladakh, Thinlas (p. 67), having broken through local gender stereotypes, went on to co-found the Ladakhi Women's Welfare Network (LWWN). The group aims to help women in different ways to empower and educate them on their legal rights and to build confidence in them. In a few short years, this group has given voices to women and girls who were not being heard. In Chapter 8 we saw how Nepali entrepreneurs, having succeeded themselves, wanted to share the benefits and lift other women out of poverty. In Mexico, a successful potter wanted to support other women and chose those who needed her help (see Chapter 5). This is not only the case with entrepreneurs, as Fiona Bakas et al. in Chapter 4 report: significant statistical research from a large study shows that women managers put more gender equality measures in place.

Furthermore, in local government, there was a notable change when two consecutive mayors of Metepec were women, and a female official was appointed. Female artisans were registered, allowing them access to public aid, training and competitions – some of these benefits brought about by these women were reversed when the mayor was replaced by a man (Chapter 5).

Cultural and Institutional Barriers

This book has explored the barriers from global to local perspectives. As Lucy Ferguson documents in Chapter 2 there has been a lack of will and leadership for change at the global level. Programmes set up by the UNWTO for gender equality training are still 'being designed' nearly 10 years after the programme was announced! In Chapter 3, Daniela Moreno Alarcón explored the resistance she had experienced as a consultant, and the typical language used and the importance of gender mainstreaming action plans on gender and tourism at the national level. Even in Mexico, one of the countries that has legal and policy frameworks that call for the promotion of gender equality and women's empowerment in tourism planning, these goals have not been implemented. Paola Vizcaino Suárez exposes this in Chapter 5 through her exploration of Metepec potters. Giota (p. 12) faced both institutional and cultural barriers in Greece as she was not able to open a cottage industry because she didn't have a home caring role and because she was a woman choosing to live alone. Meanwhile, in Morocco, Leila (p. 106) faced hotels refusing her rooms and buses leaving her behind. Both Chapter 4 and Chapter 7 speak to industry resistance, with male managers not recognizing their roles for gender equality and the tour operators disempowering township women with their truncated tours. However, as we have seen, in examples from Ladakh (in Chapter 6), Nepal (Chapter 8), Cape Verde (Neusa's Story, p. 33) and Thailand (Nukul's Story, p. 23), some women have overcome cultural

challenges and are making their own change despite limited support from authorities.

Hope and Fear

Tourism can bring hope but also fear. The women in Soğanli (Chapter 11) hoped that tourism income would be enough to send their children to school, whilst also hoping that this would mean they were the last generation of doll-makers. Perrine's work (p. 44) not only gives hope to the guides who can make a new life for themselves, but also educates children on the other side of life for people who share their modern city. The township women (Chapter 7) also had hopes that tourists would help them in some way. Women's independence brought about through their tourism roles is one of the benefits tourism can clearly bring. As one of the women in Los Tuxlas explained, independence from her husband meant she didn't have to 'endure situations that make you feel unhappy and you are not okay' (Chapter 10). However, despite the hope encapsulated by so many of the women in the tourism stories, the underlying structural inequalities mean that women are constantly vulnerable. The fact that 'violence against women is a global health problem of epidemic proportions' (WHO, 2013) means that women are constantly under the shadow of sexual assault. The Ladakhi women in Chapter 6, who pride themselves on breaking gender stereotypes on the one hand, continue to acquiesce to the patriarchal norms that blame women for the violation of women's safety, on the other.

Gender and (In)decent Work

When the UNWTO suggests that tourism can empower women in multiple ways by the provision of jobs, we have to ask ourselves what kind of jobs? As Heather Jeffrey suggests in Chapter 9 in relation to Tunisia, most tourism jobs are in hotels and many women's jobs will be in housekeeping. As a recent report from Oxfam painfully describes, 'housekeepers earn poverty wages, enjoy little to no job security and face serious risks to their health and safety'. Under constant time pressure, they must clean as many rooms as possible, and 'they face significant physical, biological, chemical, sexual and psychological hazards'. The high rate of injury makes housekeeping even more precarious. Workers have to take days off to recover, often with no pay, and risk dismissal when they have to request modified work duties. The power dynamic created by the contrasting social and economic status of housekeepers and guests means sexual harassment is a common occurrence. A survey of 500 Chicago housekeepers by the union UNITE HERE revealed half of housekeepers had been sexually harassed by guests (UNITE HERE, 2016).

However, housekeeping can provide for decent and stable employment. In workplaces where they have managed to organize, housekeepers earn decent wages and benefits, have greater job security and experience less stress and fewer injuries. As the comparison between New York and London in UNITE UK's (2016) report clearly highlights, where the workforce is unionized, workers have far better treatment. The city of Seattle even went so far as to require hotels to provide panic buttons and post signs in hotel rooms denouncing harassment and informing guests of the buttons, which give housekeepers a greater sense of security and empowerment (UNITE HERE, 2016).

As Moreno (2017) explains, the appalling conditions found in so many places 'impoverishes employment in tourism as a whole, both for women and men, because the principles of decent work are not respected. If we improve the situation of female tourism workers, that is to say if we invest wisely, we are supporting the whole industry.'

Although improved profits should not be the sole reason for improving gender equality in the workplace, it is known to pay financial dividends. As TUI (2016) suggests, studies have shown that gender equality between male and female employees makes for better quality of service – especially in the tourism sector. In the same report, the world's biggest tour operator boasts diversity in their workforce in one paragraph, only to admit that although over 60% of their employees are female, only 30% of their managers are – and even less at senior management level. Although studies show increasing the number of women on boards increases profitability (Norland and Moran, 2016), the increase in women at the top is stubbornly slow in tourism companies, especially given the number of female employees. In 2013, Equality in Tourism reported women are not in decision-making positions. Out of 78 leading tourism companies, across four key sectors of the tourism industry, women make up 15.8% of all board members. In 21 of the companies and professional associations surveyed, there was not a single female board member (Equality in Tourism, 2013). While some (e.g. Catalyst) suggest increasing bonuses for those who promote women, I suggest the route taken by Unilever, which encourages men to take flexi-time, will make a greater difference.

Intersectionality

As laid bare in Oxfam's report, gender and race are compounded for many women. 'Many of the women in the hotel industry's insecure jobs are immigrants or migrants, and/or women of visible minorities. The feminization and racialization of such occupations tend to trigger a further decline in wage rates, job security and social value' (Oxfam, 2017, p. 4). Seventy per cent of London's hospitality workers are migrants (UNITE UK, 2016). Intersectionality explores how categories of identity such as gender, race, ethnicity, ability, age, sexuality, etc. are mutually constructing and interrelated, and shape systems of power, producing complex social inequalities that vary over time and space (bel Hooks, 1989). The use of intersectionality as a framework has been limited in tourism, but in other sectors has been used to highlight how capitalism, patriarchy and ethnicity inform women's subordination. As I explore in my water, gender and tourism work about Labuan Bajo (Cole, 2017), poverty compounds gender inequality and this is related to ethnicity. Tourism is outcompeting residents for water supplies. The research demonstrated how patriarchy, ethnicity, life stage and proximity to water supplies informed women's subordination. Thus, as Chapter 9 highlights, women's rights are context-dependent and there is a complex interplay of multiple factors to be unpicked. Discrimination takes many guises. Nukul faced prejudice because she came from an ethnic minority. Chapter 7 speaks to residual insidious effects of colonialism, while Heather Jeffrey (Chapter 9) demonstrates it's even down to how women dress, and how veiling has consequences for women's (in)equality.

Steps Towards a Transformation in Gender Relations

While the stories in this book point to the ways women can take advantage of tourism opportunities to increase their own agency – and in some cases autonomy and authority – structural barriers mean that there is limited impact at the ultimate level of control. So, what actions are required to increase the speed of the very 'slow revolution' we have signalled? As a recent London School of Economics (LSE) report suggests with regard to the UK, 'there is much work to be done, even in mainstream public and social life, to unearth and subject to critical scrutiny the gendered assumptions on which individual actions, regulatory norms and institutional designs still tend to be based' (LSE, 2017, p. 14). But there are some clear steps in tourism that will help:

Gender equality as a human right

As Fiona Bakas *et al.* suggest in Chapter 4, gender equality needs to be better defined – many of the issues women in tourism face are not a matter of increased equality but human rights issues. This should not be a case of encouraging or 'nudging towards them', but rather these should be demanded and enforced. Agenda 2030 emphasizes,

'It is not possible to realize the full human potential and achieve sustainable development if half of humanity is still denied the full enjoyment of their human rights and their opportunities'. While the UN points out, 'regardless of where you live, gender equality is a fundamental human right. Advancing gender equality is critical to all areas of a healthy society, from reducing poverty to promoting the health, education, protection and the well-being of girls and boys.' I question the same document's reference to empowerment. As we have argued in this book, the power has been hollowed out of empowerment, and gender equality can only be achieved when there is a lasting change in the power and choices women have over their own lives, rather than just an increase (often temporary) in opportunities (Woodroffe and Smee, 2012). It can only be achieved when women's awareness is such that their responses no longer automatically and habitually maintain, reproduce and legitimize the patriarchal structures that lie at the roots of their inequality. Cornwall and Rivas (2105) argue that gender equality and empowerment have become analytical and political cul-de-sacs and argue for a paradigm transformation to reclaim the gender agenda. They suggest a reframing around human rights centred on the concepts of accountability, inclusion and non-discrimination offers a powerful set of entry points around which to refocus. A transformative agenda needs to address the structural causes of gender inequality. As Wendy Hillman and Kylie Radel suggest in Chapter 8, emancipation for individuals is dependent on developing a deep understanding of the processes of power, and requires that people gain the tools, knowledge and capacities for questioning and subverting the social rules of status and class, and thereby transcending the structural constructions of gender. Some of the women presenting their stories in this book, for example, Perrine (p. 44) and Arzu (p. 130) have begun that process. Tourism scholars have been slow to explore gender (Swain, 2016) – let us hope we are not so slow in relinquishing the political cul-de-sac of empowerment. Achieving gender equality requires a transformation in gender relations.

Current understandings of the economy need to be broadened to include the reproductive sector and unpaid care work

Reconciling earning money and keeping up with domestic life is the commonest challenge for women. This is a consequence of not including, not counting and thus devaluing all the work that they contribute to family, community and society but that does not contribute to wallets, profits or gross domestic product (GDP), as argued extensively in the literature on feminist economics and feminist political economy, on which many of the authors of this book draw. As Paola Vizcaino Suárez discusses in relation to Mexico (Chapter 5) women carry the burden for domestic responsibility on top of income-generating responsibilities. Meanwhile in Ladakh the trekking guides didn't challenge the social norms in the private sphere and continued to assume the responsibilities for domestic work even when away from home and working and staying with guests in homestays. As Maria (p. 55) explains, women without family to help with childcare are unable to progress with tourism roles, or, in Priscilla's case (p. 80), she has to make all the preparations for her children before departing for her hotel manager position, despite being the main family breadwinner. While some of the women were able to negotiate more equitable distributions of housework, most were like Ica (p. 94), who, despite her tourism management position and her multiple volunteer roles, still made time to prioritize her son.

As long as reproductive labour is not counted, it will not be valued. Until the importance of this work is recognized, its sharing will not be prioritized. If men and women are equal stakeholders in a family, change will occur. Gender-friendly working patterns are needed, that is, the introduction of measures so people have time to care without adverse implications for job choices and career development, such as part-time work and eradication of long hours. When men take children to school or finish early to pick them up as much as women do, greater flexibility will be offered to all workers and caring will be better shared. As Fiona Bakas *et al.* (Chapter 4) report, when men have caring duties the invisibility of child-care comes to light. Furthermore, men as well as women should have time to care without penalties. According to Krivkovich and colleagues' (2017) 'Women in the workplace' report, women with a partner are 5.5 times more likely than their male counterparts to do all or most of the housework. Furthermore, research has also shown that men are perceived as more responsible when they have children, while women are seen as being less committed to work. Fatherhood results in a wage bonus, as it 'is a valued characteristic of employers, signalling perhaps greater work commitment, stability, and deservingness', whereas motherhood has a wage penalty (Budig, 2014). This bias requires gender awareness training.

Gender awareness training including unconscious bias

As Daniela Moreno Alarcón discusses in Chapter 3, gender inequality is not a random, unfortunate occurrence – it is a systematic problem, and for tourism development policy to be sustainable it requires understanding and training about gender relations. As Arzu (p. 130) argues, the training that's needed is not to train women as entrepreneurs but rather to express their opinions, ask the right questions and suggest ideas, to engage and thus to have power. Turban *et al.* (2017) highlight that gender inequality is due to bias, and this is worse for women of colour than for white women. Catalyst, the non-profit organization promoting inclusive workplaces for women, defines unconscious bias as an implicit association or attitude about race or gender that operates out of our control, informs our perception about a person or group of people and can influence our decision-making and behaviour towards a person or group of people. Research has shown that it is possible to establish procedures and strategic actions that help diminish implicit biases (Devine *et al.*, 2012). However, without these concerted actions, prejudices and stereotyping will be perpetuated and bias-based decisions made. As Isis

Díaz-Carrión suggests in Chapter 10, gender awareness programmes are needed to change male attitudes. Very few tourism organizations are working to confront unconscious bias, but some are. Tour operator Intrepid, for example, has pledged unconscious bias training for all employees (Robyn Nixon, 2017, personal communication).

Inclusion of women's voices and action plans

Development policies lack gender mainstreaming and decisions are being made without the voices of women. The women in Ladakh attended meetings but did not speak out; in Mexico women's voices were excluded through the Ejido assemblies (local decision-making forums) because they were not landowners (see Chapter 10), and the situation was similar in Nicaragua (Moreno, 2017). As my work in Labuan Bajo demonstrates, this goes further than decisions that are obviously about tourism. Women's lack of voice in water supply decision-making was one of the causes of the community missing out on water to the hotels (Cole, 2017). Arzu's Story (p. 130) is an example of how, with the right training, women can succeed in having their voices heard and that tourism can be the prism through which this happens. As Paola Vizcaino Suárez suggests in Chapter 5, 'to transform regulative ideals into tangible efforts, it is necessary to bring women's voices to the forefront of national and local policy debates'. Daniela Moreno Alarcón (in Chapter 3) explains why a good gender analysis requires a feminist approach, and suggests action plans as a practical tool to make gender analysis a reality – by partnering with local women's organizations and including the voices of local women the causes of gender discrimination can be identified and the gaps can be closed.

Gender auditing and impact analysis

As Lucy Ferguson discusses in Chapter 2, one of the reasons the UNWTO's work has lacked any action is that no mechanism was put in place for monitoring and evaluating the implementation of the recommendations. This lack of impact analysis is one of the drags on the speed of change. While participatory gender audits are 'globally considered a powerful tool for organizational transformation and to help identify organizational strengths and challenges towards integrating gender within specific workplaces' (Business Essentials, 2017), tourism organizations have been resistant to take on this essential work. Equality in Tourism has first-hand experience of this as organizations, hotels groups and tour operators have all declined the suggestion that they might like to conduct a gender audit to help them improve their gender equality. Such audits would help them spotlight gender (in)equality and identify systems, policy, processes and organizational culture that would need to be changed to make improvements. Without destinations, organizations and nations conducting impact analyses, we will not know the impacts tourism is having on women. Bakas and colleagues' study, part of which is reported in Chapter 4, has some powerful findings about gender and tourism in Portugal. Conducting gender analysis requires sufficient resources, leadership and political will, and must be based on targets that transform social relations and tackle the root causes of inequality.

Spreading the word about what makes a difference

When improvements are made everybody needs to know about them. Countries and destinations compete and if there were a competition to be more gender equal, measures would be put in place and companies and countries would shout about it. If gender equality were more central to responsible tourism and prizes were given for those companies doing better, they would receive more publicity. Then, if this were combined action from the platforms that market and sell tourism, customers could make their choices. So far this is not mainstream, although there are a few websites that high-light the issues, such as Equality in Tourism, Gender Responsible Tourism, which presents options for and from women and fair hotels in the USA. Far more disclosure of actions taken to promote gender equality would accelerate change.

Future Studies

This book is one of only a handful to explore gender and tourism and, while it has added to the debates, it has also identified gaps in the bigger picture. Three of the most significant areas for further study are as follows.

Tourism and gender-based violence

The reports about sexual harassment and the violence faced by housekeepers in hotels referred to above make stark reading. There are indications from my own work in Labuan that emancipated women face more violence. Three out of the seven women in managerial positions in Labuan were single, having escaped domestic violence. Many of the women in the stories presented here are single but we do not know how many of them were fleeing domestic violence. We do know that tourism has been important in providing independent incomes for women, but more studies are required to explore whether women emancipated through tourism face more gender-based violence or improved harmony at home. Certainly, studies in other areas suggest that 'the restructuring of the global economy and expansion of women's rights' has increased violence against women (Wright, 2006). As Gamlin and Hawkes (2017) discuss in relation to Mexico, a decline in traditional male occupations and concomitant growth in female employment – albeit precarious – are breeding grounds for new forms of gendered violence.

Changing masculinities

This book about gender equality has focused on women and their stories. Men are the other half of our shared humanity. Many of them too face exploitation in the workplace and their human rights are also abused. However, without changes by men there will be no change. We know apathy, fear and ignorance about gender issues are barriers for men to support gender equality measures (Prime and Moss-Racusin, 2009), but it's important to understand how they experience moves towards greater gender equality. 'Many men don't fully grasp the barriers that hold women back at work. As a result, they are less committed to gender diversity, and we can't get there without them' (Krivkovich *et al.*, 2017). In relation to tourism, there is a clear lack of research on the topic; exceptions include Ferguson (2010a; 2010b). To increase the pace of change we need a better understanding of how men see their role in the changes and how we take them on the journey with us.

Women excluded from tourism in destinations

This book has concentrated on women in tourism, but there is a gap to explore how life changes for those people in tourism destinations who are not part of tourism, directly or indirectly. If tourism can be an enabler to emancipation for women who work in tourism, does this cascade to others around them? Does the increased confidence and pride set tourism workers apart, or can this diffuse through to other women in their communities? Again this is a missing part of our puzzle. For tourism to fulfil its promises, it must work beyond those who become employees and entrepreneurs or suppliers. However, if the accumulation of changes for women in tourism can spread, if consciousness can be increased through their networks, perhaps we can increase the pace of our slow revolution.

Final Words

Putting this book together has been a huge privilege and an inspirational journey. Working with such a wise, experienced and supportive group of women has been pure pleasure. Our sharing goes to show just how much the debates and actions about gender equality in tourism have moved on. This collection has not only shown how, despite the structural barriers, the patriarchal norms and inequitable global system, women are using the power that tourism can bring. Using their strength and resilience women are overcoming stereotypes, helping one another, finding hope and putting the power back into empowerment. Change is happening, countries are making gendered action plans, companies are conducting unconscious bias training, dedicated websites are emerging. For many of us the transformation is too slow; we are eager for the pace to move up a gear. Hopefully the stories in this book will go some way to encouraging this, to motivate others to take steps to put policies in place, to implement, evaluate, monitor, audit, disclose and celebrate every effort to put gender rights higher on the agenda. There is no sign of tourism slowing down, let us use it as a force to improve gender equality.

References

Budig, M. (2014) The fatherhood bonus and the motherhood penalty: parenthood and the gender gap in pay. Available at: www.thirdway.org/report/the-fatherhood-bonus-and-the-motherhood-penalty-parenthood-and-the-gender-gap-in-pay (accessed 1 March 2018).

Business Essentials (2017) The importance of participatory gender audits for the world of work. Available at: www.businessessentials.co.za/2017/06/12/importance-participatory-gender-audits (accessed 1 March 2018).

Cole, S. (2017) Water worries: an intersectional feminist political ecology of tourism and water in Labuan Bajo, Indonesia. *Annals of Tourism Research* 67, 14–24.

Cornwall, A. and Rivas, A. (2015) From 'gender equality and 'women's empowerment' to global justice: reclaiming a transformative agenda for gender and development. *Third World Quarterly* 36(2), 396–415.

Devine, P., Forscher, P., Austin, A. and Cox, W. (2012) Long-term reduction in implicit race bias: a prejudice habit-breaking intervention. *Journal of Experimental Social Psychology* 48, 1267–1278.

Equality in Tourism (2013) Sun, sands and ceilings: women in the boardroom in the tourism industry. Available at: http://equalityintourism.org/wp-content/uploads/2013/07/Sun_Sand_Ceiling_F.pdf (accessed 1 March 2018).

Ferguson, L. (2010a) Tourism development and the restructuring of social reproduction in Central America. *Review of International Political Economy* 17(5), 860–888.

Ferguson, L. (2010b) Interrogating 'gender' in development policy and practice: the World Bank, tourism and microenterprise in Honduras. *International Feminist Journal of Politics* 12(1), 3–24.

Gamlin, J. and Hawkes, S. (2017) Masculinities on the continuum of structural violence: the case of Mexico's homicide epidemic. Social Politics: International Studies in Gender, State & Society. Available at: https://doi.org/10.1093/sp/jxx010 (accessed April 2018).

Hooks, b. (1989) *Talking Back: Thinking Feminist, Thinking Black.* South End Press, New York.

Krivkovich, A., Robinson, K., Starikova, I., Valentino, R. and Yee, L. (2017) Women in the workplace 2017. McKinsey Report. Available at: https://www.mckinsey.com/~/media/McKinsey/Global%20Themes/Gender%20Equality/Women%20in%20the%20Workplace%202017/Women-in-the-Workplace-2017-v2.ashx (accessed 12 March 2018).

London School of Economics (LSE) (2017) Confronting gender inequality: findings from the LSE Commission on Gender, Inequality and Power. LSE Knowledge Exchange HEIF 5. LSE, London.

Moreno, D. (2017) Tourism and gender: an essential approach in the context of sustainable and responsible tourism development. Unpublished PhD thesis. University Complutense of Madrid, Spain.

Norland, M. and Moran, T. (2016) Study: firms with more women in the C-suite are more profitable. *Harvard Business Review.* Available at: https://hbr.org/2016/02/study-firms-with-more-women-in-the-c-suite-are-more-profitable (accessed 12 March 2018).

Oxfam (2017) Tourism's dirty secret: the exploitation of hotel housekeepers. Available at: https://www.oxfam.ca/sites/default/files/file_attachments/tourisms_dirty_secret_-_oxfam_canada_report_-_oct_17_2017.pdf (accessed 1 March 2018).

Prime, J. and Moss-Racusin, C. (2009) Engaging men in gender initiatives: what change agents need to know. Available at: www.catalyst.org/system/files/Engaging_Men_In_Gender_Initiatives_What_Change_Agents_Need_To_Know.pdf (accessed 1 March 2018).

Swain, M.B. (2016) Embodying cosmopolitan paradigms in tourism research. In: Munar, A.M. and Jamal, T. (eds) *Tourism Research Paradigms: Critical and Emergent Knowledges*. Emerald, Bingley, UK, pp. 87–111.

TUI (2016) Future opportunities for young women in the tourism sector. Available at: www.tui-politiklounge. com/en/policy-blog/2016/december/future-opportunities-tunisia (accessed 1 March 2018).

Turban, S., Freeman, L. and Waber, B. (2017) A study used sensors to show men and women are treated differently at work. *Harvard Business Review*. Available at: https://hbr.org/2017/10/a-study-used-sensors-to-show-that-men-and-women-are-treated-differently-at-work (accessed 12 March 2018).

UNITE HERE (2016) Hands off pants on: sexual harassment in Chicago's hospitality industry. Available at: https://www.handsoffpantson.org/wp-content/uploads/HandsOffReportWeb.pdf (accessed 1 March 2018).

UNITE UK (2016) Unethical London: global hotel chains – making London an unethical tourist destination through 'standard industry practice'. Available at: www.unitetheunion.org/uploaded/documents/(JN7544)%20 A4%20Unethical%20London%20Brochure%20(2)11-27954.pdf (accessed 1 March 2018).

United Nations World Tourism Organization (UNWTO) (2015) Goal 5: Achieve gender equality and empower all women and girls. Available at: www.un.org/sustainabledevelopment/gender-equality (accessed 1 March 2018).

Woodroffe, J. and Smee, S. (2012) Women's empowerment and gender equality in the post-2015 framework. Gender and Development Network, London. Available at: https://static1.squarespace.com/static/ 536c4ee8e4b0b60bc6ca7c74/t/54b54681e4b0177640af55c7/1421166209765/Achieving+gender+ equality+and+women%27s+empowerment+in+the+post+2015+framework.pdf (accessed 1 March 2018).

World Health Organization (WHO) (2013) Global and regional estimates of violence against women: prevalence and health effects of intimate partner violence and non-partner sexual violence. Available at: http://apps.who.int/iris/bitstream/10665/85239/1/9789241564625_eng.pdf (accessed 1 March 2018).

Wright, M. (2006) *Disposable Women and Other Myths of Global Capitalism*. Routledge, New York.

Index

Page numbers in **bold** type refer to figures, tables, boxed text and 'women's story' sections.

CABI – who we are and what we do

This book is published by **CABI**, an international not-for-profit organisation that improves people's lives worldwide by providing information and applying scientific expertise to solve problems in agriculture and the environment.

CABI is also a global publisher producing key scientific publications, including world renowned databases, as well as compendia, books, ebooks and full text electronic resources. We publish content in a wide range of subject areas including: agriculture and crop science / animal and veterinary sciences / ecology and conservation / environmental science / horticulture and plant sciences / human health, food science and nutrition / international development / leisure and tourism.

The profits from CABI's publishing activities enable us to work with farming communities around the world, supporting them as they battle with poor soil, invasive species and pests and diseases, to improve their livelihoods and help provide food for an ever growing population.

CABI is an international intergovernmental organisation, and we gratefully acknowledge the core financial support from our member countries (and lead agencies) including:

 Ministry of Agriculture
People's Republic of China

 Australian Government
Australian Centre for
International Agricultural Research

 Agriculture and
Agri-Food Canada

 Ministry of Foreign Affairs of the
Netherlands

 Schweizerische Eidgenossenschaft
Confédération suisse
Confederazione Svizzera
Confederaziun svizra

Swiss Agency for Development
and Cooperation SDC

Discover more

To read more about CABI's work, please visit: **www.cabi.org**

Browse our books at: **www.cabi.org/bookshop**,
or explore our online products at: **www.cabi.org/publishing-products**

Interested in writing for CABI? Find our author guidelines here:
www.cabi.org/publishing-products/information-for-authors/